THE FATHERS
OF THE CHURCH

A NEW TRANSLATION

VOLUME 114

THE FATHERS
OF THE CHURCH

A NEW TRANSLATION

BARSANUPHIUS AND JOHN

LETTERS
VOLUME 2

Translated by

JOHN CHRYSSAVGIS

THE CATHOLIC UNIVERSITY OF AMERICA PRESS
Washington, D.C.

Copyright © 2007
THE CATHOLIC UNIVERSITY OF AMERICA PRESS
All rights reserved
Printed in the United States of America

The paper used in this publication meets the minimum requirements of the
American National Standards for Information Science—Permanence of Paper
for Printed Library Materials, ANSI z39.48–1984.

LIBRARY OF CONGRESS CATALOGING-IN-PUBLICATION DATA
Barsanuphius, Saint, 6th cent.
[Biblos psychophelestate periechousa apokriseis. English]
Letters / Barsanuphius and John ; translated by John Chryssavgis.
p. cm. — (The fathers of the church ; v. 114)
Includes bibliographical references and index.
ISBN-13: 978-0-8132-0114-6 (cloth : alk. paper)
ISBN-10: 0-8132—0114-4 (cloth : alk. paper)   1. Spiritual life—
Orthodox Eastern Church.   2. Asceticism—Orthodox Eastern Church.
3. Monastic and religious life.   I. John, the Prophet, Saint.
II. Chryssavgis, John.   III. Title.   IV. Series.
BR60.F3B2513 2006
[BR65.B273]
270 s—dc22
[270
2006006979

CONTENTS

CONTENTS

INDICES

ACKNOWLEDGMENTS

The first draft of this translation was prepared during a sabbatical at the Center of Theological Inquiry in Princeton, New Jersey. I am indebted to the brotherhood of The Holy Transfiguration Monastery in Brookline, Massachusetts, for their insightful counsel. The Rt. Rev. Bishop Sava of Troas has provided guidance throughout the project.

Ms. Melissa Lynch generously offered her time in the compilation of the scriptural index, while Ms. Roberta Powers graciously assisted in the preparation of the general index. The entire publication has benefited enormously from the editorial skills and invaluable suggestions of Dr. Carole Burnett, staff editor at The CUA Press.

Any portions of this translation that also appear in my previous volume, *Letters from the Desert*, are used by permission of St. Vladimir's Seminary Press, Crestwood, New York 10707, www.svspress.com.

ABBREVIATIONS

GCS   Die griechischen christlichen Schriftsteller der ersten drei Jahrhunderte. Leipzig.

PG   Patrologia Graeca, ed. J.-P. Migne. Paris.

PL   Patrologia Latina, ed. J.-P. Migne. Paris.

PO   Patrologia Orientalis. Paris.

ROC   *Revue de l'orient chrétien*. Paris.

SC   *Sources chrétiennes*. Paris.

SELECT BIBLIOGRAPHY

Texts and Translations

Barsanuphe et Jean de Gaza: Correspondance. Edited with notes and index by F. Neyt and P. de Angelis-Noah. French translation by L. Regnault. *SC* 426–27 and 450–51. Paris, 1997–2001.

Barsanuphius. *Doctrina.* PG 86: 891–902. [Teaching on Origen, Evagrius, and Didymus]

Barsanuphius and John: Questions and Responses. In *Philokalia.* 3 vols. Thessalonika: Byzantion Editions, 1988–1989.

Barsanuphius and John: Questions and Responses. Greek Fathers of the Church. Thessalonika, 1988. [In Greek]

Barsanuphius and John: Discerning and Hesychastic Texts; Questions and Responses. 3 vols. Kareas, Athens: Holy Monastery of St. John the Forerunner, 1996–1997.

Chitty, D. J., ed. and trans. *Barsanuphius and John: Questions and Responses.* PO 31, 3 (Paris, 1966): 445–616. Also published by New Sarov Press, Blanco, TX, 1998. [Partial critical edition of the Greek text with English translation]

Dorotheus. *Questions and Responses.* PG 88: 1811–22. [Incorporated among his *Instructions*]

John Rufus. *Plerophoriae.* Edited by F. Nau. PO 8, 1 (Paris, 1912).

Lovato, M. F. T., and L. Mortari, eds. *Barsanufio e Giovanni di Gaza: Epistolario.* In *Collana di Testi Patristici* 93. Rome, 1991.

Mark the Deacon. *The Life of Porphyry, Bishop of Gaza.* Translated by G. F. Hill. Oxford, 1913.

―――. *Vie de Porphyre, évêque de Gaza [par] Marc le Diacre.* Edited and translated by H. Gregoire and M.-A. Kugener. Paris, 1930.

Nikodemus of Mt. Athos. Βίβλος ψυχωφελεστάτη περιέχουσα ἀποκρίσεις διαφόροις ὑποθέσεσιν ἀνηκούσαις, συγγραφεῖσὰ μὲν παρὰ τῶν ὁσίων καὶ θεοφόρων πατέρων ἡμῶν Βαρσανουφίου καὶ Ἰωάννου, ἐπιμελῶς δὲ διορθωθεῖσα καὶ τῇ τῶν ὁσίων βιογραφίᾳ, καὶ πλατυτάτῳ πίνακι πλουτισθεῖσα παρὰ τοῦ ἐν μοναχοῖς ἐλαχίστου Νικοδήμου τοῦ ἁγιορείτου. Venice, 1816. [Also contains a substantial introduction by Nikodemus himself]

Pachomius Hieromonk. *Opisanie roukopisei solovetskago monastyria nakhodiachlchikhsia v biblioteke Kazanskoi doukhovnoi Akademii I.* Kazan, 1881.

Prepodobnykh ottzev Varsanoufiia Velikago I Ionna roukovodstvo k doukhovnoi zisni, v otvetakh na voprocheniia outchenikov. Perevod s gretcheskag. Moscow, 1883.

Regnault, L. *Maîtres spirituels au désert de Gaza: Barsanuphe, Jean et Dorothée.* Selected texts and introduction. Sable-sur-Sarthe: Abbaye de Solesmes, 1967.

Regnault, L., Ph. Lemaire, and B. Ottier, trans. *Barsanuphe et Jean de Gaza: Correspondance.* Sable-sur-Sarthe: Abbaye de Solesmes, 1971. [Complete French translation from the Greek and Georgian]

Rose, S., ed. *Saints Barsanuphius and John: Guidance toward Spiritual Life. Responses to the Questions of Disciples.* Platina, CA: St. Herman of Alaska Brotherhood, 1990. [Partial English translation from the Russian edition, *Rukuvodstvo k Duchovnoi Zhizni,* Moscow, 1855]

Schoinas, S., ed. *Vivlos Psychopelestate . . . Varsanoufiou kai Ioannou* [as above in the book by Nikodemus]. Volos, 1960. [In Greek; English translation of full title as follows: "Most edifying book, containing responses on various matters written by our holy and God-bearing Fathers Barsanuphius and John"]

Soterchos, P. M. *The Great Old Man Barsanuphius and his Disciple Saint John the Prophet.* Athens, 1988. [Selections from the two elders, in Greek]

Sozomen. *Historia ecclesiastica.* GCS 56. Edited by J. Bidez and G. C. Hanson. Berlin, 1960.

Barsanuphius and John: Secondary Sources

Angelis-Noah, Paula de. "La méditation de Barsanuphe sur la lettre *êta.*" *Byzantion* 53, fasc. 2 (1983): 494–506.

Binns, J. *Ascetics and Ambassadors of Christ: The Monasteries of Palestine 314–631.* Oxford: Clarendon Press, 1994.

Brown, P. *The Body and Society. Men, Women and Sexual Renunciation in Early Christianity.* New York: Columbia University Press, 1988.

Cameron, A. "On the date of John of Gaza." *Classical Quarterly,* n.s. 43 (1993): 348–51.

Chitty, D. *The Desert a City: An introduction to the study of Egyptian and Palestinian monasticism under the Christian Empire.* Oxford: Blackwell, 1966. Reprint, Crestwood, NY: St. Vladimir's Seminary Press, 1995.

———. "The Books of the Old Men." *Eastern Churches Review* 6 (1974): 15–21.

———. "Abba Isaiah." *The Journal of Theological Studies,* NS, 22 (1971): 47–72.

Chrestou, P. *Greek Patrology.* Thessalonika: Patriarchal Institute of Patristic Studies, 1976. [In Greek]

Chryssavgis, J. *Soul Mending: The Art of Spiritual Direction.* Brookline, MA: Holy Cross Press, 2000.

Festugière, A. J. *Les moines d'Orient.* Paris, 1961–. See especially vol. 4, 1965.

Garitte, G. "Le menée georgien de Dumbarton Oaks." *Le Muséon* 77 (1964): 29–64, esp. 43 and 55.

Hausherr, I. "Barsanuphe (saint)." *Dictionnaire de spiritualité.* Vol. 1. Paris, 1937.

————. *Direction spirituelle en Orient autrefois. Orientalia Christiana analecta* 144. Rome: Pontificium Institutum Orientalium Studiorum, 1955. See also the English translation: *Spiritual Direction in the Early Christian East.* Translated by Anthony P. Gythiel. Kalamazoo, MI: Cistercian Publications, 1990.

————. "Noms du Christ et voies d'oraison." *Orientalia Christiana analecta* 157. Rome: Pontificium Institutum Orientalium Studiorum, 1960.

Hevelone-Harper, J. L. *Disciples of the Desert: Monks, Laity, and Spiritual Authority in Sixth-Century Gaza.* Baltimore, MD: Johns Hopkins University Press, 2005.

Janin, R. "Barsanuphius." *Dictionnaire d'histoire et de géographie ecclésiastiques.* Vol. 6. Paris: Letouzey et Ané, 1912–.

Neyt, F. *Les lettres à Dorothée dans la correspondance de Barsanuphe et de Jean de Gaza.* Doctoral diss., University of Louvain, 1969.

————. "Citations 'Isaiennes' chez Barsanuphe et Jean de Gaza." *Le Muséon* 89 (1971): 65–92.

————. "Précisions sur le vocabulaire de Barsanuphe et Jean de Gaza." *Studia Patristica* 12 (Berlin, 1975): 247–53.

————. "Un type d'autorité charismatique." *Byzantion* 44, fasc. 2 (1974): 343–61. Also appeared in English as "A Form of Charismatic Authority," in *Eastern Churches Review* 6 (1974): 52–65.

————. "L'*Apsephiston* chez les Pères de Gaza." *Uberlieferung der geschichtlichen Untersuchungen.* Berlin: Akademie-Verlag, 1981.

Perrone, L. *La chiesa di Palestina e le controversie cristologiche: dal concilio di Efeso (431) al secondo concilio di Constantinopoli.* Brescia: Paideia, 1980.

————. "Εἰς τὸν τῆς Ἡσυχίας Λιμένα. Le lettere a Giovanni di Beersheva nella corrispondenza di Barsanufio e Giovanni di Gaza." Pages 463–86 in *Memorial Dom Jean Gribomont (1920–1986).* Rome, 1988.

————. "Le lettere a Giovanni di Beersheve nella corrispondenza di Barsanufio e Giovanni di Gaza." *Studia Ephemeridis Augustinianum* 27. Rome, 1988.

————. "Dissenso dottrinale e propaganda visionaria: Le Pleroforie di Giovanni di Maiuma." *Augustinianum* 29 (1989): 451–95.

————. "Monasticism as a Factor of Religious Interaction in the Holy Land during the Byzantine Period." Pages 67–95 in A. Kofsky and G. G. Stroumsa, eds. *Sharing the Sacred: Religious Contacts and Conflicts in the Holy Land. First–Fifteenth Centuries CE.* Jerusalem: Yad Izhak Ben Zvi, 1998.

Rapp, C. "'For next to God, you are my salvation': Reflections on the Rise of the Holy Man in Late Antiquity." Pages 63–81 in J. Howard-Johnston and P. A. Hayward, eds. *Essays on the Contribution of Peter Brown.* Oxford: Oxford University Press, 1999.

————. "Monasticism, Prayer and Penance in Late Antiquity." *Bulletin of Saint Shenouda the Archimandrite Coptic Society* 6 (2000–2001): 83–93.

Regnault, L. "Dorothée de Gaza." *Dictionnaire de spiritualité.* Vol. 3. Paris, 1954.

————. "Théologie de la vie monastique selon Barsanuphe et Dorothée."
Pages 315–22 in *Théologie de la vie monastique: Études sur la tradition patristique.* Paris: Aubier, 1961.

————. "Jean de Gaza." *Dictionnaire de spiritualité.* Vol. 8. Paris, 1974.

Vailhé, S. "Jean le Prophète et Séridos." *Echos d'Orient* 8 (1905): 154–60.

————. "Les lettres spirituelles de Jean et de Barsanuphe." *Echos d'Orient* 7 (1904): 268–76.

————. "Saint Barsanuphe." *Echos d'Orient* 8 (1905): 14–25.

Vamvakas, D. Τὸ ἐν παντὶ εὐχαριστεῖν τῶν ὁσίων καὶ θεοφόρων πατέρων ἡμῶν Βαρσανουφίου καὶ Ἰωάννου. Hagion Oros: Karyai, 1991. [In Greek]

Veselinovich, K. A. *Barsanuphius the Great, John the Prophet and Dorotheus the Abba.* Doctoral diss. Athens, 1941. [In Greek]

Voulgarakis, I. A. "Missionsangaben in den Briefen der Asketen Barsanuphius und Johannes." In A. Kallis, ed. *Philoxenia.* Munster, 1980.

General References

Abel, F.-M. "Gaza au VIe siècle d'après le rhéteus Chorikios." *Revue biblique* 40 (1931): 5–31.

————. *Histoire de la Palestine depuis la conquête d'Alexandre jusqu'à l'invasion arabe.* Paris: J. Gabalda, 1952. See esp. Part 3, 267–406.

Aharoni, Y. *The Land of the Bible.* Rev. ed. Philadelphia: Westminster Press, 1979.

Anderson, G. *Sage, Saint, and Sophist: Holy Men and their Associates in the Early Roman Empire.* London and New York: Routledge, 1994.

Avi-Yonah, M. *The Madaba Mosaic Map.* Jerusalem: Israel Exploration Society, 1954.

Bottini, G. C., L. Di Segni, and E. Alliata, eds. *Christian Archaeology in the Holy Land: New Discoveries. Essays in Honour of Virgilio C. Corbo.* Jerusalem: Franciscan Printing Press, 1990.

Brown, P. "The Rise and Function of the Holy Man in Late Antiquity." *Journal of Religious Studies* 61 (1971): 80–101. Reprinted as pages 391–439 in Martin, J., and B. Quint, eds. *Christentum und Antike Gesellschaft.* Darmstadt, 1990.

Brun, P.-M., ed. *La vie de saint Dosithée.* In *Orientalia Christiana* 26. Rome, 1932. Pages 85–124. Also published in *SC* 92. Edited by L. Regnault and J. de Préville. Paris, 1963.

Bury, J. B. *A History of the Later Empire from Arcadius to Irene (395 A.D.–800 A.D.).* London and New York: Macmillan and Co., 1889. Unaltered reprint, Amsterdam: Adolf M. Hakkert, 1966.

Canivet, P. "Dorothée de Gaza est-il un disciple d'Evagre?" *Revue des études grecques* 78 (1965): 336–46.

Chryssavgis, J. *In the Heart of the Desert: The Spirituality of the Desert Fathers and Mothers.* Bloomington, IN: World Wisdom Books, 2003.

Dan, Y. "On the ownership of the land of the village of Thavatha in the Byzantine period." *Scripta Classica Israelica* 5 (1979–1980): 258–62.

Garitte, G. "Chronique." *Revue d'histoire ecclésiastique* 60 (1965): 287–88.

Glucker, C. A. M. *The City of Gaza in the Roman and Byzantine Periods.* BAR International Series 325. Oxford: B.A.R., 1987.

Guillaumont, A. *Aux origines du monachisme chrétien.* Spiritualité orientale 30. Bégrolles-en-Mauges: Abbaye de Bellefontaine, 1979.

Guy, J.-C., ed. *Les Apophtegmes des Pères du désert.* Bégrolles-en-Mauges: Abbaye de Bellefontaine, 1966.

———. *Les Apophtegmes des Pères,* I–IX. SC 387. Paris, 1993.

Hirschfeld, Y. *The Judean Desert Monasteries in the Byzantine Period.* New Haven: Yale University Press, 1992.

Jones, A. H. M. *The Cities of the Eastern Roman Provinces.* Revised by Michael Avi-Yonah. 2d ed. Oxford, 1971.

Miller, J. I. *The Spice Trade of the Roman Empire: 29 B.C. to A.D. 641.* Oxford, 1969.

Mortari, L. *Vita e detti dei Padri del Deserto.* Rome: Città Nuova, 1971.

Nau, F. "Histoire des solitaires égyptiennes." *ROC* (1907): 43–69, 171–89, and 393–413; (1908) 47–66 and 266–97; (1909) 357–79; (1912) 204–11 and 294–301; and (1913) 137–46. English translation in B. Ward. *The Wisdom of the Desert Fathers.* Oxford: SLG Press, 1975.

Regnault, L., ed. *Les sentences des Pères du désert. Nouveau recueil.* 2d ed. Sable-sur-Sarthe: Abbaye de Solesmes, 1977.

———. "Les *Apophtegmes* des Pères en Palestine aux Ve et VIe siècles." *Irénikon* 54 (1981): 320–30. Later appeared as pages 73–83 in Regnault, L. *Les Pères du désert à travers leurs apophtegmes.* Sable-sur-Sarthe: Abbaye de Solesmes, 1987.

Resch, Alfred. *Agrapha; aussercanonische Evangelienfragmente.* Leipzig: J. C. Hinrichs, 1889.

Roll, I. "The Roman Road System in Judea." In *The Jerusalem Cathedra.* Vol. 3. Edited by L. I. Levine. Jerusalem: Yad Izhak Ben-Zvi Institute; Detroit: Wayne State University Press, 1983.

Rubin, Z. "Christianity in Byzantine Palestine: missionary activity and religious coercion." In *The Jerusalem Cathedra.* Vol. 3. Edited by L. I. Levine. Jerusalem: Yad Izhak Ben-Zvi Institute; Detroit: Wayne State University Press, 1983.

Stemberger, G. *Juden und Christen im Heiligen Land: Palästina unter Konstantin und Theodosius.* Munich, 1987.

Vailhé, S. "Repertoire alphabetique des monastères de Palestine." *ROC* 4 (1899): 512–42; and 5 (1900): 19–48, 272–92.

———. "Saint Dorothée et Saint Zosime." *Echos d'Orient* 4 (1901): 359–63.

———. "Un mystique monophysite, le moine Isaïe." *Echos d'Orient* 9 (1906): 81–91.

Van Parys, M. "Abba Silvain et ses disciples." *Irénikon* 61 (1988): 315–30.

LETTERS

VOLUME 2

LETTERS TO VARIOUS BROTHERS (349–398)

A brother heard from another brother about the warfare of the latter; so he advised him as much as he could, although he had not reached the measure to give such advice. As a result, the warfare immediately turned upon himself. When he saw himself burdened and knew that he was suffering this because he had not admitted his own weakness to his brother, and that it is necessary to seek the counsel of the fathers, he announced this to the Other Old Man. The latter responded in this way.

ROTHER, THERE is no other way for a person except to blame himself for what he has said, and God will grant forgiveness.

The brother was at once relieved of the warfare and gave thanks to God.

LETTER 350

Question from the same [brother] to the same [Old Man]: "If one is confronted by two things, both of which are harmful to the soul, and it is by all means necessary to submit to one of them, what should one do?" Response by John.

When comparing two harmful things, one should choose the lesser harm. It is written in the fathers that someone was once approached by another brother seeking to borrow some money, but the former did not give him any, saying: "I do not have any to give you." When later asked why he did not give anything, he replied: "If I had given him some money, we would both have faced harm to the soul. So I chose to transgress one commandment in order not to lose my soul entirely."[1]

---

1. Cf. *Sayings,* John the Persian 2.

1

LETTER 351

A brother who was progressing in godly virtue announced to the Great Old Man: "Give me a word, abba;[2] for I am afflicted." Response by Barsanuphius.

The holy Apostle Paul understood the power of patience, and wrote: "Indeed, you need endurance, so that when you have done the will of God, you may receive what was promised."[3] Therefore, anyone who wishes to ascend with Christ on the cross must become a partaker of his sufferings in order always to have peace. I, too, say to you: "Struggle to acquire thanksgiving in all circumstances,[4] and 'the power of the Most High will overshadow you,'[5] and then you shall find rest."

LETTER 352

Question from the same brother to the same Old Man: "What should I do with the filth that I have, as well as with the pretense to rights and the forgetfulness that intensely afflict me?" Response by Barsanuphius.

Anyone who has filth within himself painlessly throws himself into filth whenever he wants; moreover, anyone who is steeped in filth[6] very painfully drags himself out of that filth. The one who is steeped is worse than the one who has it within.

As for the pretense to rights, evil never suppresses evil. Therefore, remember that the pretense to rights never justifies a person, and you will find rest. As for forgetfulness, "there are two kinds of forgetfulness, and one is opposed to the other. So one who reaches the point of forgetting to eat his bread from the sound of his sighing will not be dominated by the forgetfulness of the enemy."

---

2. This is frequently the opening sentence addressed by a visitor to an elder in the *Sayings of the Desert Fathers*.
3. Heb 10.36.
4. Cf. 1 Thes 5.18.
5. Lk 1.35.
6. Cf. Ps 68.3.

LETTER 353

Request from the same [brother] to the same Great Old Man: "Add more of your mercy and remove me from the belly of the lion, which has swallowed me. Have compassion on my soul, as God from above; for you have received the authority to do so: 'Whatever you loose on earth shall be loosed also in heaven.'[7] Do not abandon my soul to Gehenna in order that I may not die in sin. Finally, give me a word according to my strength, so that I may become a partaker of your labor." Response by Barsanuphius.

"May the God of peace himself sanctify you entirely, and may your spirit, soul, and body be completely preserved sound and blameless at the coming of our Lord Jesus Christ."[8] What more comforting word could I send you than these words of the Apostle? Strive to acquire whatever I have written you, and I shall labor even more than you, praying to God night and day[9] until you attain to these. Brother, learn this, too: as you know, I would sacrifice my life for you gladly and my prayer for you is unceasing.

LETTER 354

A brother was sent out on a mandate on behalf of the monastic community. So he asked the Other Old Man whether he should accept the invitation of his friends to eat with women. The Old Man replied that he should certainly not eat with women. The brother said: "But how do I know, when I am invited by someone, whether a woman will in fact come to eat with us, in order that I not accept the invitation?" The Old Man told him: "Ask the person who has invited you whether there is any woman there. If he says yes, then excuse yourself, saying: 'Forgive me, but I have been commanded not to eat with a woman.'" The brother said: "If I happen to go there and am taken by surprise before even asking or thinking that women might come to the table, what should I do?" The Old Man replied as follows.

7. Mt 18.18.   8. 1 Thes 5.23.
9. Cf. 2 Tm 1.3.

You should take aside the person who invited you and tell him: "Forgive me, but I have been taken by surprise and have not told you that I have in fact been ordered not to eat with a woman. Please allow me to leave." If he happens to ask the woman to leave, then stay; otherwise, depart and do not transgress the command in order that you are not caused to die on account of your disobedience.[10] And do not be afraid; for this will not be the source of any scandal, but only of edification.

LETTER 355

Question from the same [brother] to the same [Old Man]: "If I am sent out on some mandate without the blessing to eat anywhere and someone asks me to eat with him, persisting and arguing and even forcing me, even after I have told him that I am unable to do so, since I do not have the abbot's blessing, what should I do?" Response by John.

Since argumentation gives rise to nothing good, if it is not a matter of harming the soul, then accept the invitation and announce it to the abbot on your return, seeking forgiveness for your sin. If the matter is harmful to your soul, then even if this brother should argue ten thousand times, do not stay; for admittedly, this is the work of the devil.

LETTER 356

Question from the same [brother] to the same [Old Man]: "I was sent out to the Holy City [of Jerusalem] on a mandate, and I went down to the Jordan in order to pray; however, I did so without asking for a blessing from the abbot about this. Did I act well or not?" Response by John.

You should go nowhere without an explicit blessing; for whatever takes place according to one's own thought, even if it appears to be good, is in fact not pleasing to God. On the other hand, keeping the command of the abbot who sent you constitutes prayer and service to God, who said: "I have come down

10. Cf. Rom 5.19.

from heaven, not to do my own will, but the will of him who sent me."[11]

LETTER 357

Question from the same [brother] to the same [Old Man]: "If I travel a great distance and happen to lose my way, where should I stay if I neglected to ask my abbot about this? What should I do in this case?" Response by John.

You should pay attention to all things that happen in order that you may do everything for the benefit of your soul. In so doing, you should act as if transgressing the commandment [of your abbot] and not as doing any good at all. For in this way, the abbot will be assured about forgiving you.

LETTER 358

Question from the same [brother]: "If the abbot specifically commands me not to do something, but in my human weakness I am overcome by temptation, what should I do?" Response by John.

Repent both before God and before your abbot, and strive to correct yourself henceforth. God will forgive you your sin.

LETTER 359

A brother, who was entrusted with guarding the door of the monastic community, grew tired because he was alone. So he asked the Great Old Man whether he should take another brother with him or not. Response by Barsanuphius.

Brother, whosoever wishes to come to the Lord and to travel the way of salvation should expect temptations, affliction, and suffering all the time; for it is said: "Son, when you come to serve the Lord, prepare yourself for testing."[12] The Lord also said: "If any come to me, let them deny themselves and take up their cross daily and follow me."[13] Therefore, whosoever wants to become his disciple must practice obedience until death.[14]

11. Jn 6.38.
13. Mt 16.24; Lk 9.23.
12. Sir 2.1.
14. Cf. Phil 2.8.

Being alone, then, and laboring a little is of more benefit to you than having someone else. When necessary, you will always have the assistance of someone else; however, in that case, boldness will not abound as much when a brother assists you [for a while] as it would if you were together all the time.

Therefore, do not despair at the labor, and you shall find humility; and if you find humility, you shall also receive forgiveness of sins. For it is said: "Consider my humiliation and my affliction, and forgive all my sins."[15] If you are humbled, you will receive grace; and if you receive grace, this grace will assist you. For the holy Paul labored more than all of the apostles, and yet he said: "It is not I, but the grace that is with me."[16] If you believe without hesitation, then you will be strengthened not only to guard the monastery door but also to perform other needs. Therefore, pay attention to the work of God in hope; and he shall arrange the matter in a way that you do not know. May the Lord be with you. Amen.

LETTER 360

Question from the same [brother]: "Father, pray for me, that I may receive understanding and strength from God; for I am ignorant and weak. When I happen to leave the kitchen or cellar carrying something, I sometimes encounter certain fathers or other important people. What should I do? Pray also that I might be delivered from the impurities that occur to me." Response by Barsanuphius.

If only you can believe that from the sterile stones "God is able to raise children for Abraham,"[17] and that he who opened the mouth of the ass[18] is also able to open, illumine, educate, and strengthen you, God grants you everything, brother, and you simply do not know what he gives you. The door of the monastic community is the door of God, and God knows that his servant, the doorkeeper, needs wisdom, prudence, knowledge, strength,[19] assistance, and discernment. For it is said: "Your Father in heaven knows what you need, even before you ask it of him."[20] If you

---

15. Ps 24.18.   16. 1 Cor 15.10.
17. Mt 3.9.   18. Cf. Nm 22.28.
19. Cf. Is 11.2–3.   20. Mt 6.8.

have the strength to be patient, your soul will be blessed. When you happen to be walking about or carrying something from the kitchen or elsewhere, and meet up with certain fathers or other important secular people, calmly put down whatever you are holding and receive them with humility and fear of God. And God will make your encounter to be an occasion for the glory of his name[21] and for the edification of all, through the prayers of the saints. Amen. As for the impurities, if your heart is humbled, reckoning yourself to be earth and ashes,[22] then—after God— humility will protect you.

LETTER 361

A brother asked the Other Old Man, saying: "Tell me, father, whom I should ask about my thoughts. And should I consult a second person in regard to the same matter?" Response by John.

You should ask the person whom you trust, knowing that he must bear your thoughts; trust in him as if in God. As for consulting another person in regard to the same thought, this is a matter of faithlessness and temptation. For if you believe that God has spoken through his saint, then why is it necessary to test God by posing the same question to someone else?

LETTER 362

Question from the same [brother]: "If my thought persists in afflicting me, even after asking the fathers, [what should I do then]?" Response by John.

It does not persist without reason, but because you did not purely and carefully apply the command that you heard. So you ought to correct your fault and apply whatever you heard with purity. For if God is speaking through his saints, then God would not lie.

LETTER 363

Question from the same [brother]: "Should I ask the same person about the same matter a second time, or not? I know, father,

21. Cf. Ps 95.8.   22. Cf. Gn 18.27; Jb 42.6.

that I was once told not to do something; and, when I asked the same person again about this same matter, then I was told that I should in fact do it. What does this mean?" Response by John.

Brother, "the judgments of God are like a profound abyss."[23] God places in the mouth of him who is responding [that which is] in accordance with the heart of him who is asking. Sometimes this occurs in order to test one, or else because one's heart has changed and demands a different response. Or perhaps certain others who are involved may have changed, and so God speaks differently through his saint for their sake. In this way he spoke through Isaiah to Hezekiah the king. For after telling him: "Arrange your affairs; for you are about to die," the king's heart changed, and he became sorrowful. Then he said to him through the same Isaiah: "Behold, God has added another fifteen years to your life."[24] Now, had he spoken through another person, the matter would have been the cause of scandal to people, thinking as they may that the saints supposedly speak differently. Again, he spoke through Jonah in accordance with the hearts of the Ninevites, saying: "After three days, I shall destroy the city."[25] When, however, their hearts were changed by repentance, God showed his great loving-kindness and left the city alone, since it changed for the good. This is why one should never change the saint whom one consults, but should ask the same one again in case God needs to change the response for some reason; and, when this happens, then there would be no scandal.

LETTER 364

Question from the same [brother]: "Master, I had some sort of problem with someone else, and it was necessary for me to go with him to the magistrate. Therefore, I asked the advice of the fathers on this matter, and they told me what I should do when I go. So I did what I thought was my best not to transgress their words to me. Since the result was not as they had told me, how-

---

23. Ps 35.7.   24. 2 Kgs 20.1–6; Is 38.1–5.
25. Cf. Jon 3.4.

ever, I was greatly afflicted and did not know what to do. Should
I transgress? I feared to disobey. Should I wait? For the result
was not the same as they had said. What does this mean, father?
Moreover, what should I have done or thought after falling into
such dismay and need? Could it be that the fault was mine, without my knowing it?" Response by John.

This question is like your first. How can this be the case? Listen. You received a mandate in regard to something: "Go and
do that," you were told, and you found the circumstances to be
different. First, you should blame yourself, in case your heart
took pleasure in the matter and you did not leave the matter
entirely up to God. This is perhaps why God did not allow the
matter to occur in accordance with the mandate of the fathers.
So the cause of the problem is in fact due to you, while you attribute it to their mandate. Indeed, Elisha confidently sent his
disciple to raise the dead person, but he was unable to.[26] The
reason for this, however, did not come from the person who
sent him, but from the person who was sent. Otherwise, how
is it that he was later able to raise him? Therefore, you should
do your best to make sure that things occur in accordance with
the mandate that you received. If, however, after striving to do
so, still this does not occur, then learn that there was probably
some change that occurred in one of the factors, and this is why
God is changing the details of the mandate.

Let me give you an example. Let us suppose that someone
owes you ten coins but is unable to repay them all. So you ask
your elder: "What should I demand from him?" He replies:
"What is fair is to ask for all ten coins." The elder was assured in
his response to you not to forgive [your debtor] because the latter was hard-hearted. Having heard, then, that you were about
to demand these, he repented and prayed to God, saying: "Master, I am unable to repay the ten coins; please inform the magistrate not to force me to repay it in full, and I shall strive to
please you for the rest of my life." So the compassionate God
changes his judgment, while you are not actually aware of this.

26. Cf. 2 Kgs 4.28–32.

Therefore, since [your elder] is not physically close by in order
for you to ask him, you should pray to God and invoke the name
of your elder, saying: "God of my elder, do not allow me to wander away from your will or from your servant's mandate, but inform me as to what I should do." Then you should do whatever
he informs you, believing that God actually spoke through the
saint and is guiding you; furthermore, you should be aware that
some change has certainly occurred in order for God to have
changed the details of the mandate itself.

LETTER 365

Question: "My master, how many times must I pray so that my
thought may be assured about this?" Response.

When you are unable to ask your elder in regard to this, then
you should pray three times about everything. Afterward, you
should observe where your heart inclines, even to the slightest
degree, and act accordingly. For the assurance is clear and certainly becomes apparent to the heart.

LETTER 366

Question from the same [brother]: "Should I pray three times
on different occasions or on one and the same occasion? For
sometimes, it happens that there can be no delay in the matter."
Response by John.

If you have some leisure time, then pray three times on three
different days. If, however, it is a matter of urgency, then take as
your example the hour in which the Savior was betrayed—when
it was certainly very urgent—and recall how he withdrew three
times in order to pray the same thing.[27] And if it appears that we
have not been heard, since the divine economy certainly has to
occur, we are nevertheless taught in this not to grieve when we
pray and are not heard for the time being. For he knows even
more than we do what is beneficial for us.[28] Let us not cease giving thanks, and we shall be saved.

27. Cf. Mt 26.44.
28. Cf. 1 Cor 6.12.

LETTER 367

Question from the same [brother]: "If, after praying, the assurance delays in coming, what should I do? Indeed, if it is my fault that this is concealed from me, how will I understand this?" Response.

If the assurance does not come to you after praying three times, then you should know that the fault clearly lies with you. If this failure is not apparent to you, then blame yourself, and God will have mercy on you.

LETTER 368

Question from the same [brother] to the same [Old Man]: "How should one behave in approaching the fathers with a question? Should one perhaps carry out all of the responses without the least transgression?" Response by John.

No, one is not obliged to carry out all of them, but only the ones given in the form of a command. For simple, godly advice is one thing, and a command is another. Advice is counsel without compulsion, revealing to a person the straight way of life; a command, on the other hand, is an inviolable bond.

LETTER 369

Question from the same person: "Father, you showed me the difference between a command and godly advice. Give me also the signs of each: how are they recognized and what is the power of each?" Response by John.

If you approach a spiritual father in order to ask about something not so much because you wish to receive a command but only in order to hear a godly response, and you are told what you should do, then you should still keep to this [word] by all means. If, in so doing, you are tempted as a result of this affliction, then do not be troubled; for this is happening for your benefit. Now, if you do not want to do [what you have been told], you should not think that you have transgressed a command; for you did not receive it as a command. It seems, however, that you are overlooking what is beneficial to you, and so you should blame yourself for this.

Indeed, you should consider everything that comes out of the mouth of the saints as being for the benefit of those who hear them. The same applies even if you did not ask anything, but the elder's thought was inspired by God to speak to you of his own accord, something which actually happened once. For one of the elders once sought to visit a city. Another elder said to him of his own accord: "If you visit the city, you shall fall into fornication." Nevertheless, he disobeyed, visited the city, and as a result fell [into this sin].[29]

If you inquire about a specific matter, wanting to receive some command, then you should perform a prostration and ask for a command to be given to you. When the command is received, you should again perform a prostration, so that the one who gave you the command may bless you. Say to him: "Bless me, father, even as I receive the command; and pray that I might keep it." Learn this, too, brother, that the command is not given without reason, and so the one who gave the command will assist you in supplication and prayers, in order that you might be able to keep it. Now, if you are distracted and do not perform a prostration in order to receive a blessing, nevertheless do not think that the command is given without any reason. For it even holds if you happened to receive it without cause or consequence. So, if you can, labor [in this], and do not hesitate to go and perform your prostration in order to receive the blessing. If, however, you are unable to do so, then consider that you have received the command with negligence.

LETTER 370

Question: "If I ask to receive a command, but the elder does not intend to give me one—or perhaps the opposite even occurs, and I did not ask to receive one, and yet he still gives me one—is this reckoned as a command, and should I keep it by all means? Since there are ecclesiastical canons and certain sayings of the fathers, which are written documents, are we also obliged to ob-

29. Cf. *Sayings*, Nau 187.

serve these as strictly and in the same way as the command?" Response by John.

If the person asked did not intend to offer a command, then this is not actually reckoned as a command for you, even if in fact you asked for a command. If, however, he thought it was wise to offer you a command, even if you did not happen to request one, then this is in fact a command and you are obliged to keep it.

One should also accept as a command whatever the dogmatic canons have prescribed and the responses of the fathers expressed in the form of a statement. Nevertheless, give assurance to your thought in regard to these matters by asking the fathers; for you are not always able to understand the proper meaning of their words. Therefore, you should be convinced by their response and by that alone, which you should keep without transgression, with the assistance of the kind and loving God and through the prayers of the saints. Amen.

LETTER 371

Question from the same person to the same Old Man: "If I am tempted and happen to transgress the command, what should I do?" Response by John.

If you receive a command from the saints and happen to transgress it, then do not be disturbed or despair to the point of invalidating it. Remember what is said of the righteous, that "though they fall seven times a day, yet they will rise again,"[30] and also the words of the Lord to Peter: "Forgive your brother seventy times."[31] Therefore, if he commanded mortals to forgive so many times, how many more times would he forgive everything,[32] when he is rich in mercy and compassion? He cries out each day through the prophet: "Return to me and I shall return to you; for I am merciful,"[33] and again: "Now, O Israel."[34] Watch out that, upon hearing that the command has not actual-

---

30. Prv 24.16.
32. Cf. *Sayings*, Poemen 86.
34. Dt 10.12.

31. Cf. Mt 18.22.
33. Jl 2.13; Zec 1.3.

ly been invalidated, you do not become indifferent and come to the point of neglect; for this is indeed a grave sin. Furthermore, do not despise the command for the sake of what appear to be small details; even if you happen to become neglectful in these details, you should still strive to correct yourself. For through indifference in such small details, one is [later] led to greater sins.

LETTER 372

Question from the same [brother]: "My thought suggests that I should not ask the saints, in case I learn something and then happen to despise this on account of my weakness, and then I sin." Response by John.

Such a thought is really terrible. So do not tolerate it at all. For if one learns something and then sins, one will surely incur condemnation. If one has not learned anything and still sins, then one will never incur condemnation;[35] in this way, one's passions will continue to be unhealed. This is precisely why the devil suggests this to us, in order that our passions may remain unhealed. When your thought suggests this, namely, that you are unable to fulfill the command on account of your weakness, then pose the following question: "Since I want to practice this, tell me, father, what is beneficial for me. Nevertheless, I know that whatever you tell me to do, I am unable to fulfill it and keep your words. Yet I still want to learn, for this reason alone, so that I might incur condemnation for overlooking what is beneficial for me." This, too, is a sign of humility on your part. May the Lord enlighten your heart to hear and adhere to this through the prayers of the saints. Amen.

LETTER 373

A brother asked the same excellent Old Man: "What is knowledge falsely so called?"[36] Response by John.

Knowledge falsely so called is trusting in one's own thought that things are exactly as they appear to us. One who wishes

35. Cf. Rom 2.1.
36. Cf. 1 Tm 6.20.

to be delivered of this should not trust in one's own thought, but [always] ask one's elder. If the elder responds and his response is precisely what the brother thought it would be, then he should still not trust in his own thought, saying: "I was ridiculed by the demons in order to be persuaded by my thought that I possess true knowledge, so that once I have believed this, [the demons] might lead me in other ways to fall on my head. The elder has spoken the truth because he speaks from God; for he is not at all ridiculed by the demons." I have said what I could to you, my brother; in the final analysis, however, I do not know if this is how it is. Pray for me.

LETTER 374

A brother asked the same Old Man: "When I am burdened by my thoughts and ask the elders to pray for me, if I listen to what they say, then my soul is immediately relieved." Response by John.

When the ship is troubled by the stormy waves, if it has a captain, then he will save the ship through the wisdom that was given to him by God, and the passengers will rejoice that the ship has been saved. Moreover, a sick person is not a little gladdened when he recalls his doctor, and especially the skills of his doctor. In addition, a traveler who is in danger of being attacked by robbers is strengthened by the mere voice of the guards; how much more so by their presence? If all this is true, how much more gladness should the response of the fathers bestow on all those who listen to them? Especially when this is mingled with intense prayer to God, who said: "Pray for one another, so that you may be healed,"[37] and when we appropriate the suffering of one of our own members,[38] crying out to Jesus, our own Master, saying with the sweetest tears: "Master, save us; for we are perishing."[39] Moreover, how can all this not cause gladness to the [brother] who hears: "The prayer of the righteous is very powerful and effective"?[40]

Therefore, let us not hesitate to entreat [the fathers] to pray for us, even if we are unworthy. For God shows favor to his ser-

37. Jas 5.16.
39. Mt 8.25; Lk 8.24.
38. Cf. 1 Cor 12.26.
40. Jas 5.16.

vants, as he has already done: "Indeed, he shall fulfill the desires of all those who fear him,"[41] and so forth. Often, brother, thieves happened to hear the responses or the voice of the
more powerful and have fled. The same occurs when the spiritual thieves hear the responses or the voice of the more powerful, who have heard from their Master and Protector Jesus:
"Take courage; I have overcome the world."[42] And again: "See, I
have given you authority to tread on snakes and scorpions, and
over all the power of the enemy; and nothing will hurt you."[43]
They flee with trembling and in shame. Therefore, let us entreat the saints to pray for us; and let us appropriate them for
ourselves; for we shall benefit not a little from them. Pray, then,
also for me, so that I, too, may practice this, lest the labor from
the left-hand side might dominate me. May the Lord be with
you. Amen.

LETTER 375

Question from the same [brother] to the same [Old Man]: "You
once told me that freedom is a good thing, at least when it comes
to asking about one's thoughts and about one's actual conduct.
Tell me how I can possibly be free when I have [questions] to
ask." Response by John.

Freedom in the matter of thoughts implies that the one asking completely reveals his thought to the person who is being
asked, without concealing anything at all from that person, and
without transforming the thought out of embarrassment or presenting it as being the thought of some other person, but only
as one's very own, just as it in fact is. For transforming it in this
way is especially harmful.

LETTER 376

Question from the same [brother] to the same Old Man: "Master, tell me what sort of freedom exists in one's actual conduct
and how one should make use of this." Response by John.

41. Ps 144.19.   42. Jn 16.33.
43. Lk 10.19.

Freedom is truth manifestly expressed. Imagine that someone needs food or clothing or anything else. This person must ask these things of the person who is able to give them. We should ask this freedom of people who are not in fact scandalized by it; for not everyone is edified by it. Someone who possesses discernment will be edified and rejoice; another who does not have discernment may be scandalized. Anyone who uses such freedom should not use it passionately, in order to satisfy the passion that troubles him, but only in order to fulfill his need. If no one else is scandalized, and if one's own passion is not satisfied, then the freedom here is good. One should also pay attention not to use such freedom before another person who may be easily scandalized by it. If it is possible, then, one ought to ask whatever one wants privately from the person who is able to give it, in order for another brother's thought to remain unharmed. Take another example. It may happen that, being tired, you need to eat quickly. Yet, when your brother hears this, he is actually scandalized. Or perhaps you may ask about something, and your brother is not in fact edified.

Therefore, as we have said, freedom is good when it occurs in godly fear. If you require something but do not inquire about it, then you may wait for that person to offer it of his own accord; yet he may not happen to know that you need it, or he may know but happen to forget that you need it; or, again, perhaps he wishes to test you and keeps it in order to see if you have patience. Nonetheless, you are the one found to be grumbling against him and scandalized by him, and therefore in sin. Now, if you in fact openly tell him what you want, none of this would happen. Prepare your thought in advance, however, so that, even if after asking for what you want you still do not receive this, you may not be afflicted or scandalized or grumble. Simply say to your thought: "Either he is unable to give me what I want, or else I am unworthy and therefore God did not allow him to give it to me." Be careful also that you do not look to the impending failure and consequently cut off your freedom with regard to that person. For then, you will not be able to approach him again in order to ask for something else that you happen to need. In every way, keep yourself calm in failure. Now, on the other hand, if someone should ask you whether you actually need something, then tell him the truth. If you are distracted and happen to say that you do not in fact need it, take hold of yourself and say: "Forgive me; for I was taken by surprise; however, in fact I do need to receive it."

LETTER 377

Question from the same person: "What happens when I am unsure as to who is actually being scandalized by such freedom? What should I do then?" Response by John.

You are able to test him in order to see whether he is scandalized or not. For instance, if you need to eat, do not say: "Give me some food." Rather, say: "I see that I am hungry for one reason or another." When he hears this, he will reveal himself; and in this way, you will learn his disposition, as to whether or not he is scandalized.

LETTER 378

Question from the same person to the same Old Man: "How is it that, when the Great Old Man was asked by brother John whether he should abstain from eating dried fruit, he permitted him to partake of whatever he was offered, but advised him not to ask to receive any? Does it seem, then, that he was preventing him here from exercising his freedom?" Response by John.

The thought was suggesting to brother John not to eat at all. When the Great Old Man was asked about this, he told him that this was suggested by the demons. Wanting to rebuke them, he said: "Do not ask for anything of your own accord, and you will understand the evil of the enemy." For the one telling you not to eat at all is the same one who suggests that you grumble if you receive only a little piece instead of the entire portion. Therefore, this is precisely why he responded in this way. In any case, he did not give him a command. Wherever there is no command, then it is always beneficial to practice freedom.

LETTER 379

A brother asked the Great Old Man: "I pray you, lord abba, on account of my soul, which is wounded; I have long wanted to entreat you about this but was afraid, saying: 'Perhaps I will not apply his words and am merely putting the Spirit of the Lord to the test.'[44] Yet my abba told me that not asking is in fact a great fall for the soul. I entreat you, therefore, to pray to the Lord for me and to declare to me how I might be saved. And forgive me." Response by Barsanuphius.

Brother, you have woken up a little late, long after your wounds have grown foul and festered.[45] Nevertheless, if you wish to be saved, repent and cut off all those seeds of death, and say with David: "Now, I am beginning."[46] From now on, then, cut off all of your desires and your pretense to rights, as well as your scorn and neglectfulness. And in their place, acquire humility, obedience, and submission. Reckon yourself as being completely annihilated in all things, and you will be saved. If you guard these things, then you will be guarded from every evil;[47] otherwise, it is up to you. For you will be interrogated on that terrible day. You will not only be condemned for the times when you asked scornful questions, but also all these things will be demanded of you, now and for the future. Therefore, pay attention to yourself and do not lose your reward,[48] or rather your opportunity, by neglecting your own salvation, which the Lord loves.

LETTER 380

Question by the same person to the Other Old Man: "What does it mean to cut off one's own will?" Response by John.

Cutting off one's own will is precisely what progress according to God is all about. It implies cutting off one's individual will in good things and doing the will of the saints; in regard to evil things, it implies avoiding anything improper of one's own accord.

44. Cf. Acts 5.9.   45. Cf. Ps 37.6.
46. Cf. Ps 76.11.   47. Cf. Ps 120.7.
48. Cf. Mt 10.42.

LETTER 381

Question from the same person to the same Old Man: "When-ever I ask about subtle thoughts, my thought grows arrogant, thinking that it possesses some acuity with regard to such mat-ters." Response.

If you want to ask some of the fathers about subtle thoughts without feeling arrogant, remember that one is first required to correct the greater thoughts, which are forbidden by the Apostle, such as fornication, debauchery, envy, and the like.[49] Subsequently, we should also not despise the subtle ones. For someone who strives in regard to the subtle thoughts and ig-nores the greater ones resembles a person who has a filthy house, filled with shameless materials, and yet in the midst of them there also lie some wisps of straw. Then, in an effort to clean the house, this person begins by removing the straw but leaves behind the rocks and other materials over which he is literally tripping. Now, even if he removes the straw, the house assumes no beauty; but if he removes the rocks and other mate-rials, then he would not even be able to leave behind the straw because this would detract from the house's beauty. This is how our Savior reproached the Pharisees and the Sadducees, when he said to them: "Woe to you! For you tithe mint, dill, and cum-min, and have neglected the weightier matters of the law, which you ought to have practiced without neglecting the others."[50]

LETTER 382

A Christ-loving layperson asked the same Old Man: "If someone asks an elder about some matter and the elder tells him to do something, but then the same person hesitates—whether out of apparently difficult or contradictory circumstances—is that per-son still condemned as lacking faith?" Response by John.

If the person asking is a struggler, then he will denounce his own lack of faith, believing that the Holy Spirit does not lie

49. Cf. Gal 5.19–21.
50. Cf. Mt 23.23.

when it speaks through the mouth of its saints, as it wills; for it is said: "God has spoken through his saint[s]."[51] Indeed, if that person does not believe that God is the one speaking through the mouth of the one who is being asked, then the person asking is indeed lacking in faith and condemned from the outset. If, however, he believes but afterward hesitates, then he should correct himself, hearing Ecclesiastes saying: "The righteous person falls and rises seven times a day."[52]

One should also pay attention to the fact that, often, God has spoken through the sacred Scriptures about his servants; yet, at least from what is apparent, the opposite occurred to them. For example, God said: "I shall glorify those who glorify me";[53] nonetheless, we find some of the saints still living in dishonor and great affliction until their death. Could we say, then, that God did not in fact glorify these? Indeed, he glorified them exceedingly; however, those who do not see with the eyes of the heart[54] are unable to see their glory.

For it is through such humility that Job was exceedingly glorified. Although in the human eyes of his friends, he was reckoned to suffer what he deserved, later he heard from the divine voice: "Will you even put me in the wrong? Will you condemn me that you may be justified?"[55] Lazarus, too, who was a pauper sitting at the gate of a rich man in great contempt and bodily affliction, exceedingly glorified God through his patience. While we have observed that God glorifies those who glorify him,[56] yet it appeared that the opposite happened to Lazarus, who remained in great affliction until his death. Later, however, it was revealed how God glorified him, placing him in the bosom of Abraham.[57]

Indeed, what can we say about the holy Paul, who was deemed worthy of contemplating[58] the very Son of God and of hearing his divine voice?[59] About him, God bore witness that he would

---

51. Cf. Ps 59.8 and 107.8.   52. Prv 24.16.
53. 1 Sm 2.30.   54. Cf. Eph 1.18.
55. Jb 40.8.   56. Cf. 1 Sm 2.30.
57. Cf. Lk 16.20–22.
58. Lit., "receiving a vision of" (ἀξιωθέντος τῆς θεωρίας).
59. Cf. 1 Cor 15.8.

be "a chosen vessel."[60] Then he was taken up into the heavens, which no person had seen, where he heard ineffable[61] words.[62] Nevertheless, this same person was let down twice in a basket and in a net;[63] was this not worthy of scandal for those who were lacking in faith or discernment? Yet this was precisely the same Paul who was deemed worthy of divine grace. This happened for the testing of many, in order to see whether they would keep the same faith in the Apostle.

The same thing happened also to the rest of the saints for the benefit of those who approach them.[64] Why, however, do we even speak of mortals, when the Savior himself prayed, saying: "Father, if it is possible, let this cup pass from me."[65] When the apostles heard this, they were scandalized, not knowing that everything in fact occurred according to dispensation for the benefit of us humans.

Therefore, the same thing is happening here. It is not occurring for the weakness of the person being asked or praying, but for the testing and confirmation of the faith in those who approach, in order to see whether they would remain firm in their faith to the very end. For if they remain firm in this up to the final conclusion of the situation, they shall indeed see God's glory coming upon them. There are some who ask in the hope of achieving something fleshly, and not in fact for the benefit of the soul. Such people may quickly achieve [what they want]. Yet why do we not instead pay attention to those who were around Azariah and Hananiah? These placed their trust in God, who could save them from the furnace; so they said to the king: "We have our God in the heavens, who is able to deliver us from the furnace of blazing fire and out of your hand, as long as we do not worship your gods."[66] Nevertheless, God did not immediately glorify them; rather, he left them until they offered themselves to the furnace. Then, as their total trust in God became apparent to everyone, he delivered and glorified them, leaving them behind as an example for those who doubt the toler-

60. Acts 9.15.
61. Lit., "unspeakable" (ἄρρητα).
62. Cf. 2 Cor 12.4.
63. Cf. Acts 9.25; 2 Cor 11.33.
64. Cf. Heb 7.25 and 10.1.
65. Mt 26.39.
66. Cf. Dn 3.16–17.

perfect in every way both for assistance and for the salvation of
our soul. If, after receiving a mandate, we come across torment
and affliction in the situation at hand, or else if God allows us to
fall into temptation along the way, let us not despair or regard
those who gave us the mandate as being weak, or be scandalized in them because after their mandate we lost something or
were physically hurt.[85] Rather, let us remember that the sacred
Apostle himself, who was strong, perfect, and holy, fell into all
of these things, boasting: "What dangers I have endured! Yet
the Lord rescued me from all of them";[86] remember also that:
"Many are the afflictions of the righteous, but the Lord rescues
them from them all,"[87] and that: "It is through many persecu-
tions that we must enter the kingdom of heaven."[88] Again: "The
untempted is also untested and unproven."[89]

Let us also bear in mind that no good thing is perfected without affliction; for it has the devil's envy opposing it. Now, if we
happen to come out without affliction, let us not become arrogant, believing that we were worthy of being saved from affliction; rather, [let us believe] that God knew our weakness, and
that we are unable to endure affliction, and so he protected us
from affliction by means of the saints' mandate. Indeed, about
those who endured in affliction or temptation, it is also written: "Blessed is the one who endures temptation; such a one has
stood the test,"[90] and so on.

Moreover, be careful not to travel negligently on your way,
simply because you have a mandate from the saints. Rather, if
you hear anything along the way either about robbers or anything else, you should protect yourself and do your best not to
fall among such circumstances. Instead, pray to God and remember the mandate of the saints; and be sure to journey that
way together with others or else to ask in what way you might
pass by there safely, perhaps through some other route. If, however, you wish to pass by that way for some pious reason or else
to visit the holy fathers, and you happen to hear about robbers

85. Cf. 2 Cor 6.5.   86. 2 Tm 3.11.
87. Ps 33.19.   88. Acts 14.22.
89. *Agraphon*, no. 90.   90. Jas 1.12.

or other dangers on the road, do not presume to travel along that way without any security, so that you might in this way avoid pride and danger. One should not voluntarily place oneself in temptation, but only gratefully endure the temptation that comes one's way by God's permission. For we also have the example of certain saints, who wanted to travel and visit certain other saints that lived in the deeper desert; however, when they heard about robbers and other afflictions, they delayed their journey. This is how we acquire humility. So, if you either know or have heard that a particular road will cause you affliction, try to ask your abbot, saying: "What do you think I should do?" And do whatever he tells you. Now, if you happen to forget to tell him and find yourself on the road for some mandate, and then on the way you remember that you forgot to tell him, it is not necessary to return. Nevertheless, pray to God, saying: "Master, forgive my negligence, and through the mandate of your saint and the goodness of your compassion, teach me to do your will,[91] save me and protect me from every evil and every wicked thing.[92] For your name is glorified to the ages. Amen."

LETTER 387

From the same [brother] to the same Old Man: "Is the faith of one person able to benefit another who does not have faith, just as the paralytic was helped by the faith of those who bore him?"[93] Response.

If the paralytic was not also faithful, then he would not have allowed them to bear him and let him down; so it is the faith of both that in fact saved him. Therefore, unless a person places his faith in God, he receives no benefit. Do not, then, pretend that you can do nothing and cast your entire burden onto others.[94] For even though Jeremiah believed that God would be merciful to the people, yet he still prayed for them. Because, however, the people did not also contribute their faith to his, this is why he was not heard.[95] Where, too, was the faith of the prophet?

91. Cf. Ps 142.10.
93. Cf. Mk 2.3–5.
95. Cf. Jer 11.14.
92. Cf. Ps 120.7.
94. Cf. Lk 11.46.

Did he not have the same faith as those who carried the paralytic? Surely, the fault lay with the people. The same applies to other similar cases. For it is not without reason that it is said: "The prayer of the righteous is very powerful and effective."[96]

LETTER 388

Question from the same [brother] to the same [Old Man]: "Father, I ask you to tell me how it is that the daughter of the Canaanite woman[97] and the servant of the centurion[98] contributed [to their faith] in order that they may be healed. Even the other paralytic only asked for bodily health, and yet he first received forgiveness of sins.[99] Therefore, where is their contribution in this case? The Lord, too, says to the apostles: 'Whatever you loose on this earth shall also be loosed in heaven,'[100] and: 'If you forgive the sins of any, they are forgiven them.'[101] He did not say: 'If they contribute.' So please explain this to me." Response.

Brother, affliction comes to those who do not understand how things are. For the daughter of the Canaanite woman and the servant of the centurion had lost their minds: the first from madness, the second from the danger of the illness. So they were unable to contribute to the faith of those who were praying for them. The paralytic contributed his faith to the healing of body and was deemed worthy of receiving something greater through the loving-kindness of the Master. For the Savior himself, in order that people may believe that he had come, from the very outset performed signs without the cooperation [of those healed]; and yet people were healed gratuitously, in order that the word of the prophet might be fulfilled: "He has borne our infirmities and carried our diseases."[102]

Therefore, people were justified of their sins and were healed by his grace, without their contribution being demanded, except insofar as they should keep this afterward, as it is said: "Behold, you have been made well; do not sin any more, so that nothing worse happens to you."[103] About him, John again says: "Behold,

96. Cf. Jas 5.16.
98. Cf. Lk 7.2.
100. Mt 18.18.
102. Is 53.4.

97. Cf. Mt 15.21–28.
99. Cf. Mt 9.2–6.
101. Jn 20.23.
103. Jn 5.14.

the Lamb of God, who takes away the sin of the world."[104] Look at what he says: "Of the whole world." Those who did not accept him, however, did not receive healing; and about these, the word is fulfilled: "If the unbeliever separates, let it be so."[105] He also gave to the apostles the authority to heal and to forgive the sins of those who contributed with their prayer.[106] Let James himself, who received such an authority, convince you, when he says: "The prayer of the righteous is very powerful and effective."[107] Therefore, the prayer became effective in the case of the apostles and the other saints; but it was different in the case of the Savior. In his case, all those who accepted him were saved and healed. Those who did not accept him, but instead pushed him away, perished. Let us, then, become established in the faith in order that we may be saved in the name of God, to whom is due glory to the ages. Amen.

LETTER 389

Question from the same person to the same [Old Man]: "Master, I entreat you to teach me what was the fault of the disciple of the holy Elisha, that the dead man was not raised. Moreover, why did the prophet send him, when he knew in advance what would happen? Or why did he not correct him in advance before sending him?"[108] Response.

Could it be that Elisha sent his disciple in order to despise him? Surely not, but he did so in order to teach him that it is a good thing not to despise a person, thereby bringing him to repentance, that he might believe and raise the dead. Yet the disciple remained in the same condition; and so, on account of his lack of faith, he was in fact unable to raise the dead. The prophet knew of course that he would not raise the dead; however, in order to remove any excuse from him, since he had been advised but had not understood, he did send him.

The same thing happened with the Lord, who knew that Judas was a traitor, and yet he did not despise him until his last

---

104. Jn 1.29.
106. Cf. Mt 10.1; Jn 20.23.
108. Cf. 2 Kgs 4.29–31.

105. 1 Cor 7.15.
107. Cf. Jas 5.16.

breath. Instead, he advised him without ignoring him, until he perished entirely; for people are endowed with free will. In order also to reveal that neither God nor the saints are the cause of evils, but rather people are themselves to blame for their own evils, he allowed them their freedom so that they may be without any excuse on the day of judgment, when each would accuse the other.

LETTER 390

Certain brothers living in a monastery, who were delivered of many temptations through the prayers of the holy fathers, heard about an impending assault by robbers and were going to leave the monastery. So they asked the Great Old Man about this. Response by Barsanuphius.

We have the experience of the loving-kindness of our Master and God, who has delivered us from many afflictions and temptations. Let us now also not doubt that he will deliver and protect us from every evil.[109] Therefore, let us cast [all] our anxiety and hope upon him;[110] wherever you may happen to live, through the prayers of the saints, do not be concerned about any evil. Instead, stand firm in the faith of Christ,[111] chanting with the prophet David: "The Lord is my help, and I shall not fear what any mortal can do to me,"[112] and so on, as well as: "The Lord will keep you from all evil; the Lord will keep your life. The Lord will keep your going out and your coming in, from this time on and forevermore."[113]

Be careful, then, in order that people do not learn that, while you have God, yet you still fear people. "Even though I walk through the shadow of death, I shall fear no evil; for you are with me."[114] Tell the soul that is lacking in faith to acquire courage. The Lord of hosts is with us; the God of Jacob is our protector. All of us greet you in the Lord, saying: "It is I; do not be afraid."[115]

---

109. Cf. Ps 120.7.
111. Cf. 1 Cor 16.13.
113. Ps 120.7–8.
115. Mt 14.27.

110. Cf. 1 Pt 5.7.
112. Ps 117.6.
114. Ps 22.4.

LETTER 391

A brother, who heard about this response, declared to the same Old Man: "I entreat you to tell me: should someone, then, who lives in a place where there are robbers, have such confidence as to live there without fear?" Response by Barsanuphius.

We should always have confidence in Jesus, who "does not allow us to be tested beyond our strength."[116] Nevertheless, since he himself taught us, saying: "Pray that you may not come into temptation,"[117] we should not throw ourselves into temptation; for this would be transgressing the commandment of God, and we would be delivering ourselves unto death. Instead, we should guard ourselves. If, however, we are living in a peaceful place and happen to hear about an assault by robbers, we should not be troubled, because we have the protection of God. For God sees that we have not led ourselves into temptation or transgressed his commandment. Rather, we have kept this commandment, crying out day and night: "Do not lead us into temptation, but deliver us from the evil one."[118]

Therefore, if we are praying in this way and some temptation or assault by robbers befalls us, we should not surrender; for this is happening in order to test us, and God is allowing it to happen for our benefit. If, then, it is allowed to happen, we have the support of the teaching of the Apostle, who says: "God is faithful, and he will not let you be tested beyond your strength; but with the testing, he will also provide the way out, so that you may be able to endure it."[119]

For if we leave one place for another on the basis of hearsay, the devil is able to prevent us from being able to remain in any one place. When, however, we know with certainty about a particular place, where there is suspicion of danger, we should also protect ourselves. If the place is peaceful and temptation suddenly arises, God will see that it is not our fault and will protect us according to his will.

Indeed, there is temptation that is provoked by us, and there

116. 1 Cor 10.13.   117. Mt 26.41.
118. Mt 6.13.   119. 1 Cor 10.13.

is temptation that is permitted by God. The one provoked by us is harmful to the soul; it is about this that James the apostle cried out, saying: "No one, when tempted, should say, 'I am being tempted by God'; for God cannot be tempted by evil,"[120] and so on. The one permitted by God is beneficial for the soul and occurs to people in order to test them. "And endurance leads a person to hope, and hope does not disappoint us,"[121] according to what is written. Whosoever is not disappointed has been saved, in Christ Jesus our Lord, to whom be the glory to the ages. Amen.

LETTER 392

Question from the same person to the same [Old Man]: "It is said: 'Prove me, Lord, and test me';[122] and again: 'Whenever you fall into trials of any kind, rejoice';[123] and elsewhere: 'Lord, do not lead us into temptation';[124] as well as: 'Pray that you may not enter into temptation.'[125] Are these texts contradictory? Moreover, I entreat you to teach me the difference between the various temptations." Response by Barsanuphius.

The phrase: "Prove me, Lord, and test me"[126] belongs to someone who is struggling and who is asking to be tested through temptation with God's permission, so long as such a person is able to maintain patience in the affliction of the temptation. Indeed, patience in trials, as already said, also leads a person to the remainder of goods.[127] Here precisely is where joy and progress are found. For the will of the person struggling does not consent but in fact resists; and so he gives himself to labor in order not to be conquered by the temptation. The phrase: "Do not lead us into temptation"[128] signifies the following: "Do not allow us to be tempted by our own will and desire." For falling into such temptation gives rise to death. In regard to this, the Savior says: "Pray that you may not enter into temptation."[129] This is why a righteous people will offer both prayers, asking on

120. Jas 1.13.   121. Rom 5.4.
122. Ps 25.2.   123. Jas 1.2.
124. Mt 6.13.   125. Mt 26.41.
126. Ps 25.2.   127. Cf. Rom 5.4.
128. Mt 6.13.   129. Mt 26.41.

the one hand to be tempted with the permission of God in order to be tested for salvation, while asking on the other hand not to be tempted by their own wills and desires in order not to lose their souls.

Question from the same [brother]: "How can I acquire unswerving godly fear in my hard heart?[130] Moreover, when I am doing something, even before completing it, I transfer my intellect from that to something else, supposedly on the pretext of godly fear. Is this a good thing or not?" Response.

Those who want always to keep the fear of God in their hearts may understand [how to do this] through the following example. When someone wants to travel somewhere, one wears sandals. For Scripture says that sandals are a sign of preparation.[131] It is also written: "I was prepared and was not troubled."[132] Therefore, if one understands that one is about to perform some task, then that person should learn from this fleshly preparation how to prepare spiritually. Wearing spiritual sandals means being prepared with godly fear and remembering that everything should be done with fear of God, thereby preparing the heart to invoke God in order that he might bestow on us the fear of him.[133] For in placing such fear before our eyes in everything, it gradually becomes unswerving in the heart as well.

One should also be careful not to transfer one's intellect from the task at hand to some other matter, pretending that this is out of godly fear. For this is not in fact the correct way;[134] instead, it is distraction and deceit by the enemy. Rather, in every important task, one should strive hard to have godly fear within oneself. It is also necessary to be attached to the holy fathers in order that, from their example, word, sighing, and good life, we may be filled with compunction according to God. (For even the sheep of Jacob, which paid attention to the rods in the water, conceived and gave birth in accordance with the

130. Cf. Ex 13.16; Prv 17.20. 131. Eph 6.15.
132. Cf. Ps 118.60. 133. Cf. Ps 85.11.
134. Cf. Ezek 33.17.

rods.)[135] If we impress on ourselves their examples, in order to deal with matters in the same way, we shall not delay in traveling the same journey as they.

LETTER 394

Question from the same [brother] to the same Old Man: "Often the memory of godly fear comes to me, and immediately I remember the judgment and am touched by compunction. How, then, should I receive such a memory?" Response.

At whatever time such a memory comes to you, namely, compunction over what you have done wrong either in knowledge or in ignorance, be careful lest this occurs to you through the action of the devil unto greater condemnation. And if you say: "Then, how do I distinguish genuine compunction from the one caused by the devil?" listen. Whenever such a memory comes to you and you strive to show correction in your deeds, this is genuine compunction, through which sins are forgiven. If, however, you see that you are touched by compunction after this memory, and yet you still fall into the same sins or even worse ones, then you should know that this memory comes from the enemy, who suggests this memory to you only in order to condemn your soul. Therefore, behold, the two ways are clear for you. If you want to fear condemnation, avoid its works.

LETTER 395

Question from the same [brother] to the same Old Man: "When is it the proper moment to assume the memory of godly fear in one's intellect, in order thereby to be touched by compunction and to correct one's sins?" Response.

Fire is by nature warmer; so one who wants to use fire will not always kindle it but will want to conceal the fire in order to be able to kindle it for warmth when one wishes. The same must be done in this case, too. For suggestions appear from the enemy, who sows his seed inopportunely by transforming himself[136]

135. Cf. Gn 30.37–40.
136. Cf. 2 Cor 11.13–15.

into godly fear, desiring either to throw us into sorrow or else to trouble our intellect, while we have no opportunity to discern the origin of the thought, on the basis of the pretext of being preoccupied with the task at hand. For such is also the art of those who pillage people's houses. If they do not find them preoccupied with something else, they are unable to empty their house.

Always remember Ecclesiastes, which says: "There is a time for everything,"[137] and say to yourself: "I shall first do what is at hand with fear of God, and then I shall be at leisure to carry out whatever I have thought of, not through my own wisdom but with the strength and energy of God, who tests hearts and minds."[138] You should determine an appropriate time for this, in the morning or evening, in order to discern your thoughts with regard to what happened during the night or day. And if you notice some mistake, then strive to correct it, with the assistance of Christ.

LETTER 396

Question from the same [brother] to the same [Old Man]: "Often, forgetfulness comes upon me and disperses the memory of many of my sins; there are times when I cannot even remember them at all. What should I do?" Response by Barsanuphius.

There are some people who are unlettered but who have genuine associates, in whom they have confidence, and who, should they forget something, always remind them, saying: "We shall repay you whatever you think we owe you." Are you perhaps able to find some associate that is more genuine than God, who knows even those things that have not occurred? Commit to him, then, all those faults that you have forgotten, and tell him: "Master, this, too, is a mistake, namely, forgetting my own transgressions; for it is before you alone, who know the heart, that I have sinned in every way.[139] Forgive me everything according to your loving-kindness. Indeed, this reveals the majesty of

---

137. Eccl 3.1.   138. Cf. Ps 7.10.
139. Cf. Ps 50.6; Acts 1.24.

your glory, inasmuch as you do not treat sinners according to their sins. For you are glorified to the ages. Amen."

LETTER 397

Question from the same [brother] to the same [Old Man]: "There are times when I am scandalized by something, and at once it is revealed that I was not right to be scandalized; so, afterward, I am embarrassed by this. Is this perhaps from God for my correction, or is it from the devil for my condemnation?" Response by Barsanuphius.

If we pay attention to the meaning of the previous response, we shall find that the response is similar in the case of this question. It was said in that response that unless we manifest in our deeds the memory of godly fear and the compunction that results from this, then we are condemned. The same, then, applies here. For if we correct in our deeds that of which we are ashamed, then this derives from God for the sake of our salvation; otherwise, it is the suggestion of the devil unto even greater condemnation.

LETTER 398

Question from the same [brother]: "If I lose something and yet, for fear of condemnation, do not at first accuse anyone of possessing it, but afterward if I suspect that some person has it, is it improper to test whether in fact he does have it? For I cannot bear losing it." Response by Barsanuphius.

It is not improper to test whether he has what you lost. If, however, he is found actually to have it, then do not try to shame him, but be content with its recovery.

LETTERS TO LAYPERSONS AND
TO MONKS (399–462)

LETTER 399

A Christ-loving layperson confessed his sins to the same Old Man, also requesting forgiveness for them. In response, the Old Man said the following.

HOEVER manifests his sins is justified of these, according to the Scripture that says: "Admit your sins first, so that you may be justified."[1] And again: "I said, 'I will confess my transgressions to the Lord,' and you forgave the impiety of my heart."[2] Therefore, brother, let us henceforth guard ourselves; however, as for our previous sins, behold, God has forgiven them.

LETTER 400

The same person asked the same Old Man: "Tell me, father, how it is that my soul has many wounds but does not weep." Response by Barsanuphius.

Anyone who perceives what he has lost will want to weep for that. Anyone who desires something will endure many travels and tribulations in order to achieve that which is desired.

LETTER 401

The same person asked the same Old Man: "If one wants to do something good, but does so for one's own benefit or else for some other personal desire, is this still counted as righteousness for him?" Response by Barsanuphius.

1. Is 43.26.
2. Cf. Ps 31.5.

We know that when someone is fasting and mixes this fasting with anything at all from his own will, or else looks for human glory and profit from this, then his fasting is an abomination to God. For the Israelites, too, fasted, but because they enacted injustices during the days of the fast, fulfilling their own desires, God reproached them through the prophet Isaiah, saying: "Such is not the fast that I have chosen, says the Lord."[3] So it is in this case. Every good deed that is not performed for—and only for—the love of God, but rather for one's own will, is found to be something polluted and causes God to flee.

We learn this also from the divine law; for it is said: "You shall not sow your vineyard with mixed seed, and you shall not wear clothes made of wool and linen woven together."[4] And if we wish to know that this is actually written about the workers [of virtue], Ecclesiastes shows us when it says: "Let your garments always be white."[5] This means that our work must always be pure. Nevertheless, if what is done also contains something from our own will, then that work is polluted and is unpleasing to God. The Lord, too, spoke to his disciples about such works: "Beware of false prophets, who come to you in sheep's clothing, but inwardly are ravenous wolves. You will know them by their fruits."[6] Therefore, let us strive to perform the work of God for no other reason but for God alone; for if this does not so occur, then God has no need of us to perform his own work. God is never short of people through whom he wishes to perform his work without reproach. In doing good, then, let us be vigilant, lest we render our toil worthless through our own will.

LETTER 402

Question from the same [brother] to the same [Old Man]: "Although I am slow in learning, nevertheless I am able to learn the Psalms more quickly. Tell me whether this has happened to me from God, or else from the demons in order that I might come to vainglory." Response by Barsanuphius.

---

3. Cf. Is 58.5.   4. Cf. Dt 22.9–11.
5. Eccl 9.8.   6. Mt 7.15–16.

Whatever God grants you, receive it with humility. For to learn the words of God easily does not actually come from the devil, but they are·in fact a seed from God. If, however, one is not careful, then the devil, too, sows his own tares. If you want to humble your thought, give it the following example: "If one receives from the master certain silver coins, as in [the story of] those servants,[7] but does not make some profit or increase, then what will happen?" And your thought will respond: "Whatever happened to that servant who hid the silver of the master."[8] Then you can say to your thought: "So do not feel proud, filling the air with fruitless words, because these shall be to my condemnation."

LETTER 403

Question from the same [brother] to the same [Old Man]: "If good comes from God, and it is also given to sinners, then why is it given to the latter?" Response by Barsanuphius.

Every good gift, as it is evident, comes from God.[9] For since he is good, everything good comes from him. Good things, however, are granted to the righteous as being worthy and to sinners as a benefit to help them to come to repentance, according to the holy Paul, who says: "I am the first among sinners, but for that very reason I received mercy so that in me, as the foremost, Jesus Christ might display the utmost patience."[10]

LETTER 404

Question from the same person to the same [Old Man]: "How is it possible to give thanks [to God] worthily?" Response.

People who are nothing forgive others for even a wretched deed, or relieve others from terrible afflictions, so that they profess their gratitude and proclaim to everyone the good [that was received]. How much more so, then, should we give thanks, who receive benefits from God in every way! With what words can we ever thank him, who before all else created us, then offered us

7. Cf. Mt 25.14.   8. Cf. Mt 25.24–30.
9. Cf. Jas 1.17.   10. 1 Tm 1.15–16.

assistance against our enemies by giving us prudence of heart, health of body, light in our eyes, breath of life, and, above all, a place of repentance as well as the reception of his body and blood for the forgiveness of sins and the establishment of our heart. For it is written: "Bread to strengthen the human heart."[11] And if anyone thinks that this refers to material bread, then how is it that the Spirit again says: "One does not live by bread alone, but by every word that comes from the mouth of God"?[12]

So if people give rewards and thanks for material and corruptible things, what can we ever give in return to the one who was crucified for us, if we in turn wish to be grateful? We should endure everything for him until death. Do not, then, toil in your effort to understand the gratitude that people, and especially sinners, owe to God; for he died for them. If someone goes to prison for you, you will want to thank that person exceedingly. How much more so for the one who dies for you? Learn this, too; we never come to the point of thanking God worthily. Nevertheless, let us thank him as much as we can, with our mouth and heart, and he is so kind and loving toward us that he will count and number us with the two copper coins of that widow.[13] Enough, however, for the sinners who want to give thanks; because the righteous give more than thanks, even when they are cut up and put to death, according to the holy Paul, who says: "Give thanks,"[14] obviously to God. To him be the glory to the ages. Amen.

LETTER 405

Question from the same person to the same Old Man: "Is it possible for the demons to do good to anyone? And how is it revealed whether this good comes from the demons? And what is the difference between this and a divine gift?" Response by Barsanuphius.

There is a possibility, theoretically, that good can come to someone from the evil one with the purpose of deceit. Every good, however, that comes from the devil in order to deceive us,

11. Ps 103.15.   12. Dt 8.3.
13. Cf. Mk 12.42.   14. 1 Thes 5.18.

upon closer examination, is found only to be disguise. For he is a liar, and one cannot find truth in him, as the final result will display. Indeed, the final result of his light is darkness, according to the Apostle, who says about the angels of the devil that they can be disguised into ministers of righteousness: "Their end will match their deeds";[15] and according to the Savior, who says: "You will know them by their fruits."[16]

So if you investigate with knowledge and discernment, you will certainly find that, in the supposed good that comes from the devil, there is no trace of good but only vainglory or turmoil or something else similar; on the other hand, God's good always abounds in illumination and humility of heart, bringing us to calmness. Now, if we unknowingly suffer some harm from the deceit of the evil one, and later learn about this temptation, let us return to ourselves and take refuge in the one who alone can abolish this temptation. It is also necessary to know that the saints immediately and easily perceive this difference, whereas sinners only perceive it at the end. Just as when an experienced goldsmith receives gold, he is able to say what it is even before putting it through fire, whereas an inexperienced person will know only after putting it through fire.

LETTER 406

Question: "Once the supposed good of the demons is exposed, explain to me how one can escape the danger that derives from it." Response.

We are always obliged to regard good as being good. If, however, the good is tested in practice and found in fact to be evil, then it is necessary to reject it in the same way as someone who finds something to drink and thinks that it is good, but upon tasting it discovers it to be bitter. And immediately one spits it from one's mouth, even while one's mouth becomes numb through bitterness. The same happens with chestnuts, almonds, and the like. Of course, that person is not to blame for the taste. If, however, the same person learns about its bitterness and still persists in consuming it, filling his stomach with the bitterness,

15. 2 Cor 11.14–15.   16. Mt 7.16.

then one can only blame oneself. The same also applies here. Therefore, if a person is deceived but afterward learns and says: "I have been deceived; Lord Master, forgive me," he will forgive that person; for he is merciful. Learn this, too, beloved one: God does not allow us to be tested beyond our strength.[17] So in all things, let us offer supplication to him, and he will distinguish for us the good from the supposed good. To him be the glory to the ages. Amen.

LETTER 407

Question from the same person to the same [Old Man]: "If something appears to me to be good, but an opposing thought contradicts it, preventing me from putting it into practice, as not in fact being good, how can I perceive whether it is truly good?" Response.

If the matter appears to you to be according to God and an opposing thought contradicts this, then this is the way of testing whether it is truly from God. If, while we are praying, our heart is strengthened for doing good, and the good increases rather than decreases, then even if the opposing thought persists in afflicting us or whether it does not persist in doing so, we should know that this matter comes from God. For the envy of the devil causes affliction in order to oppose everything good, whereas good increases abundantly through prayer. If, however, the supposed good has been suggested by the devil, which is the reason also for its resistance, then this supposed good will decrease together with the apparent resistance. For the enemy appears to be resisting the thought suggested by it, in order that we may be deceived by it, and in order that we might believe it to be good.

LETTER 408

Question: "So what happens when good occurs without any affliction; is it not from God? And when I happen to perform a small act of charity and find that my thought is not afflicted, have I done this in vain, and will the deed not please God? Please enlighten my heart, father." Response.

17. Cf. 1 Cor 10.13.

If someone does something good and finds that the thought has not been afflicted, then that person should not feel confident that it will completely pass without affliction. For every good comes from God's way; and God is not lying when he says: "The road is narrow and hard that leads to life."[18] Indeed, even if the affliction does not occur at the time of enacting the good, nevertheless one must certainly undergo affliction after the fact. And when one performs the good deed eagerly, then that person may not even perceive the affliction, nor again does that person perceive the variety of ways in which this affliction may occur. If, however, we are willing to examine closely, we shall certainly find it either concealed through vainglory—for this, too, is a result of afflictions—or else in some person who hinders us, or again through our need afterward of the goods that we have given away in charity. Since we do not have it in our hands, we regret [having given it]. And then? Where do we find the thought that is without affliction?

Therefore, this is why we should not become too confident. For to those who lack prudence, the devil preserves the affliction for the very end. Yet one who is always prudent expects at all times to find affliction, whether today or tomorrow, and therefore is never troubled. "I prepared myself," it is said, "and was not troubled."[19] And blessed is the one who always holds before one's eyes the phrase: "The earth is the Lord's, and all that is within it,"[20] believing that he is powerful enough to take care of me, his servant, as he wills. Such a person does not regret what he has given away. And so, if we find affliction, let us learn that God has allowed this in order to test us. For he never overlooks those who fear him, and especially those who do anything for his name.

LETTER 409

Question from the same [brother] to the same [Old Man]: "Does a person ever think anything good of one's own will?" Response.

18. Cf. Mt 7.14.   19. Cf. Ps 118.60.
20. Ps 23.1.

It often happens that a person can think of something good from a movement of the natural thought. It is necessary, however, to ascribe this as well to God; for nature is his creation. And we should know that we cannot even bring it to fruition except through the command of God. For when we hold this command before our eyes, then our heart is strengthened in it to fulfill that good thought.

LETTER 410

Question from the same person to the same [Old Man]: "When I do something good, how should I humble my thought? And how can I bear blame on myself when I have done something good?" Response by Barsanuphius.

In order to humble your thought, when you do what is good and keep all the commandments, remember him who said: "When you have done all that you were ordered to do, say, 'We are worthless slaves; we have only done what we ought to have done.'"[21] How much more so, when we have not yet reached the point of fulfilling even one commandment! This is what you must always think, as well as bearing the blame in regard to the good deed, saying: "I do not know if it will be pleasing to God."[22]

Doing the will of God is a great thing, but fulfilling it is an even greater thing; for it is the completion of all the commandments. Indeed, doing God's will is only a partial deed; certainly it is less than fulfilling it. This is why the Apostle said: "Forgetting what lies behind and straining forward to what lies ahead."[23] So then, as long as one strains forward, there is no stopping, but one always considers oneself as lagging behind, and therefore one continually progresses. For he also said: "Those of us who are mature are of the same mind," namely, in regard to [spiritual] progress; and he added: "If you think differently about anything, this, too, the Lord will reveal to you."[24]

---

21. Lk 17.10.   22. *Sayings*, Agathon 29.
23. Phil 3.13.   24. Cf. Phil 3.15.

LETTER 411

Question: "When I keep a commandment, how can I avoid pride, so that I may know that I have done a good thing and yet at the same time remain estranged from it?" Response.

Brother, we ought to regard good things as indeed good, and hasten toward them as being good. For we should not regard a good thing as being evil, unless one does not practice this good in a manner that is pleasing to God; and then we discover that the good has occurred as evil only on account of the [faulty] discernment in that person. One ought to make every effort always to do what is good, and afterward the grace of God will assist that person to act according to the fear of God. So, when some good is done through you, give thanks to him who grants good;[25] for he alone is good. And blame yourself, saying: "If I had properly performed this task, I would have participated in the good." Then you will find yourself praying to God with compunction, in order that he may render you worthy of the good performed by you.

LETTER 412

Question from the same person to the same [Old Man]: "If I happen to be patient in something, my thought grows proud; what, then, should I think?" Response.

I have already told you that, if you happen to do anything good, you should know that this is a gift from God and comes from his own goodness; for he is merciful to all. Pay attention to yourself, lest on account of your weakness you lose the mercy that comes to you from him, as indeed it also comes to all sinners. So, if he gave it to you well, make sure that you do not lose it inefficiently. The way that you can lose it is as follows: by praising yourself when you are patient, and by forgetting God's benefits to you. As if this were not enough, you also bring judgment on yourself by daring to ascribe this to yourself instead of offer-

---

25. Cf. Jas 1.17.

ing due thanks to God, who is known for his loving-kindness. For the Apostle says: "What do you have, that you have not received? And if you have received it, then why do you boast as if you did not receive it?"[26]

Say to the thought that praises you in any given situation: "Those who sail at sea, even if they happen upon calm weather, yet while they are in the ocean, always expect storm, danger, and shipwreck. Therefore, they could never benefit from a short period of calm. Then, and only then, do they feel safe, when they actually enter the harbor; in fact, many have been shipwrecked even at the entrance to the harbor." In the same way, a sinful person who is still in the world must always tremble at the thought of shipwreck. Therefore, do not be deceived by believing the thought that praises you for a good deed. For good belongs only to God, and we can never be confident that he will stay with us for the sake of our negligence. Therefore, how can we dare to grow proud?

LETTER 413

Question: "If I say to my thought, wanting to humble it, that my patience has not come to me from God but from the evil one, in order to deceive me into feeling proud, am I not irritating God by doing this, since everything good comes from God?" Response.

It is not something very serious to say that this patience has not come from God, and that God is not irritated by this. After all, you are saying this in order to banish the evil thought from you. For indeed, one of the saints once told some people who were visiting him all about their donkey, which died on their way there. Amazed by this, they asked him how it is that he knew, and he told them: "The demons informed me."[27] Although he actually knew from God what had happened, yet for their benefit he responded in this manner; and [as a result] he did not irritate God.

26. 1 Cor 4.7.
27. *Sayings*, Antony 12.

LETTER 414

Question: "If a sinner should acquire certain visions, should that person not believe at all that these are from God?" Response.

When this happens to a sinner, it is clear that it has come from the demons, in order to deceive the wretched soul of that person into destruction. Therefore, one should never believe in these, but one should rather come to know one's own sins and weaknesses, in order always to lead a life in fear and trembling.

LETTER 415

Question: "So should one also turn away from these visions, even when they appear in the form of the Master Christ?" Response.

It is especially then that we should turn away from and anathematize their wickedness and deceit even more so. Brother, never be deceived, therefore, by such demonic assurance. For divine visions certainly occur to the saints, but they are always preceded by calm, peace, and joy in their hearts. Indeed, the saints are always aware of the truth and regard themselves as being unworthy [of such visions]. How much more, then, should sinners never believe these visions, when they are aware of their own unworthiness?

LETTER 416

Question from the same [brother]: "Master, tell me how it is that the devil dares to display our Master Christ or holy Communion, whether in a vision or in our imagination?" Response by Barsanuphius.

The devil can display neither our Master Christ himself nor holy Communion, but rather he lies and assumes the form of any person and of mere bread. He certainly cannot, however, in any way display the holy cross; for he cannot find a way to present it in some other form. He knows that we understand the true sign and shape [of the cross], and so he does not dare to use this. In this sign, his strength was destroyed, and through it he was dealt a mortal wound.

Nevertheless, since we do not know the Master Christ in flesh, therefore the devil is able to tempt us with his lies in order to persuade us that it is truly [Christ], so that we may be destroyed through believing in his deceit as being the truth. Thus, when you see the sign of the cross in your sleep, know that it is a true sign and that this dream comes from God. Nevertheless, strive hard to acquire discernment from the holy fathers, and do not trust your own thought. May the Lord illumine the eyes of your intellect, brother, in order to escape every deceit of the enemy.

LETTER 417

Question: "My thought tells me: 'If the holy cross appears to you, you will be found unworthy, and so you will feel proud.' And yet, afterward, it causes me cowardice and fear." Response.

Do not be concerned about this; for if the holy cross actually appears to you, it will abolish any puffing sense of pride. For wherever God is, there evil is not.

LETTER 418

Question: "I have heard that if a dream appears three times, then it is true. Father, is this so?" Response.

This is not true either. Nor should you believe in any such dream. For the one who appears to us once in the form of a lie can also achieve the same thing three times or even many times. Therefore, do not be ridiculed, brother, but pay close attention to yourself.

LETTER 419

Question: "There are times when I can see in my heart that evil thoughts are surrounding my mind like beasts, without, however, any of my thoughts being harmed in any way. What does this mean?" Response.

This is deceit from the enemy, concealing within itself a sense of pride in order to persuade you that evil thoughts cannot bring any harm to you, and in order that your heart may be thus elated. You should not, however, be deceived; rather, remember your own weakness and sins. And invoke the holy name of God in order that he may assist you against the enemy.

LETTER 420

Question from the same person: "Can one say that the Holy Spirit dwells within a sinner? And if, father, you should say that this is not possible, then how is it that sinners are protected?" Response.

The saints are rendered worthy to possess the Holy Spirit, and they become his temple: "I will place my dwelling in your midst," it is said, "and I will walk among you."[28] Sinners, however, are alienated from the Holy Spirit, in accordance with the words: "Wisdom will not enter a malignant soul."[29] Yet, at the same time, they are protected by the goodness of God. Therefore, let us offer thanks in all circumstances to his ineffable loving-kindness. To him be the glory to the ages. Amen.

LETTER 421

Question: "When I am afflicted in regard to something and am praying, if the ineffable goodness of God assists me, my thought is elated as having been heard. So what should I do?" Response.

When you have been praying and feel that your prayer has been heard, if indeed you are elated, it is clear that you have neither prayed according to God nor have you received the help of God, but rather the feeling that worked in you was from the demons so that your heart might be elated. For whenever assistance comes from God, the soul is never elated; instead, it is always humbled.

The soul will be amazed at how the great mercy of God condescends to show mercy on sinners, who are unworthy and who always irritate him. And that soul offers exceeding thanks to his glorious and ineffable goodness; for he has not handed us what accords with our sins, but rather, in his great forbearance, he shows long-suffering and mercy. And so the soul is no longer elated, but [only trembles] and gives glory.

---

28. Lv 26.11–12; 2 Cor 6.16.
29. Wis 1.4.

LETTER 422

Question: "Father, when I asked you about patience, you said that it, too, like every other good deed, is a gift from God. Yet now you have said, in regard to prayer, that the assistance is not in fact from God. Therefore, please clarify the difference between the two." Response.

If the good deed, namely, prayer, occurred according to vainglory from the very outset, then it was undoubtedly diabolical. Nevertheless, if vainglory was not its beginning, but was in fact received only later, then in this case what originally was begun as good has been destroyed through vainglory, just as when someone builds a wall and then turns around to tear it down. If, however, vainglory has beset you, and you did not consent to receive it, then it did not harm you at all.

LETTER 423

Question: "Often, as I recite the Psalms, I feel that I am growing proud. What, then, should I say to my thought?" Response.

When the heart is elated during recital of the Psalms, remember what has been written: "Let the rebellious not exalt themselves."[30] Rebellion signifies that we are not in fact reciting the Psalms prudently and with fear of God. Examine, then, whether your thought wanders during the recital of the Psalms. You will surely discover that it is indeed distracted, and that you are therefore provoking God.

LETTER 424

Question: "When my thoughts are burdened, whether during recital of the Psalms or else outside of psalmody, and I invoke the name of God in order to assist me, the enemy suggests to me that [God] is causing this elation so that one may think one is doing something good by unceasingly remembering God the Master. What, then, should I make of this?" Response by Barsanuphius.

30. Ps 65.7.

We know that those who are unwell always have need of a doctor and of medication; likewise, those journeying in a storm always hurry to some harbor in case they might be brought to shipwreck. This is also why the prophet cries out, saying: "Lord, you have been our refuge in all generations."[31] And again: "God is our refuge and our strength, a well-proved help in our troubles."[32] If, then, he is our refuge, let us remember that he says: "Call on me in the day of trouble; I will deliver you, and you shall glorify me."[33]

So let us learn that, when the day of trouble arrives, we must invoke the merciful God without ceasing. Moreover, when we invoke the name of God, let us not be elated in our thought. For unless one is utterly foolish, someone who stands accused can never be elated. Since we always have need of God, let our thought never be elated; instead, let us invoke his name for assistance against the enemies. And unless we are crazy, we should never be elated in our thought. For it is in our need that we actually invoke him; and it is in our afflictions that we in fact take refuge in him.

In addition to all this, we learn that unceasingly naming God is like a medicine that dispels not only all of the passions but even the [sinful] act itself. For just as the doctor recommends some medicine or perhaps plaster for the wound of a patient, and this acts within the patient without one even realizing how this occurs, so also the name of God dispels all of the passions when it is invoked, even without us knowing how this actually occurs.

LETTER 425

Question: "When it seems that our thought is calm and not being afflicted, is it not a good thing at that time to refrain from invoking the name of our Master Christ? For my thought suggests to me that, since we are now calm, there is no need for this [invocation]." Response.

31. Ps 89.1.
32. Ps 45.1.
33. Ps 49.15.

We should never have such peace, if we actually consider ourselves as being sinners. For it is said: "There is no peace for the wicked, says the Lord."[34] So if there is no peace for the wicked, then what sort of peace are you experiencing? We should in fact be afraid, because it has been written: "When they speak of peace and security, then all of a sudden destruction comes upon them, as labor pains come upon a pregnant woman, and there will be no escape."[35]

There are also times when the enemies craftily allow the heart to find a little rest, in order that it may not invoke the name of God. For [the demons] are not ignorant of the fact that they are unnerved by the invocation of God's name. Therefore, knowing this, let us not cease invoking the name of God for assistance; indeed, this is the best prayer. Moreover, it is also said: "Pray unceasingly";[36] and "unceasingly" implies without end or limit.

LETTER 426

Question: "When other people, or else even the thoughts in my heart, praise me, and I see that I am being burdened by this, what should I say to myself?" Response.

When your thought praises you and you cannot bypass it without harm, then strive to invoke the name of God; say to yourself: "It has been written: 'My people, those who praise you mislead you, and confuse the course of your paths.'"[37] That this praise, my brother, is nothing else but deceit is made evident in the cry of the prophet: "All people are grass, and a person's glory is like the flower of the field."[38] Anyone who receives praise from others receives no benefit at all; for this is also made clear by our Master: "How can you believe in me, when you accept glory from one another?"[39] And if something occurs according to God, then we should remember: "Let the one who boasts, boast in the Lord."[40] Even the Apostle himself, who reached

34. Is 48.22.
36. 1 Thes 5.17.
38. Is 40.6.
40. 1 Cor 1.31; 2 Cor 10.17; Jer 9.24.

35. 1 Thes 5.3.
37. Is 3.12.
39. Jn 5.44.

such great heights [of perfection], would not boast in himself, but only cried out, saying: "I am what I am by the grace of the Lord."[41] For truly his is the glory in all things and the majesty to the ages. Amen.

Question: "If, while I am reciting the Psalms or praying or reading, some inappropriate thought arises, should I pay attention to it, interrupting my psalmody or prayer or reading in order to oppose it with the appropriate thoughts?" Response.

Show contempt for the thought, and pay close attention to your psalmody, prayer, and reading in order that you may be able to receive strength from the words recited. For if we consent to spend time with the thoughts of the enemy, then we would never have time to do anything good, which is precisely what the enemy is looking for. Indeed, when you notice that you are so congested by such thoughts, that they interfere with your psalmody, prayer, or reading, even then do not struggle against them; for this is not something within your control. Rather, strive to invoke the name of God, and he will come to your assistance, abolishing the machinations of the enemies. For his is the power and the glory to the ages. Amen.

Question: "How can one acquire compunction in prayer, reading, and psalmody?" Response.

Compunction comes to a person from the continuity of remembrance.[42] Therefore, when one is praying, one must prayerfully recall one's actions to memory, remembering how those who do these things are judged, and hearing the fearful voice: "Depart from me, you that are accursed, to the eternal fire,"[43] and so on.

When I speak of remembrance of sins, I do not mean the recollection of specific individual sins, in case the adversary in-

41. Cf. 1 Cor 15.10.
43. Mt 25.41.

42. Cf. *Sayings*, Syncletica 20.

trudes again and brings us into some other form of captivity. I simply mean the remembrance of the fact that, as sinners, we are in fact debtors. And if the hardness remains even after all this, then do not surrender; for often this continuance is prolonged by God for our testing, in order to see if we will endure.

As far as reading and psalmody go, one must keep one's intellect alert to the words of the text and assume within one's soul the meaning[44] concealed in them. If the words are about good deeds, then we should strive to perform good deeds; if they are about the punishment of evil deeds, then we should strive to avoid the expected threat against those who do evil. And by persisting in such recollections, do not surrender if the hardness also happens to persist. For God is merciful and long-suffering, and he awaits our ascetic struggle. Always remember the psalmist, who says: "I waited patiently for the Lord, and he inclined to me,"[45] and so on. As you spend time on these matters, hope that the mercies of God will come upon you quickly.

LETTER 429

Question: "When I try to pay close attention to the meaning of the words of the psalmist, it often happens that they cause me evil thoughts." Response.

If you see that the enemy has craftily used the very words of the Psalms to bring warfare upon you, it is not necessary to stay too closely attached to the meaning of the words, but simply recite these with vigilance and without distraction. For even if you are merely repeating the words, the enemies know their meaning and will not be able to resist you. Then your psalmody will become not merely a supplication to God, but also an abolition of the enemies.

LETTER 430

Question: "When I am reciting the Psalms or else happen to be with other people, and I am afflicted in my thought, if I say the name of God in my heart, since I cannot do so with my mouth, or

---

44. Lit., "power" (τὴν δύναμιν).
45. Ps 39.1.

even if I simply remember his name, is this perhaps not enough to receive divine assistance?" Response by Barsanuphius.

If you are standing in the choir while it is chanting the Psalms, or if you happen to be with other people, and the thought comes to you to say the name of God, do not suppose that, because you are not saying it with your mouth, you are not in fact naming God. Remember that he knows people's hearts and is paying attention to your heart. So go ahead and say his name in your heart. For this is what is said in the Scripture: "Shut your door and pray to your Father, who is in secret."[46] This means that we are to shut our mouth and pray to him within the heart. Therefore, they who shut their mouths and say God's name, or else pray to him in their hearts, are fulfilling this Scripture. Even if you do not mention his name in your heart, but simply remember him therein—indeed, this is still more powerful than saying the name aloud—it is certainly sufficient for you to receive divine assistance.

LETTER 431

Question: "So is it good for someone to meditate or pray constantly in the heart, even if the tongue does not fully cooperate? When this happens to me, my thought sinks and I feel burdened, so that I think I am seeing or imagining things, and I even live in my dreams." Response.

This belongs to the perfect, who are able to direct the intellect and keep it in godly fear, so that it may not deviate and sink to the deepest distraction or imagination. Those who are unable always to maintain their concentration on God, however, grasp hold of themselves and connect the meditation to the tongue as well. For the same occurs with those who swim at sea. Some are experienced swimmers and confidently throw themselves into the water, knowing that the sea cannot sink those experienced in swimming. Yet those who are still novices at these skills, who feel the waters causing them to sink and are afraid of drowning, remove themselves from the ocean to the shore. And

46. Mt 6.6.

after regaining their breath a little, they will again lower themselves into the deep water and continue to make every effort to acquire the skills of swimming completely, until they reach the level of those who have previously mastered them.

LETTER 432

Question: "What does it mean when one of the fathers says that it is not for the thoughts which enter [our intellect] that we are judged, but for handling them badly? Abba Joseph said to one of the brothers: 'Cut off your thoughts quickly'; while to another brother, the same Abba said: 'Let them enter, and exchange conversation with them, in order that you may be tested.'"[47] Response.

When thoughts enter [our intellect], it is like seed being sown, but this is not to our condemnation. When, however, we consent to these thoughts, that is, when we handle them badly, this is certainly to our condemnation. As for the difference between allowing thoughts to enter and cutting them off, it is as follows. Anyone capable of resisting or waging warfare against, and not being defeated by, these thoughts allows them to enter; however, anyone who is weak and unable to do so, possibly even giving one's consent to them, should cut them off in order to flee toward God.

LETTER 433

Question: "Whenever I am in some place where there are relics of holy martyrs, my thought is troubled so that I want to approach and venerate them many times. And whenever I pass by them, my thought suggests that I should bow my head. Is this what I ought to be doing?" Response.

It is not necessary to do this. If you venerate them once, it is sufficient. So do not dwell on this thought, especially if you have already venerated three times of your own accord without being troubled. For we have heard that everything that comes with turmoil and sorrow, as well as anything extreme, comes

47. *Sayings*, Joseph of Panephysis 3.

from the demons.[48] Likewise, bowing your head once, or at most three times, is also enough; but, even then, you should not be constrained by what your thought suggests.

LETTER 434

Question: "When the devil suggests cowardice to me, should I use this as an excuse to enter [my cell] and pray?" Response.

On the excuse of cowardice, do not enter [your cell] to pray; but only do this at the proper time, entering on the excuse that you require prayer in order to implore God and the saints for your salvation.

LETTER 435

Question: "You told me not to enter for the sake of cowardice. When, however, I want to enter [the cell] and pray for my own salvation, [the devil] suggests cowardice to me in order to prevent me from prayer; after all, the order that you gave me was not to enter on the excuse of cowardice." Response.

No, do not take it like that, but enter and pray. For you should not give any consideration to cowardice at all, whether it moves you to prayer or else moves you away from prayer; but simply do everything in its proper time and with fear of God.

LETTER 436

Question: "The same thought troubles me to perform the sign of the cross many times, both during the night as well as during the day." Response by Barsanuphius.

If we are vigilant, then performing the sign of the cross just once—whether during the night or during the day—is sufficient for our protection and salvation. For if we believe that the first sign we perform is clearly valid, then there is no need to do so a second time. Seeking to perform it a second time signifies that we do not reckon the first as being valid. We can see this even in worldly matters. For if one seals a treasure and the first

48. Cf. *Sayings*, Poemen 129.

seal is firm, then there is no need for another seal. Nevertheless, the demons cause this in order to lead us to despondency and carelessness, so that we do not do anything at all with vigilance, instead of performing it only once with purity. This is why we should do the little that we do with godly fear, and this will benefit us more than doing it many times with the turmoil of the enemies. For it is said: "Better is a little that the righteous person has."[49] I say this about the times when they bring disturbance to our vigilance, forcing us to do something inopportunely. Indeed, when we see our thought performing the sign of the cross with joy, neither on account of cowardice nor on account of any other disturbance, then we should understand this as occurring with godly fear; for what we do voluntarily is certainly pleasing to God.

LETTER 437

Question: "If I perform the sign of the cross with my left hand, because I am unable to do so with my right hand, is this improper?" Response.

Well, as for me, whenever I want to perform the sign of the cross over my right hand, I certainly have to use my left hand to do so.

LETTER 438

Question: "When I am praying about a number of important matters, should I remember each of these matters individually in my prayer?" Response.

If you want to pray about many important matters, since God knows what we need,[50] then use the following words: "Master Jesus Christ, guide me according to your will." If you are praying about the passions, simply say: "Heal me according to your will." And if you are praying about temptations, say: "You know what is beneficial to me; help me in my weakness, and grant, according to your will, an end to this temptation."

49. Ps 36.16.
50. Cf. Mt 6.32.

Question: "If I delay in my prayer, should I persist in the same words?" Response.

Not necessarily; but persist in their meaning. This alone is what is necessary to keep to, namely, the will of God, who alone can grant all things. This should be the sole purpose of your prayer, namely, that what is being requested may be in accordance with the will of God.

Question: "If someone wants to handle certain matters in a pious manner, namely, by leaving them to another person, according to God's pleasure, yet the latter does not know how to handle them and cannot find any direction among the fathers, what should he say in prayer?" Response.

Let him pray thus: "Lord, I am in your hands; you know what is beneficial to me; guide me according to your will, and do not allow me to be misled into misusing anything. For all things are yours, and you are Lord of all and of us also. As our Master, then, see that everything occurs in your fear. For yours is the glory to the ages. Amen."

Question: "When I am sitting down, whether reading or doing my handiwork, and want to pray, I am not sure if I should in fact be sitting. The same happens even if I have my head covered. And when I am walking about and want to pray, my thought demands that I turn eastward in order to do so. What should I do, father?" Response.

Whether you are sitting down or walking about, whether you are working or eating, indeed whatever else you are doing—in fact, even if you are performing your bodily need!—then, whether you happen to be turned toward the east or toward the west, nevertheless do not hesitate to pray. For we have been commanded to pray without ceasing[51] and to do so in every place.[52] Again, it has been written: "Prepare the way for the one who rides toward the west; his name is the Lord,"[53] which shows precisely that God is everywhere. Moreover, when you have your head covered, still do not cease praying. Simply make sure that you are not doing so in contempt.

LETTER 442

Question: "My thought tells me that I am sinning in everything [that I do], and that I must say with every word, deed, and thought: 'I have sinned.' For if I am not [continually] confessing my sin, then I might consider myself as being without sin. And I am greatly grieved with both these thoughts. For it is not possible for me to say this every time; yet if I fail to do so, I feel as if I have not sinned." Response by Barsanuphius.

We should always be convinced that we are in all things sinful, alike in deed, word, and thought. But to say every time: "I have sinned" is not possible. In fact, this is an act of the demons, who want to throw us into despondency. Likewise, we should not feel confident to say, each time, that we have not sinned. Instead, let us remember the words of Ecclesiastes: "There is a time to speak and a time to keep silent."[54] And in the morning with regard to the night, as in the evening with regard to the day, let us say with compunction in prayer to God our Master: "Master, forgive me everything for the sake of your holy name, and heal my soul; for I have sinned before you." And this will be sufficient for you. Just as someone who has an agent, from whom one receives various amounts of money, cannot keep full account each time, but simply pays him in full, the same occurs in this case.

LETTER 443

Question: "When I recite the Psalms, my mind wanders or else is distracted. What should I do?" Response.

51. Cf. 1 Thes 5.17.   52. Cf. 1 Tm 2.8.
53. Cf. Ps 67.5.   54. Eccl 3.7.

If your mind wanders, then resume the same Psalm from the last word that you remember. And if this happens once, or twice, or three times, and you cannot even recall which point or find any word that you remember in the part you have just recited, then resume the Psalm from the very beginning. If it happens that you have read through most of the Psalm, in order not to be further interrupted or else fall into despondency, then recite from the following Psalm. For the aim of the enemy is to prevent us from giving glory through forgetfulness. So, then, starting from the following Psalm is a form of doxology; but as for not being distracted, this belongs only to those who have purified senses, whereas we are still weak. When, however, we become conscious of the distraction, let us at least keep vigilant in order to understand the words from that point onward, so that they are not to our condemnation.

LETTER 444

Question: "If I am distracted during prayer, what should I do?" Response.

If you are praying to God and become distracted, struggle until you begin praying without distraction. And keep your intellect alert in order that it does not become too lofty. Nonetheless, should this actually occur, since we are weak, persist to the very end of your prayer; then prick your heart and say with compunction: "Lord, have mercy on me and forgive all of my offenses." And afterward you will receive forgiveness of all your offenses as well as of the distraction that occurred during your prayer.

LETTER 445

Question: "When another brother is reciting the Psalms, sometimes my thought is peaceful and at other times it is distracted. What should I do?" Response.

When your thought is at peace, and you observe that you are receiving compunction from the brother's recital of the Psalms, then take advantage of this. When, however, you notice that your intellect is being held captive by some other thoughts, then prick your intellect in order that it may pay attention to the brother's doxology.

LETTER 446

Question: "What then happens, however, is that, by wanting to understand the words being recited by my brother, I am actually tempted against him." Response.

This, too, is a form of captivity; for the enemy transfers the intellect from one place to another. Nonetheless, prick yourself again when you notice this temptation arising; and tell your intellect with reproach: "Where are you going, wretched one? Remember your future torments, reserved for those who do or think these things." For did not Job make an inopportune offering for his children, saying: "It may be that my children have sinned in their hearts against God."[55] And with these words, apply your intellect to the words of the Psalms being recited. If you notice that this happens again, then rebuke your intellect; and do this on a third occasion as well. If, however, it continues to persist, then remove your intellect from there. But do not leave it idle; think about the judgment and about eternal punishments. And pray the holy name of God, saying: "Lord Jesus Christ, have mercy on me."

LETTER 447

Question: "If one is standing with the rest of the brothers during the chanting of the Psalms, but does not know how to recite the Psalms with them, what is it better to do: to listen to them being recited, or to recite the verses of the Psalms that one happens to know?" Response.

If one does not know the Psalms being chanted by the choirs, instead of simply listening to them, it would be more profitable to chant those verses that one knows; for mere listening often causes distraction.

55. Jb 1.5.

LETTER 448

Question: "Whenever an evil thought comes to me, my heart is moved and jumps as soon as it senses this, fearing that it might be dominated by the evil thought on account of its weakness. And when this happens, I feel a great burden in my soul, and so I am grieved. Make me worthy, father, of hearing from you what I should do before the shamelessness of this evil thought, and how it may be averted." Response.

The way to do this is not to be convinced by and not to give consent to the evil thought, but simply to hurry toward God without turmoil. And do not say: "I am troubled, lest it ambush me." Indeed, learn the meaning of all this from the following example. If someone brings some accusation against another in regard to some matter, and the person accused learns that he cannot respond to the former, then he will surely feel what you describe in the second part of your question. If, however, that person knows an established landowner, then he will confidently approach him, in order to be defended by the landowner, and thus he will not be troubled inasmuch as he trusts that landowner. Or again, if someone is ever taken by surprise and falls into the hands of a robber on some road, if he stays there long enough to resist and does not allow the robber to take anything from him, then all is well and good. If, however, the robber does take something, then that person need only be able to recognize the face of the robber and the place of the robbery; then he will run to the magistrate, and the latter will judge the matter. Indeed, the magistrate will not only make the robber return what he has stolen, but even punish the robber himself.

Therefore, if this thought enters your intellect, do not be troubled. Try to understand what it wants to do; and resist calmly, invoking the Lord. For what is evil here is not the fact that a thief has entered the house, but the fact that the thief steals whatever is in the house. If, however, the thief leaves with dishonor, this constitutes an honor for the master of the house; and it is a dishonor that the thief has departed without anything. Thus, if the Lord comes to the land of Judea, namely, to the heart of a person, then he will expel the demons. So cry out to him, as the

Macedonians cried out to Paul: "Come over to Macedonia and help us";[56] and together with the disciples, cry out: "Master, save us; for we are perishing."[57] He will arise and rebuke the spiritual winds,[58] and they will calm down. For his is the power and the glory to the ages. Amen.

LETTER 449

Question: "Since you said that the way to do this is not to be convinced by the evil thought, but to hurry toward God without turmoil, then I ask you to clarify this process for me, please." Response by Barsanuphius.

If someone accuses another person of something some day, and the one being accused goes to the magistrate, there is a process in all this. It works like this: after there has been an accusation, one is moved to proceed to the magistrate. Even if these two take a long time in discussing the matter, nonetheless the accused, who approached the magistrate about this, cannot be blamed for the time that it takes to resolve the issue; that person is only concerned about the conclusion of the matter and the solution to the accusation. This is why it is said: "And you will watch his heel."[59] The heel signifies the end. May your heart be strengthened, then, in the Lord through the prayers of the saints. Amen.

LETTER 450

A brother asked the Great Old Man: "Have mercy on me, and tell me how I might be saved. For I have promised to submit my thought to the contents of your letter." Response by Barsanuphius.

If you truly want to be saved, then listen to my words and put them into practice. Raise your feet from the ground and lift your intellect toward heaven; and let your meditation stay there day and night. And as much as you can, despise yourself, struggling to regard yourself as being beneath every other

56. Acts 16.9.
58. Cf. Mt 8.26.
57. Lk 8.24; Mt 8.25.
59. Gn 3.15 LXX.

person.[60] This is the true way. Outside of this, there is no other way for someone who wants to be saved in Christ, who gives us strength.[61] Let the one who wants run! Let the one who wants run! Let the one who wants run! Let that person run in such a way as to win.[62] I am bearing this witness before the living God, who desires to grant eternal life to everyone who wants it. So, if you want, brother, apply yourself to this.

LETTER 451

Question from the same person to the Other Old Man: "Why did the good elder say three times: 'Let the one who wants run'?" Response by John.

He did so in order to demonstrate how useful this way is, and that there is no way more essential than this. This is why he repeated his words three times. For the Lord also did the same: in the Gospel according to Matthew[63] he said "Amen" once, but in the Gospel according to John he repeated it, saying: "Amen, amen, I say to you,"[64] because he was discussing things that were more substantial at that point.

LETTER 452

Question: "I would like to know why it is that despondency and sleepiness mostly occur to me during the fifty-day period after Easter, even more so than at other times." Response.

We suffer this because we resemble an empty hole and not a source; this means that we are weak and unable to remain constant, in the same condition. Therefore, the winds change and the days grow, and we suffer this; however, the perfect fathers do not suffer this.

---

60. Cf. *Sayings*, Sisoes 13.   61. Cf. 1 Tm 1.12.
62. Cf. 1 Cor 9.24.
63. See Mt 5.18, 26; 6.2, 5, 16; 8.10; 10.15, 23, 42; 11.11; 13.17; 16.28; 17.20; 18.3, 13, 18, 19; 19.23, 28; 21.21, 31; 23.36; 24.2, 34, 47; 25.12, 40, 45; 26.13, 21, 34.
64. For ἀμὴν, ἀμὴν, λέγω ὑμῖν, see Jn 1.51; 5.19, 24, 25; 6.26, 32, 47, 53; 8.34, 51, 58; 10.1, 7; 12.24; 13.16, 20, 21; 14.12; 16.20, 23. Also, ἀμὴν, ἀμὴν, λέγω σοι appears in Jn 3.3, 5, 11; 13.38; 21.18.

LETTER 453

Question: "If I notice someone doing something inappropriate, should I not judge this as being inappropriate? And how can I avoid the condemnation of this neighbor of mine?" Response.

If this matter is truly inappropriate, then we cannot but condemn it as being inappropriate. Otherwise, how can we ever avoid the harm that comes from it, according to the voice of the Lord, who said: "Beware of false prophets, who come to you in sheep's clothing but inwardly are ravenous wolves; you will know them by their fruits."[65] The one, however, who is actually doing the inappropriate deed should not be condemned, according to the words: "Do not judge, so that you may not be judged,"[66] but also because we should regard ourselves as being more sinful than all others. Furthermore, we should not ascribe the sin to our brother but to the devil, who deceived him. For in this case it is as if someone were to push another person towards a barrier, and we were to blame the person being pushed.

It may even be that someone will do something which appears inappropriate to those watching, but which is really done with a good intention. This happened once to the holy [Great] Old Man. For as he was walking past the hippodrome on one occasion, he entered it, fully conscious of what he was doing. And when he saw each of the competitors striving to overtake and triumph over the others, he said to his thought: "Do you see how the followers of the devil eagerly race against each other? How much more so should we, who are heirs of the heavenly kingdom?" And, as a result of that sight, he left that place more eager in his spiritual journey and ascetic struggle.

Moreover, again, we do not know whether through his repentance, the sinful brother will be more pleasing to God, like the publican who in an instant was saved through humility and confession. For it was the Pharisee who left condemned by his own arrogance. Therefore, in consideration of these things, let us imitate the humility of the publican and condemn ourselves

65. Mt 7.15–16.
66. Mt 7.1.

in order to be justified; and let us avoid the arrogance of the Pharisee in order not to be condemned.[67]

LETTER 454

A Christ-loving layperson asked the same Old Man: "It often happens that I am in the company of certain people among whom I am so shy that my face entirely changes and drops; indeed, I cannot look at them or speak to them with a tranquil state of mind. And this makes my heart feel saddened and perplexed. Even if I do say something, my words are filled with foolishness, disorder, and vainglory. Often laughter is also mingled with the words I utter, without anything graceful being said; and this happens against my will, and so I am greatly grieved at this. I am at a loss as to what to do. For if I speak, this is what will happen; and if I keep silent, I feel that it would be inappropriate, especially when they address me so many times. What, then, does this mean, father? May your holy prayers assist me." Response by John.

This occurs to us as a result of the devil's envy. For in wanting neither us nor those who are with us to gain any benefit, he offers us this tare in order, if possible, to scandalize those in our company. Godly fear, however, is without turmoil or any disorder and disturbance. Therefore, if we equip ourselves with godly fear prior to entering the company of others, and if we pay attention to our heart with vigilance, then there will be no reason at all to be troubled or to laugh. For in the presence of godly fear, there is no laughter. Whereas, in regard to foolish people, it is said: "They raise their voice when they laugh."[68] The words of a foolish person are both troubled and graceless. A righteous person, however, is said only to smile.[69]

Therefore, if we bring to ourselves the remembrance of God, recalling that we must be in the company of our brothers with humility and calm thought, and if, in addition to this, we also love [them] and keep the fearful judgment of God before our eyes, then these resources will expel every evil thought from our heart. For wherever there are stillness, gentleness, and humility, there also God dwells.

67. Cf. Lk 18.10–14.   68. Sir 21.20.
69. Cf. ibid.

So let us have these [as our supplies] during any company that we may happen upon. And if the enemy persists in tempting us in this matter, thinking in his shamelessness that he will trap us or triumph over us, let us not surrender, and let him not seize us.[70] And if this happens the first time, let us at least be more prudent the second time, and so forth. For it is written: "The righteous fall seven times a day, and rise up again."[71] Rising up again means that the righteous person is struggling. And anyone struggling is exactly like this: falling and rising again, until one sees what will happen later. And above all else, we know that we must invoke the holy name of God; for wherever God is, there also are all good things; at the same time, this means that, wherever the devil is, there also are all evil things. Thus it is clear that, if we speak in a troubled manner according to vainglory or in order to please people, or even speak in any other evil way, then all this comes from the devil. Let us remember also the words of the holy Paul to Timothy: "Let your speech always be graceful, seasoned with salt."[72] And if we work hard in this, the almighty God through his compassion will grant us a perfect state according to his fear. To him be the glory to the ages. Amen.

LETTER 455

Question by the same person to the same [Old Man]: "Someone once asked one of the fathers to share a meal with him, but the latter declined, claiming that he was unable to do so. Another person asked the same father to [enter and] simply say a prayer in his cell, and when the latter entered, he forced him to stay for a meal; so the father stayed because of the strong coercion. Now when the person who had first invited the father for a meal learned this, he was deeply saddened. Is this sorrow according to God?" Response.

When one is troubled, saddened, and angered against one's neighbor, even on the pretext of some supposedly reasonable or spiritually beneficial matter, then it becomes clear that this

---

70. Using the variant reading ἁρπάσῃ instead of ἁρπάζει; see SC 451, 538-39.
71. Cf. Prv 24.16.
72. Col 4.6.

is not according to God. For everything that comes from God is peaceful and beneficial, bringing one to humility and to the point of condemning oneself. For it is said: "Righteous people are the first to condemn themselves."[73] Indeed, one who appears to want something according to God, but is prevented from receiving this, while afterward condemning and slandering the one who prevented him in this, is personally exposed as not originally having the right intention according to God. For it is said: "You will know them by their fruits."[74] Therefore, someone who has the right intention according to God, and yet is still prevented, will instead humble himself, instead regarding himself as being unworthy and regarding the one who prevented him as a prophet, inasmuch as that person foresaw his unworthiness and thus prevented him [from fulfilling his intention].

So if you invite someone out of love of God to come into your cell, or if you ask for something from someone in good faith, and your request is denied—while, at the same time, another person's request is accepted and fulfilled—do not allow the demon of anger to trouble your heart. For everything accompanied by turmoil does not come from God. Rather, humble yourself, saying: "I have been found unworthy, and God has revealed my sins and unworthiness to the fathers." Then he who gives grace to the humble will also give his grace to you. For those who possess humility never desire what is beyond themselves, but always hurry downward toward humility. Think also of the centurion, who approached Jesus for the sake of his servant; he heard the words: "I shall come and heal him," yet the centurion ran toward humility, and replied: "Master, I am not worthy to have you come under my roof."[75] Who would not have seized that opportunity? Nevertheless, humility did not even seek that, instead condemning itself as being unworthy. And God, who knows the hearts of all, receiving the intentions of all, praised his faith, saying: "I have not found faith like this in all of Israel."[76] So this humility procured for the centurion great praise, in addition to the health of his servant. Many, then, are the gifts granted by humility. Let us hasten toward humility, in order to

73. Cf. Prv 18.17.
74. Mt 7.16.
75. Mt 8.5–13.
76. Cf. Mt 8.10.

receive its grace and the praise from Jesus Christ, who humbled himself and became obedient unto death,[77] thereby offering us a model of humility. To him be the glory to the ages. Amen.

LETTER 456

Question: "Father, since therefore the centurion exercised extreme humility and judged himself unworthy of the Master's presence, his faith, too, was praised by him.[78] Abraham, however, both entreated and even begged him to enter the tent,[79] although he was addressing him as a human being, not even knowing that it was the Master. So did Abraham not possess humility? And was the virtue of the centurion greater than that of the patriarch? For humility, as you always teach, enjoys primacy among the virtues. Tell me, then, the meaning of each man's virtue and the difference between the two. For one of them did not accept the Master's presence and was praised for this, while the other very warmly received it and was also praised." Response.

Both of them were perfect in their faith toward God; and both of them used this faith and humility at the appropriate moment. For the patriarch Abraham also said: "I am earth and ashes."[80] In so considering himself, he reveals that he did not reckon himself worthy even of the hospitality. Yet, since he was perfect, he accepted every person, not differentiating at all between sinners and saints. Moreover, it was also said of him and Lot: "Do not neglect to show hospitality to strangers; for by doing that, some have entertained angels without knowing it."[81] Therefore, had Abraham known that it was in fact the Master, he would have spoken with the voice of the centurion. Indeed, we cannot find anything more humble than someone who regards himself as being earth and ashes. And the centurion also exercised humility at the appropriate moment, knowing that it was the Savior. Yet we might also add that he, too, performed the work of hospitality;[82] for his faith was not without works. Nor again was Christ praising idle faith; for the centurion's faith also included works. Indeed, at a fitting time he would have prac-

77. Cf. Phil 2.8.
79. Cf. Gn 18.1–15.
81. Heb 13.2.

78. Cf. Mt 8.5–13; Lk 7.1–10.
80. Gn 18.27; cf. Jb 42.6.
82. Cf. Lk 7.4–5.

ticed hospitality toward everyone, in the same way as the patriarch Abraham extended an invitation to all. So we actually find
that both of them are perfect.

LETTER 457

Question: "Since I am sinful, I possess neither the true and genuine humility for which the centurion was praised, nor the love of
hospitality through which Abraham was made worthy to receive
God. So what should I do? Should I perhaps consider my own
unworthiness and decline the presence of the saints in order to
gain a reward from it? Or should I instead run toward them, not
for the purpose of hospitality but as a person with a sick soul that
requires their healing? For it is proper for those who are sick to
seek the presence of doctors, and this is not regarded by them
as constituting any kind of hospitality. And if they do not invite
them, they are hardly seen to possess the virtue of humility, but
rather the characteristic of foolishness. Therefore, father, teach
me whether I should invite them as requiring their presence, or
decline them as being unworthy [of their presence]." Response.

Invite them as though you are unwell and have need of a doctor. And learn that a child that is born does not become fully
mature immediately.[83] Rather, it goes through the stage of soft
food and later arrives at the stage of solid food: "for solid food
is for the mature."[84] This is why the Apostle said: "I have fed you
with milk, not solid food."[85] Therefore, when we receive guests,
let us not believe that we are fulfilling the commandment, but
that we have need of doctors because we are unwell. Exercise
these things until God brings you to perfection.

LETTER 458

Question: "What is boldness, and what is immodest laughter?"
Response.

There is one kind of boldness, and there is another kind.
There is the boldness that comes from shamelessness, and this
gives rise to all kinds of evils;[86] and there is the boldness that

---

83. Cf. Eph 4.13.   84. Heb 5.14.
85. 1 Cor 3.2.   86. Cf. *Sayings*, Agathon 1.

comes from gladness, and this does not greatly benefit the one who exercises it. While the powerful and the strong, however, are able to avoid both of these, yet we in our weakness are not able to avoid either of them. So let us only exercise the boldness that comes from gladness, being careful not to give occasion for sin or scandal to our neighbor in any way. For those who live among others, unless they are perfect, cannot be entirely free of the second kind of boldness. So, then, if we cannot be free on account of our weakness, then let it at least be for our edification and not for any scandal, especially by trying to shorten our conversations with people. For indeed, prolonged conversations are not very beneficial, even if they do not appear to contain anything inappropriate.

The same can be said about laughter; for it is caused by boldness. If one has the boldness of shameless talk,[87] it is clear that the same person will be characterized by shameless laughter. Whereas, if one has the boldness that comes from gladness, it is clear that the same person will be characterized by the laughter of gladness. And as it was said of boldness, namely, that it is not beneficial to exercise it, the same applies to its laughter. It is not necessary, however, to prolong it or give it free rein; rather, one should constrain one's thought in order to make it pass with modesty. For indeed, those who give it free rein should know that they all fall into fornication as well.

LETTER 459

Question: "Father, I implore you to tell me, what is the proper kind of gladness, and how can a sinner exercise it without exceeding one's limits?" Response by John.

The perfect pay attention to themselves completely, like the craftsman who knows his craft entirely. For if such a craftsman should be found in the company of others while working, their company—that is to say, their conversation—does not prevent him from exercising the proper skills of his craft. Instead, he can continually converse with those present, but his mind will be entirely focused on the craft at hand. Likewise, one who is

87. Cf. Col 3.8.

in the company of others should do the same. One should display a joyful countenance and conversation, but inwardly one's thought should be sighing. For it is written of such a person: "The sighing of my heart is not hidden from you at all times."[88]

Otherwise, someone who exercises gladness resembles an inexperienced craftsman, who works while in the company of others but risks destroying his craft. Therefore, such people must pay close attention to their words and to the gladness of their countenances, lest they completely deviate from the way of mourning. When such people are about to be with others, they should remind their thought about how they ought to conduct themselves, and prepare themselves accordingly. For it is written: "I was prepared and was not troubled."[89] Preparing oneself implies discernment with regard to those [who are about to come], the reason for which they wish to be in one's company, and, depending on the purpose of their visit, preparing one's thought with godly fear. If the company is gathering for the sake of greeting one another, then one should deal with this company with grace and with appropriate words. If it is a case of receiving certain fathers, then this should occur with joy, in the manner in which Abraham washed the feet of the Master and the angels, receiving them with comforting words.[90] For the expression of the gladness toward each person is indicated to us by the occasion of the gathering. Thus, when we happen to encourage our visitors in the love of God to share some food or drink, we should do so with gladness, while cutting even this short in order not to confuse our thoughts.

LETTER 460

Question: "What is a person with vainglory, and what is a person with pride? And how does one come from vainglory to pride?" Response.

One comes to vainglory by seeking to please people; and when this is increased, it leads to pride. Forgive me, brother, and pray for me.

---

88. Ps 37.9–10.   89. Cf. Ps 118.60.
90. Cf. Gn 18.1–15.

A brother asked the Great Old Man: "Tell me, father, whether the compunction that I think I possess is genuine, and whether I should live here on my own. Also, pray for me because I am troubled by bodily warfare." Response by Barsanuphius.

Brother, your weeping and compunction are not genuine at this time; rather, they come and go. For genuine weeping, which comes with compunction, becomes like a servant submitted to us without separation; and a person who possesses this does not experience warfare. It even wipes away one's former faults and washes away all spots. Moreover, in the name of God, it continually protects the person who has acquired it. It also expels laughter and distraction, while at the same time unceasingly maintaining one's mourning. For weeping is a large shield that deflects all of the fiery arrows of the devil. The person who possesses it experiences absolutely no combat, whether that person is with others or even with prostitutes! [Such a gift] is always with us and fights for us.

So I have demonstrated for you the sign of weakness and of courage. Do not think that God could not relieve you from the battle; for he could indeed have relieved you, especially for the sake of the saints who were praying for you. Nevertheless, because he loves you, God wants you to be trained through many battles and exercises in order to reach the measure of good repute. And you cannot reach this point unless you keep all that I have commanded you through my letters, vainglorious teacher that I am. As for staying by yourself, this is a very special gift. When it comes to you, I shall inform you about this myself. Apply yourself now, child, as I have told you, and I believe that you will find progress in Christ. Do not be afraid. May the Lord be with you. Amen.

Question from the same person to the Other Old Man: "I implore you, abba sir, to pray for me, that the Lord will grant me a little humility. For the fathers say that, unless one cuts off entirely the root of the passion, the same person will again fall into

that passion at some point. How does one cut off the root of fornication and of gluttony and of avarice? And since the Great Old
Man told me that my mourning is not genuine at this time, but
that in fact it comes and goes, what is the disposition that brings
it about? Should I force myself in this matter, or should I let myself be, until genuine compunction arrives?" Response by John.

Brother, God grants us humility, but we push it away; and,
then, again we ask: "Pray that God will grant us humility." Humility means cutting off one's own will in everything and being entirely carefree. In regard to cutting off the root of the
passions, which you mention, this occurs by cutting off one's
own will and by afflicting oneself as much as possible and by tor-
menting the senses in order to keep them disciplined, so that
they may not be wrongly exercised. This is how you should cut
off the root of these things and of everything else.

As for the coming and going of your present mourning, which
is not genuine, this happens because we become relaxed and
then, later, again add fervor to the thought. When the warmth
remains, compunction becomes great and permanent, while
genuine mourning also follows suit. About this, you must certainly be sure to force yourself, in order that it may come to you.

Brother, do not neglect to keep the words and the commandments of the [Great] Old Man, and you will be saved. I, too, have
babbled, brother, but it is neither out of experience nor as a result of the Spirit. I believe that, whatever the Old Man has told
you, he has spoken both from former personal experience and
also from the Holy Spirit. My conscience, however, bears witness
that I do not want to deceive you at all in any matter. This is why
I believe that neither my words nor my counsels harm you. For
he knows that I do not wish that; instead, if the Lord gives me
the strength, I want to be the ransom of your soul, in return for
all your questions and for your desire to be saved. "The Lord
give you aid from Zion. May you see the prosperity of Jerusalem
all the days of your life."[91] Pray for me, brother.

91. Ps 127.5.

TO A DEVOUT LAYMAN, NAMELY,
THE FUTURE ABBOT AELIANOS (463–482)

LETTER 463

A Christ-loving layperson[1] asked the same [Other] Old Man whether one should reflect a great deal about the sacred mysteries, and if a sinful person approaching these mysteries would be condemned as being unworthy. Response by John.

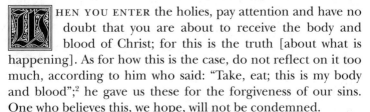 HEN YOU ENTER the holies, pay attention and have no doubt that you are about to receive the body and blood of Christ; for this is the truth [about what is happening]. As for how this is the case, do not reflect on it too much, according to him who said: "Take, eat; this is my body and blood";[2] he gave us these for the forgiveness of our sins. One who believes this, we hope, will not be condemned.

Therefore, do not prevent yourself from approaching the mysteries by judging yourself as being a sinner. Believe, rather, that a sinner who approaches the Savior is rendered worthy of the forgiveness of sins, in the manner in which we encounter in Scripture those approaching him with faith and hearing the divine voice: "Your many sins are forgiven."[3] Had that person [in this passage] been worthy of approaching him, he would not have had any sins. Yet, because he was a sinful man and a debtor, he received the forgiveness of his debts. Again, listen to the words of the Lord: "I have come not to save the righteous, but sinners."[4] And again: "Those who are well have no need of a physician, but only those who are sick."[5] So regard yourself as being sinful and sick, and approach him who [alone] can save the lost.[6]

---

1. Aelianos. See also *Letters* 571–573; moreover, *Letter* 465 mentions Aelianos by name.

2. Cf. Mt 26.26–28.   3. Lk 7.47–48.
4. Cf. Mt 9.13.   5. Lk 5.31.
6. Cf. Lk 19.10.

LETTER 464

Question from the same person: "Master, how is it that our Lord and Savior Christ allowed Judas, who was a traitor, to share in the mystical supper? For the holy John [Chrysostom], in his commentary on the Gospel according to Matthew, writes: 'The unworthy person should be prevented from approaching the awesome table of the mystery.'[7] Moreover, the holy Paul also judges that person to be liable to condemnation.[8] All of this does not allow someone with sinful conscience to dare ever approach the precious and awesome mystery and to partake of the life therein. So what should we do? For since I am a great sinner, this matter troubles me." Response.

In order for God to show his great loving-kindness and how he tolerates us to our last breath, as well as in order that we may turn from the ways of sinners and live,[9] this is why he washed the feet of [Judas] and even allowed him to participate in those mysteries, so that he might remove every excuse from him as well as from those who say that, had he been allowed to enjoy these, he might not have perished. So [Judas] condemned himself, and the words of the Apostle were fulfilled in him: "But if the unbeliever separates, let it be so,"[10] together with the words about those who sin but do not repent.

As for the matter of preventing them, according to the holy John, this would be for them to learn a lesson and in order to be chastised by using the judgment or torments [of hell]; for he did not actually speak of pushing them away or cutting them away from the church. Nor did Jesus do any such thing to Judas. If, however, they persist in their sins and approach without shame, then they are self-condemned and separate themselves from the glory of God. Whereas sinners who approach the holy mysteries, as being wounded and requiring mercy, are healed by the Lord and rendered worthy of his mysteries. For he said: "I have come to call not the righteous, but sinners to repentance."[11] And again: "Those who are well have no need of a physician, but only

---

7. St. John Chrysostom, *Homily on Matthew* 82.4-5, PG 58.743.
8. Cf. 1 Cor 11.27–28. 9. Cf. Ezek 18.23.
10. 1 Cor 7.15. 11. Lk 5.32.

those who are sick."[12] Again, however, let me return to what the
holy John says about preventing sinners from approaching the
holy mysteries, protesting that this is to their judgment. "All who
eat and drink unworthily eat and drink judgment against themselves";[13] and such people are cast out of the church of God. For
they have not partaken except unto their own condemnation.
This, then, is why he said that we should not cut them off from
the church, so that they might themselves make the decision.
Indeed, none should say that they are worthy of partaking, but
each person should only say: "I am unworthy, and I believe that
I am sanctified by partaking." This is what happens according to
one's faith for the sake of our Lord Jesus Christ, to whom be the
glory to the ages. Amen.

LETTER 465

Question to the same Old Man (the person asking is actually
Abba Aelianos, while he was still a layman): "When Judas said:
'I have sinned, by betraying innocent blood,'[14] and then threw
down the silver coins, does this not seem to be evidence of his repentance?" Response by John.

It would have been repentance for Judas, had he repented
before the Lord. For it is said: "Go and first be reconciled to
your brother,"[15] against whom you have sinned, and to no other
person. Yet Judas did even worse than this; for he went away and
destroyed himself through hopelessness. This is why his repentance was not accepted.

LETTER 466

Question: "Master, tell me, what is the will of God and what is
forgiveness? And what are the results of both?" Response.

When something grievous occurs to you, examine whether
your thought is reproaching you about any particular matter in
this regard. And if you find nothing, then this has simply occurred to you for your testing and is in accordance with the will

12. Lk 5.31.
14. Mt 27.4–5.

13. Cf. 1 Cor 11.29.
15. Mt 5.24.

of God. If, however, you do find something, then this has occurred with God's permission for the sake of your discipline. In any case, both of these are beneficial to us.

LETTER 467

Question: "It is a good thing, as you have personally taught, to surrender our will to God, which keeps us calm. One like me, however, who is weak, will sense that one is about to lose something and will either be troubled, or else, if one remains patient, will regret losing it on account of one's long-suffering. Now, which of the two, when compared, is better? And how should one be corrected? Moreover, what should one think about in order to avoid this turmoil?" Response.

The Lord said: "Rejoice whenever you face trials of any kind."[16] Therefore, among the various kinds of trials that exist, there are some for which one should rejoice. If, however, one is weak and unable to show patience and to rejoice upon the loss of that thing, casting it before the will of God, then one should first struggle against the turmoil, saying: "Pay attention to yourself, and see that you are not troubled." For if it is God's will for the thing not to be lost, then it will not be lost; but, irrespective of what happens as a result, it will be accepted gratefully. Indeèd, nothing good is achieved through our struggle, but only through the power and will of God. Yet God also demands our personal struggle that is according to God, although he does not want any evil strategy or falsehood; for these come from the evil one.

LETTER 468

Question: "When many polluted thoughts enter my intellect and I am afraid to confess any of them, what should I do?" Response.

Say to God: "Master, forgive me if I have thought anything against your will either in knowledge or in ignorance. For yours is the mercy to the ages." Amen.

16. Jas 1.2.

LETTER 469

Question: "Is it always a good thing or not to tell others about good stories found in Scripture and in the *Lives of the Fathers?*" Response.

It is well known to everyone that honey is sweet. And the words of the author of Proverbs, who said: "If you have found honey, eat only enough for you, or else, having too much, you will vomit,"[17] are also not unknown. For there are certain kinds of bags, just as there are others. There is a bag that holds one measure of corn, and another bag that holds three. So if someone tries to force the bag that holds one measure to hold up to three measures, it will not be able to contain the corn. The same applies here. Moreover, we cannot put all people on an equal footing; indeed, one person can speak without bringing any harm, while another cannot do this.

Silence, however, is always good and admirable above all else; the fathers honored and loved silence, and were glorified in it. For in order to demonstrate its beauty and show the condemnation that results from speaking, Job said: "I lay my hand on my mouth";[18] and before him, after speaking those beautiful words of comfort, the patriarch Abraham said: "I am earth and ashes, but I shall speak just once more before the Lord,"[19] indicating that he would keep silent after this.

Nevertheless, since we have not reached the point of walking the way of the perfect, on account of weakness, let us speak about those things which contribute to edification, namely, from the *Sayings of the Fathers*, rather than risking our souls by using accounts from Scripture.[20] For this matter contains a risk for someone who does not understand;[21] [the scriptural words] have been spoken spiritually, and a fleshly person will not be

17. Prv 25.16.
18. Jb 40.4.
19. Gn 18.27 and 32.
20. On the prudent reading of Scripture, see, for example, *Sayings*, Arsenius 42, Pambo 9, and Poemen 8.
21. *Sayings*, Amoun 2.

able to discern their spiritual truths.[22] It is written: "The letter kills, while the spirit gives life."[23] Therefore, let us take refuge in the words of the fathers, and we shall find benefit in them.

Yet, even so, we should be brief, remembering the one who said: "When words abound, transgression is inevitable."[24] Even if our thought tells us that the words or the stories are good, let us recall the fact that we do not practice what we speak; and so, if we suppose that we are edifying others by telling them these stories, then we are instead condemning ourselves, inasmuch as we do not practice these words. Nevertheless, let this not prevent us from godly conversation about them with others. For it is more beneficial to converse about them in a manner that is according to God than to converse about other inappropriate matters. In order, then, that we may not fall into thoughts of pride or arrogance, we should stay with the above, namely, [the recollection] that, since we have not practiced what we say, then we are doing so unto condemnation. Finally, about these as well as about other faults, let us pray to God, saying: "Do not judge me when I say these things."

LETTER 470

Question: "There are certain conversations on indifferent matters, bearing neither sin nor profit. These may include conversations with someone about, say, the prosperity of cities or their turmoil or peace, or wars about to break out, or other such matters. Is it inappropriate to speak of these matters as well?" Response by John.

If silence is more necessary even during conversations about good matters, how much more so in matters that are indifferent. If, however, we cannot keep silent, being overcome by conversation with others, let us at least not prolong the conversation in order not to fall into the snare of the enemy through chattering too much.

---

22. Cf. 1 Cor 2.15.
23. 2 Cor 3.6.
24. Prv 10.19.

LETTER 471

Question: "Well, there are many occasions when I come to such chattering by discussing matters that are indifferent; and no one escapes sin by chattering. So what should I do then?" Response.

Let us maintain some measure for ourselves in the following way. If we have noticed that we have spoken once because we were overcome by a thought, then let us try our best to prevent this from happening a second time. If we are overcome a second time, then let us at least be prepared to prevent it from happening a third time; and let us proceed in this way during every conversation. So, if the number of occasions that we are given to speak is ten, and one is overcome by temptation nine times and prevents it on the tenth, then one is found to be better than another who has been overcome by the temptation to speak ten times.

LETTER 472

Question: "Now, if I find myself among people who happen to be speaking about certain matters, whether fleshly or spiritual, what should I do then? Should I speak or not?" Response.

If you are found to be in the company of people conversing about either worldly or spiritual matters, then give the impression that you, too, are contributing something, although at the same time saying nothing that harms the soul. Bear in mind that you should avoid their praises, lest you appear to them to be silent and are later burdened by this. Even if you do this, however, make sure that you do not condemn them as speaking much, simply because you are saying little. For you do not know whether what will burden you will actually be the one word that you have spoken or the many words that they have spoken.

LETTER 473

Question: "How is it that I happen to be speaking to someone with turmoil about something, and while so often I regret this, yet I still fall back into the same thing without wanting to? Moreover, despondency also afflicts me." Response.

This occurs because we do not apply our heart to the practice of these things. So this is why we fall back into despondency as well as into many other evils.

LETTER 474

Question: "The Great Old Man said that, if one feels any turmoil in the thought, even as little as a hair, then this is from the evil one. Please clarify this for me." Response.

If you are considering doing something and notice that your thought is in turmoil, and after invoking the name of God it still persists, even as little as a hair, then you should know that what you want to do is actually from the evil one; and so you should not do it. Furthermore, if turmoil is suggested after you have considered doing something, and then the thought becomes dominated by this turmoil, once again it is not necessary to do what you had originally intended doing. For nothing that happens with turmoil is ever pleasing to God. If, however, one opposes the turmoil, then it is not necessary to consider the matter as being entirely harmful; nonetheless, one must discern whether it is good or evil. And if it is not good, then one should reject it, but if it is good, then one should do it, despising the turmoil with the assistance of God the Master.

LETTER 475

Question: "It sometimes happens that I am conversing with someone; and, after beginning the conversation, the evil one suggests turmoil. What should I do then? For if I delay the conversation to discern my words, in order to understand whether they are good or evil, the way that you have just said, then I offend the person who is listening, because all of a sudden I am silent." Response.

If it is not apparent to you that your words are sinful, then you should complete your sentence and discern only afterward whether you have actually spoken evil things. In this way, you can discipline your thought, condemning it as speaking evil in order that it may not say any more. For it is written: "Child, have you sinned? Do so no more."[25] Thenceforth, however, you should pay attention before speaking, in order to determine whether the subject is beneficial for you to join in conversation; and only then should you begin to converse. For if it is clear that the subject is sinful, then even if no turmoil is suggested, nevertheless you should strive to remove yourself, either pretending that you had forgotten about it or else transferring yourself to some other conversation that is more useful, in order not to fall into condemnation through this.

LETTER 476

Question: "Father, since you said that, before even beginning the conversation, it is necessary to examine the thought, then what happens when necessity demands that I speak immediately? For example, when I am sitting in the company of others, in order not to appear to them to be silent, I, too, want to speak on the subject. After all, I cannot notice any obvious sin in the conversation, but in fact it appears to me to be good, or at least indifferent. What do you order me to do, since I do not have the time to discern accurately whether there is any sin hidden therein?" Response.

If the conversation appears to be good, or at least indifferent, and necessity demands that you speak, then say something. If, however, you notice that your words will bring you vainglory, or that those listening will certainly praise you, then you should do everything possible to prevent your thought from accepting this vainglory. Furthermore, if you see that you are overcome by it, then it is more beneficial for you to be silent rather than to be harmed.

LETTER 477

Question: "Father, you made it clear to me how what happens with turmoil and vainglory derives from the demons. Therefore, I give thanks to the Lord, who illumined me through your spiritual teaching and granted sinners to know the way of life through his

25. Sir 21.1.

saints. But please teach me this as well: What is the pretense to rights?" Response.

Pretense to rights is something that does not contain arrogance, but rather contains the denial of fault, in the manner of Adam and Eve, as well as Cain and others who sinned, yet denied their sin in order to justify themselves.

LETTER 478

Question: "There are times when [the devil] not only suggests turmoil to my thought but even forces me to do or say something. There are other times, on the contrary, when the enemy prevents me from even completing my words or actions, and opposes me in order to interrupt these. What should I do?" Response by John.

We have already said that it is necessary to discern every thought and deed in order to see whether it is good or evil, which would help you despise everything that you are asking. So if it is something good, then do it; and if it is not, then do not do it. In order, however, that the good may not be done with turmoil, it is necessary to examine the governing thought in order to discern how this is being done. Indeed, if you examine this with fear of God, then God will not allow you to be deceived. How can he possibly do otherwise, when he swore to himself: "As I live, says the Lord, I do not desire the death of sinners, but that they should turn from their ways and live"?[26] This is especially the case when he sees you examining your thought for the salvation of your soul and for the sake of your return to God. Therefore, invoke his name everywhere, and you will find rest.

LETTER 479

Question: "There are times when I invoke the name of God, and yet a kind of weight remains on my thought as a result of this. So how many times should I invoke his name?" Response.

26. Cf. Ezek 18.23 and 32; 33.11.

You should be content with invoking it once, or at most three times. And if your thought bothers you to invoke it more times, then do not give in to it, but despise this burden; for it comes from the demons. I am saying this for the times when the subject of conversation does not prevent you from speaking or acting, inasmuch as it is either good or indifferent. For in that case, it is certainly sufficient to invoke his name once, or at most three times.

LETTER 480

Question: "Whenever I want to say or do something good but am afraid lest it cause turmoil within my heart, I avoid it. Am I doing well or not?" Response.

If you are about to do or say something, and are afraid lest some turmoil arise as a result of this, and so you avoid it, you are not doing the right thing. For you are turning your back to the enemy, and you will not avoid the turmoil. Indeed, the enemy does not find it difficult to suggest turmoil in anything whatsoever; and so the passion will become worse for you. This turmoil, however, is abolished, through God's assistance, only by doing whatever it is that you are doing with prayer and fear of God.

LETTER 481

Question: "Father, why is it that you told me that silence is good, yet when I practice it, I think I am avoiding [turmoil], and so I am harmed? How can this be?" Response.

When you come to silence by means of your ascetic struggle, then it is good. When, however, this is not the way that you come to it, but rather you keep silent out of fear of that turmoil, then it is harmful.

LETTER 482

Question: "Since God created us with free will and does not force us to do what is right, then tell me, father: How does he assist the one who suffers injustice? Why is it said: 'He brings the

counsels of the peoples to nothing; he frustrates the plans of the rulers'?[27] Moreover, pray for me, that I may be delivered from diabolical faithlessness and be vigilant in your spiritual teaching."
Response.

God does not oblige anyone to do what is right, on account of our free will. If, however, someone suffers a certain injustice, and is worthy of being delivered from this injustice, then God hinders the one enacting the injustice and does not reckon this as justification for that person, on account of the evil intention; for that person chose to fulfill every injustice. Indeed, the Chaldeans were causing injustice to those around Azariah, casting them into the fiery furnace.[28] Therefore, because the latter were worthy of being delivered, God spared them and prevented the fire from hurting them. We do not, however, ascribe this good deed to the Chaldeans, on account of their evil intention, but rather to God, who brought to nothing the plans of the nations on account of those who fear him. Yet, even if injustice is prevented for the sake of the worthy ones, nevertheless the unjust deservedly receive the recompense for the evils of their injustice. So pay attention to yourself, in order that you do not wander from the truth to which the God of glory is leading you through the prayers of the saints. Amen.

27. Ps 32.10.
28. Cf. Dn 3.21.

LETTER 483

A brother happened to be working with another brother and was struck by the latter at the instigation of the devil. Troubled by this, he sought to be relieved of working with that brother. So he asked the Great Old Man about it. And Barsanuphius responded in the following manner.

ROTHER, IN REGARD to what you have asked me, do not be troubled or do anything with turmoil, especially against a person who is already troubled by his thoughts and by the devil's envy. For you, too, have been tempted and enraged by thoughts on other occasions. And if you recall how you also were tempted at that time, you will not scorn your brother in his own time of temptation. Indeed, many people who have been afflicted with some illness involving drowsiness of the head, which comes from extremely high fever, do not know what they are thinking or saying, even when they are insulting those who are well and perhaps even those attending to them; for their illness has overcome them. The same applies now. Even if one were to tell your brother about a doctor, he would not accept healing; nor does he know what is beneficial for him, but he receives everything that one tells him as utter ravings. Furthermore, he insults others and is furious, seeking foods that harm rather than heal; for he knows not what he does.

That is what happens to a person who is tempted; even if that person's soul is being destroyed, that person is not aware of this. In fact, that person is unaware of even insulting and scorning the saints, who suffer with him for his soul; for he has become dizzy with the suffering of the illness. At the same time, the adversary always turns things against him, until he forces him to deny God himself. That is exactly what is happening here. God knows this, however, and providentially allows us to be tempted in order that we may appear to him as proven and in order that we may support our neighbor in the time of his material and spiritual weakness. For it is said: "Bear one another's burdens, and in this way you will fulfill the law of Christ."[1]

Therefore, for one who lives with a sick person, this means that what is important is not doing that person's will or giving that person something that is harmful, but rather bearing that person's insults and other burdens, as well as attending to that person and taking care not to offer anything harmful. The same can be applied in your particular case. Your concern should not be to do the will of the one who is asking, but to pray for that person. And if that person is unable to do so himself, then he should ask those who can, to implore God the Master to deliver him from the temptation that has befallen him. Then, such a person becomes like Martha and Mary, the sisters of Lazarus, who asked the Master to resurrect their brother.[2] And if one does this, one should not feel superior; for this is happening to him through others, and he should be doing the same for others. "Indeed, the measure that you give will be the measure you get back."[3]

And do not think that, because you have been struck by your brother, you have suffered something great; for the Lord of heaven and earth was also beaten, and he suffered so much more. Do not be incited to move to another place or to be separated from your brother; for this is not something according to God, but in fact constitutes the fulfillment of the devil's will. Even if you should do this, the temptation will not go away, but will only come back worse; for no good can ever come from evil. So this actually signifies lack of submission and lack of prudence. "For where there are envy and selfish ambition, there will also be disorder and wickedness of every kind."[4] No one is ever healed of these in any age, except by cutting off one's own will and struggling not to interfere with one's neighbor or ever say: "What is this?" or: "What is that?"[5] As for one who says: "I want that, too,"

1. Gal 6.2. 2. Cf. Jn 11.21 and 32.
3. Lk 6.38. 4. Jas 3.16.
5. Cf. *Sayings*, Antony 2; and Dorotheus, *Teaching* 6, 69.

that person becomes the son of the devil and is estranged from God; it is clear that such people want to fulfill their own wills and not God's. So take courage, brother. God will protect you! Pray with all your soul for your brother, and love him in Christ Jesus our Lord, to whom be the glory to the ages. Amen.

LETTER 484

A brother asked the same Great Old Man to pray for him, saying: "Forgive me for disturbing you so many times, but I believe in God that, through your prayers, he will strengthen me and I will no longer disturb you as much." Response from Barsanuphius.

All those who are children of God are by all means also heirs of his goodness, long-suffering, tolerance, loving-kindness, and love. For if they are children of God, then they are also gods; and if they are gods, then they are lords. And if God is light, then they are illuminators. Therefore, if God is disturbed and distraught when they ask something of him, then they are, too. If, however, he is not grieved when they ask, but rather rejoices when asked, then they do likewise. The Old Testament says: "Strive to love your neighbor as yourself";[6] while the New Testament shows us what perfection is, by telling us to lay down our life for one another,[7] just as the perfect one and Son of the perfect [God] laid down his life for our sake. Therefore, when the saints are asked something, they rejoice; for they are perfect, just as their Father is perfect.[8] Ask them, then, and they shall grant it to you eagerly; for they are not slack or lazy like me. Moreover, pray that I may be among them. So I ask God to grant you what you ask: first, that he might give you strength from above and love for him; second, that he might establish you in his fear and your heart in faith. So stay firm and do not hesitate, expecting to receive his mercy, and he will grant "far more abundantly than whatever we ask or imagine."[9] To him be the glory to the ages. Amen.

6. Cf. Lv 19.18.
8. Cf. Mt 5.48.

7. Cf. Jn 15.13; 1 Jn 3.16.
9. Eph 3.20.

LETTER 485

A brother asked the abbot of the monastery where the holy fathers lived to give him a cell nearby, and he consented to this. In the meanwhile, he visited another monk who asked him to make his home in a different cell. That brother told him, however, that he could not do this without the counsel of the elders and the abbot who had consented to give him the [first] cell. So he came to ask the Other Old Man about what he should do. Response by John.

Brother, the Lord decreed that we should "regard others as being better than ourselves."[10] Therefore, if it is for the love according to God that we nurture toward you, that we also said to you: "Come and live near us," then, in practice, we appear to be better than our brother. If again we now tell you: "Go and live near him," then perhaps your love may suppose that it is because we do not love you that we are urging you to go away from us. So you should go and examine the distance between the two places and the benefit of your soul in each of them; and keep the words of the Apostle: "Test everything, but hold fast to what is good."[11] I have spoken these things out of godly love. Forgive me, my brother, for the sake of the Lord.

LETTER 486

A certain monk who lived in another's cell built for himself a new cell nearby. Another brother who required a cell, however, visited him, requesting that he might reside in the newly built cell. He also wanted to receive this as a gift with a written contract. So the monk prepared an agreement for this purpose, stating that, with the permission of the elders, he would give the cell on the condition that he could draw two pots of water from the property each week. And he asked the Great Old Man about this matter. Response by Barsanuphius.

This sort of conduct is not at all appropriate for monks. For if you are seeking a contract from one another, and might in

10. Phil 2.3.
11. 1 Thes 5.21.

the future even take legal measures, then this work is not one of love. Instead, let that brother live in the cell without any contract; and if the owner of the cell wants to remove him at some point in time, then he should leave with humility without saying anything in opposition. And if the owner of the cell goes there wanting to fill two pots of water, and the one living in the cell does not give him permission to do so, then he, too, should not be troubled but make a prostration before him with humility, take his empty pot, and leave, saying: "Forgive me, brother, for the Lord's sake; for I have grieved you. And pray for me." He should also pay attention to himself in order that his thought may not be troubled afterward by anger. And God will protect both him, on account of his humility, as well as his brother from the enmity of the devil. Thus the latter will feel compunction, running after the former and making a prostration before him, in order that he might return and fill the pot, and will even carry the pot for him. Then God's love will protect both of them, and this kind and loving God will save them.

LETTER 487

Question: "What happens when the cell needs restoration? Should the one living there spend time doing this, since it is not his own, or should he wait until the time comes for him to leave for another cell?" Response.

If one believes within oneself that everything that one has belongs to God, and that all things are held in common among the faithful, and nothing belongs to one person alone, then one should not think like this; for this derives from a fleshly thought. Indeed, even if one ends up spending time restoring the cell and does not actually stay there, then the next brother who will find rest will always bless the one who restored it and labored in that place. And if we believe that there is truth in the one who says: "The measure that you give will be the measure you receive in return,"[12] and: "Return to each according to each one's works,"[13] and again: "May God grant you according

12. Lk 6.38.
13. Ps 61.13.

to your heart,"[14] then we should not allow our brother to leave prematurely, but always cry out to him continually: "I will neither fail you, nor will I forsake you."[15]

A brother asked the same Great Old Man: "Forgive me, lord father, for daring to speak. But since I observe my lord abbot apparently showing love toward certain brothers more than others, my thought afflicts me, saying that he is looking to please people. For if certain monks want something, he grants it; whereas he does not give me the same. Once I asked for one window and he did not give it to me; and another time I asked for a little lime, and again he did not give me any, while he did give some to others. How is it that he does these things? And how should I respond to my thought?" Response by Barsanuphius.

Brother, you need to have patience. For the Lord also said: "In your patience, save[16] your souls."[17] And the Apostle says: "For you have need of patience,"[18] and so on. If God wants to test whether you are able to endure anything, you will be found to have no patience. How many years have you had your cells in the current condition, and yet you have not complained? And then, once you see others doing something, immediately you, too, are burned as if by fire. Why did you not say to your thought: "I have stayed such a long time [in this cell]; can I not be patient for a few more days?" And if your thought says: "Why is he doing this for others?" then you should respond: "Because they are holy, whereas I am unworthy, worthy only of affliction."

If you consider your abbot as a people-pleaser, when in actual fact he is not, then you are losing your soul; if, indeed, he is truly a people-pleaser, then it is not you who will give account for him, but rather it is he who will give account for you. Nevertheless, whoever asks for something should examine the time, the convenience, and the delay; then, that person will understand why what he wants is not being granted. If one does not

14. Ps 19.5.   15. Jos 1.5.
16. Lit., "gain" (κτήσασθε).   17. Lk 21.19.
18. Heb 10.36.

understand the reason, then one should not blame anyone else but oneself, saying: "I am the unworthy one." In this way, you will find a way out of your thought, brother. This is the way of those who desire to be saved and to live according to God.

LETTER 489

One of the fathers, an elderly monk, once came to live in the monastery where the holy fathers dwelt. When asked by the brother attending to him: "What do you want me to prepare for you to eat?" he responded angrily: "Prepare whatever you want." And the brother was grieved, not knowing what to do. So the same Great Old Man was asked whether what was said was good or not. This is what he responded.

It is not up to me to condemn anyone; for each ultimately bears his own burden. Yet it seems to me that such a response brings affliction to the brother, even if it was spoken out of ascetic discipline. He should have spoken to the brother with humility, telling him: "Such-and-such is my custom to eat"; indeed, even if the brother prepares the food in a disgusting manner and serves him badly, he should still thank him. If, however, the brother prepares something, whether it is well prepared or not, and the visitor is moved to anger, then this is worse than all of the passions. For such a person is angered without any reason; and this is surely not through the knowledge of God, but rather through the action of the devil. Nevertheless, the brother who is attending to the visitor should also be long-suffering. For whoever bears one's brother with fear of God also receives the repose of the Spirit of God.

LETTER 490

The same brother was honored and comforted about this by the abbot and the brotherhood of the monastery, in accordance with godly fear; yet, still, he did not feel consoled. Feeling instead that he was greatly afflicted and insufficiently comforted, he left the monastery secretly. Later, when they found out where he lived, they wanted to go and implore him to return to their monastery; for they heard that he was grieved. So they asked the same Great

Old Man about this, repeating the words of the Apostle: "So that he may not be overwhelmed by excessive sorrow."[19] Response by Barsanuphius.

The Apostle said this because he had delivered that person to Satan,[20] and the latter had good reason to be grieved inasmuch as he was excommunicated by the Apostle. This is why, on seeing him repentant, he said: "They should reaffirm their love for him."[21] Therefore, if you know that you have chased him away, you should go away and make a prostration before the brother, in order that he may return. If, however, he departed of his own will, even if you find him with the help of God, his pretense to rights will always accompany him, and thus he will ever be disposed to return to the same grief. And no matter what opportunity arises, he will always say: "I was away from here, and they obliged me to return." So let him feel a little compunction in his thoughts, feeling regret for leaving; for even if he is afflicted in body [here], yet he is profiting in spirit. Indeed, when he sees himself in many sorrows, his arrogance and pretense to rights will be lifted, and he will recall the repose of the monastic community. Then he will return with humility, assuming gratitude instead of ingratitude.

LETTER 491

Question: "What happens if he should repent on the one hand, and yet be ashamed to return on the other hand?" Response.

If he should repent and bear his own blame, saying: "I am at fault in every way," then God, who said through the prophet: "Be the first to confess your iniquities, in order that you may be justified,"[22] will see that his heart has been softened and will lead him in his fear toward what is beneficial for him. For it is said: "He will lead the gentle in discerning what is right, and teaches the gentle his ways."[23] Moreover, if it happens that he is benefiting more by being in his original place, then his heart will be assured that he should return there with humility.

19. 2 Cor 2.7.
21. Cf. 2 Cor 2.8.
23. Ps 24.9.

20. Cf. 1 Cor 5.5.
22. Cf. Is 43.26.

LETTERS TO A FORMER SOLDIER,
NOW A MONK (492–502)

LETTER 492

A brother, who was a soldier in the secular world,[1] renounced everything for life in the monastery; and he asked the same Great Old Man whether he would be able to repent. Response by Barsanuphius.

ROTHER, GOD rejects no one, but rather he calls everyone to repentance. Therefore, one who approaches him should do so with all one's heart, sowing in the hope of also harvesting, and expecting temptation until one's last breath.[2]

LETTER 493

Question: "And then, will God come to the assistance of that person?" Response.

Child, the arena is open, and whosoever wants to be saved may hear Jesus crying out and saying: "Come to me, all of you that are weary and are carrying heavy burdens, and I shall give you rest. And learn from me, for I am gentle and humble in heart, and you will find rest for your souls. For my yoke is easy, and my burden is light."[3] Do you understand what you hear? "I am gentle and humble," he says, so that we may learn this from him. The one who approaches God should not be discouraged or afraid; otherwise, that person will never make a beginning in his way.

Indeed, God pays attention to the heart, and discerns our intention. And he knows our weakness, that we cannot do any-

---

1. Barsanuphius appropriately adopts military imagery in his responses to this former soldier in *Letters* 494, 495, and 497.
2. Cf. *Sayings*, Antony 4.
3. Mt 11.28–30.

thing on our own. He is everything, however; and he grants strength to the worthy person, in order to be able to do one's best. For if he holds back the strength of the powerful person, then what will become of that wretch? And if he restrains the wisdom of the wise, and changes their heart, then their wisdom will be the source of senselessness and foolishness. Therefore, let us approach him with confidence, knowing that he is the one who bestows upon us the strength for our struggle. So you should prepare your soul; indeed, more than that, you should even be prepared to receive the crown. May God assist you with his will through the prayers of the saints. Amen.

LETTER 494

Supplication from the same person to the same Great Old Man: "For the Lord's sake, since my thoughts suggest images of the world to me, inciting me to return to the world, show mercy on me, so that I may be protected by your prayers. Since I still find myself in the same sins, I asked God to deem me worthy of your protection." Response by Barsanuphius.

Beloved child, be strong in the Lord! It is God who has called you. Do not be discouraged, but be confident. The beginning of godly work includes many trials, but the Lord crushes them. The secular military service is darkness, and its heritage is eternal punishment. But the military service of God is light, and its heritage is eternal life. So, then, ponder these two crumbs [of advice]; and, afterward, choose whichever you want. Someone with a loud voice will come to you and awaken your heart, which is still cold, in order to make you run more swiftly, as you should. But do not be troubled; for it is the one who will take you by the hand to the Master, God.

LETTER 495

Supplication from the same person to the same Great Old Man: "Since the affliction of the struggle that has now come upon me was derived from me, have mercy on me, Master, in order that your prayers may abolish it. For I have lost what I had, in conceding to spend time with my brothers according to the flesh when they came to see me. Thus I have remained with the images of their company, thinking that I am still living with them. Assist, however, my great weakness and cowardice in the way of salvation. For I do not know how to pray to the God who has called me, striving instead to ignore him and in a moment to forget all his benefits. Therefore, I implore you, have mercy on me; for I have sinned greatly. And the temptations, which have arisen from my weakness and little faith, do not depart from me. Is it possible and beneficial to prevent my relatives from coming to visit me, so that they may not bring me the seductions of the world? For you know very well that it is because my heart is still cold that their visitations lead me to turmoil and in the way of temptation. Although yesterday my thoughts left me alone for a while, through your protection, today as I was sitting alone for a while in order to learn one of the Psalms, they attacked me so fiercely that I was even sweating from my discouragement. So I implore you not to abandon me to my enemies, but, with your strength, fortify my weakness and abolish my enemies; for I have had more than my fill of them. You know my heart, that I cannot bear temptations gladly. [Help me], in order that I may not be overcome on account of my weakness, or else because I am unaware of their diversity, so that I may not fall into their snares in which I was wallowing prior to taking refuge in your presence. Forgive me and pray for me, good father." Response by Barsanuphius.

Beloved brother, our Master and God holds a register on which those who approach in order to serve him sincerely are enrolled, and their names are freely inscribed thereon from the first day. I have asked him, "who does not want the death of sinners, but that they should turn from their ways and live,"[4] to place you in the rank of those who are being saved. And he has taken mercy on you, after having mercy on me. He has already ranked you there; for he is "the one who desires everyone to be saved and to come to the knowledge of the truth."[5] Therefore, you have received a free gift. It is up to you, then, either to be or not to be included in this book. And if you do want it, then you will receive the assistance of the one who says: "If you are willing and obedient, you shall eat the good of the land,"[6] and

4. Cf. Ezek 18.23 and 32; 33.11.   5. 1 Tm 2.4.
6. Is 1.19.

so forth. Behold, I have spoken. Be careful not to fall outside of this [spiritual] military service, lest you suffer an incurable wound. For if you fall away from such service, then neither will you be useful in the world. May the Lord protect you from the evil one and save you unto life eternal. Amen. Child, "let therefore the dead bury their own dead,"[7] and you shall see how God is glorified in the counsel of his saints.

LETTER 496

Supplication from the same person to the same Great Old Man: "Abba, have mercy on me, for the Lord's sake. For when I am resting alone, images arise within me, including a fear that people are assaulting me, to the point that I am afraid even when I am asleep and cannot rest. Indeed, since I am a coward by nature, the temptation swells up even more fiercely and does not allow me to sleep at all; of course, as I said, this comes from my fear and little faith. It also results in bodily exhaustion, so that I can even hardly move. Master, you surely know what is beneficial for me. So do me a favor and respond, good father. Forgive me; for I am a sinner and in a very bad state." Response by Barsanuphius.

Brother, you should give glory to God for demonstrating how Scripture is true. For it is said: "God is faithful, and he will not let you be tested beyond your strength."[8] Therefore, he allows you to be tested according to your strength; while those who are great, he tests according to their own strength with diverse temptations, and they rejoice in this. Indeed, temptation brings us to progress; and wherever there is good, there also temptation occurs. So do not be afraid of temptations, but rejoice that they are leading you to progress. Simply scorn them, and God will assist you and protect you.

LETTER 497

Supplication from the same person: "Holy father, since I am weak and sinful, I do not have the boldness to request anything from the compassionate God. Therefore, I entreat you to pray

7. Lk 9.60.
8. 1 Cor 10.13.

for me, the sinner, that I may be rendered worthy to serve him,
and that he may grant me strength and prudence—indeed, all
of these things. As your heart also knows, since I am nothing,
I request everything. Good father, I believe that your prayers
are sufficient to implore God for my sins, that he may overlook
these and render me worthy to make a beginning in the blessed
way. Thus I may, with knowledge and with the guidance of your
mercy, blessed one, travel that way and not cease offering thanks
to the kind and loving God, who counts me worthy of all good
things through you. Forgive my foolishness and boldness, and
pray for me." Response by Barsanuphius.

Brother, or rather, child, may the God of heaven and earth
strengthen you in the holy calling to which he has called you,
rendering you worthy of being ranked among those whom he
has adopted,[9] of which few are counted worthy, and establish-
ing your heart according to the heart of Hannah,[10] so that you
may give birth to fruits acceptable to God,[11] according to Samuel, that you may chant with her a new song to God,[12] and make
progress in good deeds on the way that lies before you, working for him genuinely as a proven soldier. Therefore, do not
stumble and do not collapse; but run eagerly to inherit the city
of the saints and the chosen ones. Acquire faith, hope, and love,
which will bring you to holy humility, the mother of all good
things, and you will be saved to the ages of ages. Amen.

LETTER 498

Supplication from the same person: "I am a sinner and unable,
because of my bodily weakness, to do anything good and pleasing to God. I implore you, master, pray for me who have angered
him and can do nothing; for as I have said, my weakness prevents
me." Response by Barsanuphius.

Brother, you are blessed if you are completely conscious of
your sins. For one who is completely conscious of them is dis-
gusted with them and alienates oneself from them. Part of repentance is precisely becoming conscious of one's sins and

9. Cf. Gal 4.5.   10. Cf. 1 Sm 1–2.
11. Cf. 1 Pt 2.5.   12. Cf. Ps 95.1.

requesting assistance from the fathers, in order that, through their prayers to God, one may be delivered from these sins and the torments that await one. Therefore, we are praying for you, but you must also do your best to acquire humility and submission. And do not retain in yourself any of your own will toward anything; for it is from this that anger is born. And do not judge or scorn anyone; for through this, the heart is rendered blunt and the intellect blind, and then negligence follows while hard-heartedness is born. Rather, be vigilant by all means in the study of the divine law, from which the heart receives the fervor of the heavenly fire. For it is said: "While I mused, the fire burned."[13]

Moreover, do not grieve, brother, for your calling is from God. Neither relax nor collapse; for God does not demand anything beyond your strength, but only what is according to your ability. Guard your mouth from idle talk and vain words, as well as your heart from meditating evil words. And cast your strength before God, together with the prayer of the saints, by saying: "Be merciful to me, a sinner."[14] And he shall have mercy on you and guard you, protecting you from all evil, in order that you may come from darkness to the true light, from deceit to truth, and from death to life, in Christ Jesus our Lord. To whom be the glory to the ages. Amen.

LETTER 499

Supplication from the same person to the Other Old Man: "Abba, for the Lord's sake, forgive my rashness and foolishness, and help me on account of the multitude of my sins. For if someone who commits a single sin before God requires much repentance, then what can I do when I have been raised on sin and have not ceased doing whatever I can to anger God? I need your prayers in order that sin may be taken away from me. Indeed, I continually need to be taught about this way; for having been a man of great troublemaking and numerous wrongdoings, I came here through the great compassion of God. Therefore, holy father, I implore you to take mercy on me, and, as you judge best, to guide me. Moreover, pray that I may keep the holy commandments that you have ordered me to perform." Response by John.

13. Ps 38.3.   14. Lk 18.13.

Brother, since you have come to the one who was crucified for us, you, too, should take up your cross and follow him,[15] casting your every concern on him who works "abundantly [far] more than all we can ask or imagine."[16] For he is the one who cares about us. Therefore, do not be troubled, and Christ will assist you. Only, my child, keep in your intellect the word from holy Scripture and the readiness of which it speaks: "My son, when you come to serve God, prepare your soul for testing,"[17] and also: "The untempted is also untested."[18] And again: "Blessed is anyone who endures temptation, for such a one has stood the test,"[19] and so on. I am not saying all this in order to frighten you, brother, but in order to strengthen your heart in the way of God. For this is how all of the saints progressed, namely, through temptations and afflictions; and so they became pleasing to God,[20] with the assistance also of his grace. Do not be afraid; and do not be discouraged. For we believe that God is the one who plants you and irrigates you, making you grow[21] through the prayers of the saints. Amen.

LETTER 500

Question: "Father, what should I do? For I am bothered by fornication." Response.

Torment yourself as much as you can, namely, to the best of your ability; and do not grow confident in this, but only in God's love and protection. Moreover, do not become despondent; for despondency is the impetus for every evil beginning.[22]

LETTER 501

Question: "When I speak to my brother, often I do so with anger. And if I wish to do so with love, immediately I am moved by an evil desire, which comes with shameful pleasure and bodily movement. Since I cannot even behold my brother's face with-

---

15. Cf. Mt 16.24.   16. Eph 3.20.
17. Sir 2.1.   18. *Agraphon*, no. 90.
19. Jas 1.12.
20. Using the variant reading, αὐτοῦ, instead of αὐτοῖς; see *SC* 451, 622.
21. Cf. 1 Cor 3.6.   22. See *Sayings*, Poemen 149.

out being tempted in this way, what should I do, father?" Response by John.

Speaking to your brother either with anger or with love, when your body is thus moved, is a source of death in both cases. Therefore, avoid both of these and speak to your brother normally; then God will assist you. In addition to all this, guard your eyes, and also pray for me.

LETTER 502

Question: "What should I do when I am troubled by the temptations of gluttony, avarice, and the other passions?" Response.

When the passion of gluttony tempts you, struggle as much as you can, according to God, not to give the body all that it requires. Do the same thing in regard to avarice. While the temptation troubles you, do not acquire anything more than a single garment; struggle also with any vessel, and, in fact, with the slightest object. Once you have triumphed over the temptation, with [the grace of] God, then you may acquire whatever you need, according to God. Do the same with the other passions as well.

MORE LETTERS TO VARIOUS
MONKS (503–570)

LETTER 503

A brother who dwelt with an elder asked the same Old Man, John, about his diet and sleep, as well as about the turmoil that occurred to him in regard to those things, which he felt that his elder was not doing correctly. Response.

HE ELDERS say: "Giving rest to one's neighbor is a great virtue, especially when one does not do this under coercion or with wastefulness." As for you, keep as much as your body requires; even if you eat three times a day, this is not harmful. For if one eats only once a day but does so with lack of discernment, then of what benefit is this? Therefore, try to understand the thought of your elder, by asking him about this freely. For since both of you are living according to God, he, too, is obliged to speak freely, though also with godly fear; and do whatever he says makes him comfortable; indeed, this is the will of God.

As for the matter of sleep, there are two sets of circumstances. There are times when the body is weighed down by overeating; there are other times when this occurs through weakness. When one cannot perform one's service, sleep will follow. Overeating is followed by the temptation of fornication; for this weighs one down to sleep in order to pollute one's body. Therefore, one who possesses discernment will understand how and whence this occurs. We are required, however, to do our best and no more. The protection and mercy of God are there in order to strengthen our weakness; for his is the glory to the ages. Amen. Pray for me, brother.

Furthermore, show love when you speak to your neighbor, discerning whether you are speaking without turmoil but with humility and discernment—in which case you should go on speaking; or whether in fact this is not the situation—in which case you should strangle your thought, putting it to shame in order that it may immediately cease. Do not be troubled by anything that your elder does, saying: "God knows what is beneficial," and then you will be at rest. You may bring something to his attention with humility, but let him do as he wishes.. And pray for me, most honorable brother.

Question: "If one happens to be living with an elder who is unable to respond to questions, when the brother is in fact troubled by certain thoughts, should he ask another elder, whether with or without the knowledge of his own elder? Or should one [endure and] perhaps be crushed by one's thoughts?" Response.

If one knows that one's abba will benefit the soul, one should confide in him, saying: "I have these thoughts; what do you think that I should do?" The elder, like someone who has an ill son and hurries to take him to a doctor—and, in fact, even spends all of his income in order to care for this child—will also gladly take his disciple to someone with the gift of healing, or else send him to such a person. If one knows that the elder cannot endure this, then one should not say anything but simply look for an opportunity, when God will provide an occasion, to ask another spiritual elder about one's thoughts, entreating him not to inform one's own elder because this would throw him into the passion of envy.

This of course will create great affliction for him inasmuch as one is asking another elder while not being scandalized by one's own elder for not possessing such a gift; for this gift is not given to everyone. Nevertheless, if one searches carefully, one will in fact discover that one's own elder has another gift. For the gifts of the Spirit are diverse and distributed variously among people,[1] to one in such a manner while to another in a different manner. Now, if one does not find the opportunity to ask someone else, then one should endure, praying to God for assistance.

1. Cf. Rom 12.6; 1 Cor 12.4.

LETTER 505

A brother who was easily moved to anger asked the same Old Man about this. Response by John.

If you were struggling to die unto people and to receive a little humility, you would have found rest and would easily have avoided many dangers. May your heart be humbled before God; and his goodness will come to our assistance in every circumstance.

LETTER 506

A brother asked the Great Old Man, saying: "Pray for me, father; for I am weak in both soul and body, that the Lord may strengthen me to give thanks to him. Pray also for the brother who is with me; for he, too, needs God's mercy." Response by Barsanuphius.

May the Lord strengthen you in every good deed, just as you have requested. Behold, this, too, is a good deed, namely, to be in agreement, as much as you can, with your brother who is with you. May the one who said: "I came to bring fire to the earth"[2] also kindle this fire within your heart as well as mine. May I see you flourishing as the cedars of Lebanon and blossoming as the palm trees[3] in the paradise of my God.[4] For if this happens, I, too, shall taste of your goods and rejoice in Christ Jesus our Lord. To him be the glory to the ages. Amen.

LETTER 507

Question: "Father, pray for me; for I would like to know whence such weakness has occurred to me both in my service and in my manual labor. How is it that, out of negligence, my thought inclines toward eating and sleeping?" Response.

As for the matter of praying, my child, if indeed I have any prayer, I am unable to pray for my own soul more than for yours. For I tremble when I hear: "Strive [to love] your neighbor as yourself."[5] Nevertheless, as for me, I am certainly doing my best; but the mercy is up to God, who has already shown and contin-

2. Lk 12.49.
4. Cf. Rv 2.7.
3. Cf. Ps 91.13.
5. Lv 19.18.

ues to show great mercy to us. I do not deny the fact that he has done so because that would be ingratitude.

As for the matter of weakness, and your being one way on one occasion and another way on another occasion, the right way is as follows. One walks for a while on a smooth path;[6] then one comes upon precipices, hills, and mountains; afterward, one again encounters a level path.[7] Since it is also said: "Give thanks in all circumstances"[8] and "we are debtors,"[9] then thanksgiving should always precede our eating, drinking, and sleeping. Meditate on the words of the Apostle: "Whether you eat or drink, or whatever else you do."[10] Keep this in everything that you do, and the God of thanksgiving will protect you. To him be the glory to the ages. Amen.

LETTER 508

Response by the same Great Old Man to a question from the same person about whether he should take medication.

Brother, some people use doctors and others do not. Those who do, use them with hope in God, saying: "In the name of the Lord, we entrust ourselves to doctors; for he shall grant healing through them." Those who do not use doctors, do not do so, again, with hope in his name, and he heals them. Therefore, if you do use doctors, you are not doing something wrong; and if you do not use doctors, do not be arrogant. I say this because you need to remember that when you use doctors, it is the will of God that occurs, and nothing else.[11] If, however, you wish to abide by the word of Elijah[12] in regard to thinking only about the present day,[13] then you will be carefree.

LETTER 509

Question: "Father, pray for me and tell me what it means that, when I want to chant Psalms during the night, I feel lazy, especially if it is cold. So I chant most of them sitting down and sup-

6. Cf. Is 40.4; Lk 3.5.
8. 1 Thes 5.18.
10. 1 Cor 10.31.
12. Cf. 1 Kgs 18.14–15.

7. Cf. Ps 142.10.
9. Rom 8.12.
11. Cf. Sir 38.1–15.
13. *Life of Antony* 7, PG 26.853.

posedly praying. Now since I am afraid that I suffer these things out of negligence, deem it worthy to illumine me, father, and pray that I may do whatever I am told." Response.

We have all been commanded to pray for one another.[14] Now, as for what you asked me, wanting to know what it is all about, part of it is mingled with the seed of the demons,[15] and part of it comes from the weakness of the body. Therefore, chanting the Psalms or praying while sitting down with compunction does not prevent us from pleasing God through our service. For if one stands in prayer and yet is distracted, then one's labor is in vain.[16] May the Lord help you, brother. Amen.

LETTER 510

Question: "Father, I entreat your holiness; for I am weak in both soul and body. It is now many days that my body is extremely weak, so that I eat in the morning and often even sleep on my mat. There are times when my soul gives thanks, saying: 'God has permitted this illness to befall me on account of my many sins.' Yet there are other times when I am afflicted and discouraged, saying that I am not as worthy as all the others to eat my bread once a day in peace. Then again, my thought tells me: 'Are you allowed to contradict God? Does he not know everything? Can anything happen without him? So endure this with thanks.' I entreat you, father, for the sake of God's mercies, pray for me and show me how I should avoid being consumed by sorrow." Response by Barsanuphius.

Your holiness wrote to my holiness to pray for your God-loving person. I, too, then, as an imprudent father, ask you as my prudent son to do the same, namely, to pray for me; for I am wasting my days in vain. At least you say that you give thanks to God, even if it is once; I never do so. Since, however, I am unable to keep silent, I shall offer you my suggestion. If one does not eat for the sake of pleasure but for the sake of the body's weakness, God will not condemn that person. For foods are controlled in order to avoid excessive eating and bodily arousal.

14. Jas 5.16.   15. Cf. Mt 13.39.
16. Cf. 1 Thes 3.5.

Nevertheless, whenever it is a case of illness, there one experiences a respite from such actions. For wherever there is illness, there is also the invocation of God. Therefore, I think that a person is not condemned for giving the body whatever it needs, if indeed it truly needs this, while also giving thanks for one's illness. Indeed, God does not demand of us more than we can do.[17] There, I have told you what I had to say. Of course, I do not say that I am speaking the truth. Nevertheless, I have declared to you whatever my heart had to say. So you should try it, too, and you will come to know what is beneficial for you. Forgive me, however, for never being able to keep silent.

LETTER 511

The same person was ill and unable to stand in order to perform his service or to be content with one meal a day; so he entreated the same Great Old Man to pray for him and to show him what to do about this. Response.

When the Hebrews were about to be liberated from captivity to the Egyptians, they endured constraint and great affliction between the sea and the hands of the barbarians.[18] Yet, after the signs and wonders, which their eyes beheld occurring among the Egyptians and in all of their land,[19] they forgot the God who did these things[20] and almost despaired of their salvation, seeing Pharaoh and all of his power falling upon them.[21] Now Moses was left alone before the almighty God;[22] and, since "the Lord is near to all who call on him, to all who call on him in truth,"[23] the one who knows everyone's heart[24] responded to Moses, who was crying out with his heart, even though his lips were sealed completely with a door of silence. "Why do you cry out to me? Strike the sea with the staff in your hand, and divide it, in order that the people may go into the sea, and so I will gain glory for myself over Pharaoh and all his army."[25]

---

17. Cf. 1 Cor 10.13.
18. Cf. Ex 14.9.
19. Cf. Ps 104.27–33.
20. Cf. Ps 105.13 and 21.
21. Cf. Ex 14.10–12.
22. Cf. Ps 105.23.
23. Ps 144.18.
24. Acts 1.24.
25. Ex 14.15–17.

The same also applies here. There is bodily illness and there is demonic hindrance followed by afflictions and turmoil of thoughts. Therefore, the body is slackened by illness; but it is also hindered by the weight of the demons. If Moses were to cry out in silence, that is to say, if the intellect were to cry out in vigilance—whether one is seated or standing up—he who knows the secrets of our hearts[26] will hear us, fulfilling the words: "For I am sleeping, but my heart is awake."[27] Then he will rebuke the sea, saying: "Make a way for my people." And Pharaoh and all those with him will be drowned, while the people will be calmed in order to prepare a festival for God.[28] So whether you are sitting down or standing up or [even] lying down, let your heart be alert in order to perform your service of the Psalms. If you are unable to recite the Psalms, then bow in prayer, falling down before God without ceasing, whether by night or by day. And the enemies that are tempting the soul will turn back in shame.[29]

As for the other matter of eating twice a day, let your diet be modest and in godly fear; then do not hesitate to eat twice, and you will not be condemned. This means not taking anything out of desire but only consuming what you normally do, remaining a little hungry and not completely filled after a meal. I entreat you to pray also for me, so that I may courageously and gladly travel the way that lies before me, which is level and smooth, filled with peace, joy, and gladness, with light and exaltation, with which one can never be completely filled; for there is no other way than this.[30]

LETTER 512

The same person was relieved of his illness and asked the same Great Old Man: "Father, when I partake of food, I am much weighed down. Thereafter, I am unable to fast again; for my body feels weak and I sweat a great deal. Moreover, hard-heartedness and pride drive away my tears." Response by Barsanuphius.

---

26. Cf. Ps 43.22.   27. Song 5.2.
28. Cf. Ex 12.14.   29. Cf. Ps 6.11.
30. Cf. Mk 12.31.

Brother, I greet you in the Lord, praying to him that he might strengthen you and grant you patience. You must learn, however, that this warfare comes from the devil, who weighs you down with food in order to make you relax. For he also tempted me a long time, weighing down heavily upon me, even making me vomit night after night. I began, however, to partake of a little food, and then he changed his tactic. Whenever I started to eat, just as I placed a bite in my mouth, he would make me vomit. Therefore, I began to eat every two days, in order that I might grow accustomed to the food, but that, too, was his tactic. Nonetheless, with the grace of Christ, through patience and thanksgiving, [my temptation] has ceased. I had become so weak that I cannot even describe it to you; yet I did not give up but struggled until the Lord gave me strength.[31] Brother, when I was ill, that is what I did. You should, however, pay closer attention to yourself, and God will have mercy on you. For there is only one who is envious of you, and the Lord has annihilated him.[32]

As far as fasting goes, lower your neck,[33] remembering the lives of the fathers, how they fasted and kept vigil, and be humble in your heart; if you are able to fast until the ninth hour, then do so. If not, then do not worry; try, rather, to maintain the fast of the inner self, keeping the commandment not to eat of the tree[34] and guarding yourself also from the other passions. This fasting of the inner self is acceptable to God, and he shall protect you in the matter of bodily fasting.

As for tears, you mentioned that hard-heartedness and pride drive these away from you. Remove these, and tears will then come with the assistance of the saints. As for the sweating that you suffer, it is from the cold. Warm yourself a little, and God will help you. Pray also for me; for my slackening leads me to many evils. Nevertheless, I do not despair; for I have a merciful God.

---

31. Cf. 2 Tm 4.17.
32. Cf. 2 Thes 2.8.
33. Lowering one's neck is symbolic of humility: see, among others, *Letters* 513, 535, 553, 572.
34. Cf. Gn 2.16–17.

LETTER 513

The same person fell ill and could no longer bear the pain. So he entreated the same Great Old Man to pray for him and help him. Response.

My brother and my beloved in the Lord, for the sake of assuring you of my spiritual love for you in Christ, I shall reveal to you the mysteries of God. For you know and are convinced that I pray to God day and night in order that he might save you from the evil one and receive you in his eternal kingdom. Now while I was praying in my usual manner, he said to me: "Let me test him through this bodily illness for the benefit of his soul, so that I may learn how much patience he has and decide what inheritance he shall receive through his prayers and labors." I replied: "Nevertheless, Master, treat him with mercy, as a genuine son and not as an illegitimate one."[35]

It was not necessary for me to reveal these things to you, but I have revealed them to you in order that you may learn the joy that awaits you. So do not be sorrowful; God will have mercy on you. If you cannot endure, then lower your neck, knowing what the holy martyrs endured; and sprinkle some rosewater and holy water [on your body]. Our God will take mercy on you according to his own will and according to his own pleasure. It is not pleasing for me to see you suffering, whether in soul or in body. May God have mercy on you. Pray for me.

LETTER 514

Request from the same person to the same Great Old Man for prayer and assistance in the same passion. Response.

Despondent and grumbling brother, why do you grieve? Why are you crying out? Why do you ask for prayer from a distance, when you have Jesus standing so close by, longing to be invoked by you for your assistance? Cry out to him: "Master,"[36] and he

---

35. Cf. Heb 12.8.
36. Cf. Lk 8.24.

shall respond to you. Touch the hem of his garment,[37] and he shall heal not only your one passion but all of your passions.[38] Had your intellect been where it was supposed to be, then not even the bites of venomous serpents and scorpions[39] would be able to make you feel any bodily pain. It is said: "I have forgotten to eat my bread because of my loud groaning."[40] Do not grieve, then; for the mercy of God is nearby. I greet you in the Lord; be healthy, you cry-baby.

LETTER 5 1 5

When the same person was depressed and greatly tormented, he entreated the same Great Old Man in regard to healing. Response.

My God will send you prompt healing of soul and body.[41] I have confidence in his holy name that you shall be well. Therefore, as steadfastly as you can, render thanksgiving toward him, remembering how he has loved you and shown mercy toward you through his holy discipline.

LETTER 5 1 6

As soon as this response was sent out by the holy Old Man, [the brother] was immediately healed that very hour. So he offered thanks to God and to the Old Man, at the same time asking for unceasing prayer for his progress and salvation.[42] Response.

Dearest brother, let us offer unceasing praise to our Master and God, who bestows on us the present things in order to grant us rest in our life. For by disciplining us, he is gaining us; and by tempting us, he is providing for us a way out[43] as well as strength to endure afflictions; he puts all of us to death in order to bring us to life,[44] "making of us a spectacle to the world, to angels, and to mortals."[45] Therefore, let us make him joyful through our humility, obedience, patience, gentleness, long-suffering, modesty,

---

37. Cf. Mt 9.20.
39. Lk 10.19.
41. Cf. 1 Thes 5.23.
43. Cf. 1 Cor 10.13.
45. 1 Cor 4.9.

38. Cf. Ps 102.3.
40. Ps 101.5–6.
42. Cf. 1 Thes 5.17.
44. Cf. 1 Sm 2.6.

peace, and thanksgiving. Dearest one, may you receive all that you have asked in Christ Jesus, in whom I greet you, praying that he might protect you in his name from all evil.[46] Amen.

From the same person likewise on affliction of the heart. Moreover, why is it that there still remains in him a small illness? Response by Barsanuphius.

Frivolous brother, how long will you not let the dead bury their own dead?[47] Despise the body, which is destined to be eaten by worms. In any case, you are not bringing any benefit to it, since it will be given over to decay. For it is said: "Make no provision for the flesh, to gratify its desire."[48] You should meditate on these things. As for what you have written, there still remain a small remnant of bile and a remnant of the demons. Therefore, harden your thought a little toward these, and if it is God's will, then the demonic remnant will be lifted from us, while the remnant of the bile will not harm you. As for me, I pray, with all the capacity of my weakness, that my Father and my God will not set aside your requests, but rather grant them to you in abundance and loving-kindness. It is up to him to grant you his mercy; it is up to you, however, to accept it. Think about what I am saying, and pray for me.

LETTER 518

Question from the same person to the Other Old Man: "Father, tell me whether it is necessary to assist the body whenever it needs some food that is appropriate to its illness, or perhaps to eat earlier; or else whether one should maintain the same routine and despise all of this, even if this may result in something displeasing." Response by John.

God has granted us prudence through the sacred Scriptures in order to be directed in the straight path.[49] Therefore, the Apostle says: "Test everything; hold fast to what is good."[50] There

---

46. Cf. Ps 120.7.
48. Rom 13.14.
50. 1 Thes 5.21.

47. Cf. Lk 9.60.
49. Cf. Ps 142.10.

is nothing else that a person must do except not to take or do anything in a passionate way. If one does so out of weakness or necessity, then this is reckoned to him neither as sin nor as slackness. For being healthy and seeking bodily comfort is turned into desire; whereas, when we control the body on account of necessity, then we find that it assists us in the service of our ministry.

If we take care of animals for the sake of our necessity, how much more so should we take care of the body, which is the tool of the soul? When this tool is blunt, the artisan is hindered, even if he is intelligent and experienced. The Apostle was paying attention to the weakness and the stomach of Timothy when he permitted him to use wine;[51] for he said that it was an arduous task to perform the work of an evangelist.[52] Therefore, we require discernment; and then we shall not fall quickly. Brother, forgive me, but I do not know whether I spoke well; nevertheless, it is not necessary to discuss the matter further. Whatever I had in my heart I have spoken to your love. Now do as you think best.

LETTER 519

Question: "How is it that I feel extremely tired, especially when I rise to chant the Psalms at night, as if I were unwell? Whatever I do, I do as a burden. Is this perhaps weakness, or is it from the demons?" Response.

The matter of illness is quite clear. For if the body cannot tolerate regular food, it is evident that it is unwell and one should relax one's ministry. If, however, the body accepts the customary food and does not rise for liturgy, it is evident that this comes from the demons. It is, therefore, necessary to constrain ourselves, although always according to our strength and never beyond this. If the heart is vigilant,[53] then sleep is nothing for the body; it is like a person who is almost snoring but, when he hears robbers breaking in, does everything possible to escape them. Thus, if we are able to understand, we shall see that we are exactly like this.

51. Cf. 1 Tm 5.23.   52. Cf. 2 Tm 4.5.
53. Cf. Song 5.2.

LETTER 520

Question: "Father, tell me whether an illness can come from God, and how one may recognize this." Response.

It can indeed. Therefore, when one perceives any illness and observes that no troubling passion is present, then this illness comes from God and will dispel the warfare. In this case, it is necessary to condescend a little to the body. When, however, an illness is present together with a troubling passion, then we should not condescend at all. For it is demonic, and any condescension will only increase the passion. So it is beneficial to subdue the body wherever warfare prevails, even if one succumbs to illness; nevertheless, one should not cast the soul into illness in order to support the body. On the other hand, if some illness or cause of indisposition is manifest, when, for example, the body is weakened by a journey, namely, from a heat wave, then one should condescend—always moderately and never excessively—because the demons also mingle something of their own in this.

LETTER 521

Question: "Master, teach me whether illnesses that come from negligence or disorder are natural. Moreover, for what reasons are certain illnesses inflicted on a person by God? And, as for the accidents that happen to someone, do they occur with the prior permission of God?" Response.

Illnesses that occur through negligence or disorder are natural. Those illnesses that are sent to us by God are sent for the purpose of discipline on account of disobedience. Therefore, it is up to you to be neglectful or prodigal and to fall into those, until you reach the point of correction. You are able to avoid the illnesses of discipline through repentance. As for accidents, again, some of these occur through neglect, and others for our discipline as well as for our benefit, in order that we might repent. It is up to a spiritual person to discern between the one and the other.

Question: "Tell me, father, what one should do when an illness comes jointly from nature and from demons. Above all, pray for me for the sake of the Lord." Response by John.

Anyone who wants to conquer will force oneself a little, whether in fasting, vigil, or anything else. Therefore, if one's custom is to eat nothing until the ninth hour, but illness dictates that one eats at the third hour, then one should force oneself to fast until the sixth hour. The same applies in the case of vigil. This constraint is found to hinder the action of the demons, while condescension also assists in overcoming bodily illness. The same may be said about the other matters. Thus one will spend two days practicing with discernment the fear of God. May the Lord accompany us in our weakness in all things. Pray for me.

Question: "If one is ill disposed toward regular food, what should one do?" Response.

In the case of ill disposition, there are times when one is able to force one's thought a little. If, however, this is not possible, then one should condescend a little. For this, too, is a form of weakness. Brother, strive not to forget these things. I believe that, through the prayers of the saints, you will find that you are assisted and saved by God.

Question: "Forgive me, lord abba. The fathers say that we should despise the body, and then they say that we should control the body with discernment. I entreat you to teach me the difference between the two." Response.

In regard to your question, the Apostle explains the difference between the two when he says: "Make no provision for the flesh, to gratify its desires."[54] Again, the same Apostle says: "For

54. Rom 13.14.

no one ever hates his own flesh, but nourishes and tenderly cares for it."[55] Therefore, if you notice any pleasure active [within you], then despise the body. If, however, you notice the body exhausted and miserable, then tenderly care for it and nourish it in godly fear, so that it may support you in your spiritual ministry.

LETTER 525

Question: "Since you have said that it is necessary to care tenderly for the exhausted body through proper diet, should one also avoid whatever is harmful, or not?" Response.

If one fares well in health by avoiding those foods that are harmful, this is not a sin. If another person accepts whatever comes one's way, despising possible harm to the body for the sake of God, then that person is greater than the first, unless one happens to be robbed through the door, namely, through arrogance. Furthermore, one should guard against consuming food out of passion; for this is a great loss and is more harmful than beneficial. Both health and illness come from God, who said: "I will kill and I will make alive; I will wound and I will heal; and no one can deliver from my hand."[56] Therefore, whenever God wills, he dispenses health through a doctor or, if he wants, through a mere word. As for prolonging or abbreviating an illness, this belongs to God's foresight. Thus those who submit themselves entirely to God are carefree,[57] and he does with them as he wills and as is best. Each, then, should act as one can, or rather as one believes.

LETTER 526

Question: "Father, what does the phrase 'as one believes' mean? Explain this to me." Response.

If God has sanctified and purified everything so that the faithful may partake of all, then one should receive from whatever is offered with thanksgiving and without discrimination.

55. Eph 5.29.   56. Dt 32.39.
57. Cf. 1 Cor 7.32.

Indeed, holy and pure things do not harm anyone, unless one's conscience or one's suspicion believes that one is harmed. For such a person is in fact hesitant in faith, and this is why passion abounds within. Therefore, if one believes in the one who came to heal every sickness and every weakness among his people, then that same one is able to heal not only the bodily illnesses, but also those of the inner self. If, however, one is in doubt, then one should avoid harmful foods, condemning oneself for not being able to tolerate them and for being overcome in thought, not being found to have a secure faith. In this way, one is guarded from consuming food with passion, since this is harmful for both soul and body.

LETTER 527

Question: "If someone believes that one will not be harmed, but perceives oneself to be in pain as a result of illness, what should one think in order not to fall into faithlessness?" Response by John.

If one eats with faith and the pain persists, one should not entertain doubts. For God knows that this pain would deliver one from many passions of the soul, and so he has allowed one to fall ill. Therefore, one should at that point remember the Apostle, who says: "Whenever I am weak, it is then that I am strong."[58] Nevertheless, one should not think that this has occurred because one has eaten foods that appear harmful; rather, it has been permitted by God. Indeed, even if one eats those foods that are apparently good and useful, nothing can be of benefit without God's decree.

LETTER 528

Question: "If faith is required, then how is it that Abba Isaiah said: 'If a certain food is placed on the table, even if it is harmful to you, force yourself to eat it'?[59] For in spite of one's faith, the food would prove harmful." Response.

58. 2 Cor 12.10.
59. Abba Isaiah, *Ascetic Discourse* 5.

Abba Isaiah was speaking to a scholar, who was healthy in body and able to eat of the foods offered, with a view to cutting off his own will. May the Lord have mercy on you, child, and strengthen you.[60]

LETTER 529

Question: "Father, tell me whether those who are ill but despise medicine and food have reached the measure of perfection." Response.

Those who have despised medicine and food have reached the measure of faith[61] but not the measure of perfection.

LETTER 530

Question: "If, then, someone does not have this kind of faith, should that person examine which foods are beneficial for one's illness, or merely avoid those foods that are harmful? And if it happens that a certain food is neither harmful nor extremely beneficial, should one partake of this without any fear?" Response.

One should only avoid the harmful foods. If a certain food happens to be neither harmful nor beneficial, then one should not eat to the point of satiation, but only a little. For if one eats to the point of satiation, even from food that is beneficial, one is harmed.

LETTER 531

Question: "If two kinds of food of equal amount are offered, one of these being simple and the other a delicacy, should one satisfy one's need with the simpler food? And if the simpler one also happens to be sweeter, then which one should one eat?" Response.

If two kinds of food are offered, both of equal amount, then one should eat a little of both. If only one is offered out of the

60. Cf. Eph 6.10.
61. Cf. Rom 12.3.

two, then one should choose the simpler one. If this happens to be sweet, and a delicacy is also offered, then one should prefer the latter. If a delicacy is not offered, then one should choose to eat the simpler food, even if it is sweet, struggling against its sweetness and making sure that one always eats a little less than enough. Why? Does not illness often demand something that is quite disagreeable? Yet one is obliged to take it in order to be healed. So even if the food is sweet, if one needs it, then one should eat it. One ought merely to guard oneself against being overcome by pleasure, as we have said. Nevertheless, one should always remember to blame and condemn oneself from that very moment.

LETTER 532

Question: "Since, as you have said, making use of a doctor in the name of God is not to be rejected,[62] although leaving everything up to God with faith and humility is even better, my thought tells me: 'If some physical illness comes upon you, you should show it to a doctor; for being healed without medicines is beyond your measure.' Then again, it tells me not to make use of these, but instead to use the holy water of the saints and be content with that alone. I entreat you, compassionate father, tell me to which of these I should adhere." Response by John.

Brother, since I observe that you seem to care a great deal about the healing of bodily illnesses, I should tell you that the fathers are not in fact preoccupied with these. Your second thought, then, is better than the first. For that thought has perfect faith in God, while the other [reveals] lack of faith. The second has patience, which brings one to testing of character,[63] which in turn gives rise to hope that does not shame; the other, however, contains hesitation, the sister of pusillanimity, wherein dwells faithlessness, the mother of doubt, which estranges us from God and in turn leads us to destruction. One makes us friends of God; the other makes us his enemies. One introduces us to the kingdom of heaven; the other leads to Gehenna. One

62. See *Letter* 508.
63. Cf. Rom 5.4.

raises the head,[64] granting boldness before our Master and God; the other makes us bow the head in shame and stand before God without confidence. One glorifies us; the other dishonors us. One cuts off our captivity and makes us carefree in order to cast our every concern before the Lord;[65] the other casts captivity and other evil occupations within our heart. One brings edification; the other leads to the slackening of those who consider it. One is filled with wisdom, namely, with the understanding that the one who is able to see the hidden passions will also be able to heal my own passion; the other is filled with foolishness in regard to God, wondering whether he can heal or not. One is characterized by a peaceful state and teaches the person not to despair; the other is characterized by a troubled state. One makes people travel throughout cities and towns; the other is free from all such things. One plants sorrow within the heart and consumes it; the other places thanksgiving within the heart and intercedes well for the salvation of all people before the great Doctor, who bears our sicknesses.[66]

As for me, my genuine brother, although I am completely reluctant, I have never shown myself to a doctor; nor have I taken any medicine for my wounds. I have done this not out of virtue but out of reluctance, refusing to travel to cities and towns in order not to burden anyone or trouble anyone with helping my unworthiness, fearing the future defense at the awaited hour in regard to whatever I have done. Whoever is able to endure this out of virtue is blessed; for such a person becomes a sharer in the patience of the holy Job.[67] I also remember that many women, too, courageously endured their physical illnesses, leaving everything to God. Indeed, I am ashamed even to be called a man. Thus the woman with the issue of blood renounced her former condition when she learned that worldly doctors were in no way able to help her, although she had spent all her living on them. Indeed, she assumed a different condition and hastened toward the great and spiritual, heavenly Doctor, who heals both soul and body, and so the illness disappeared even

64. Cf. Ps 109.7.   65. Cf. Ps 54.23; 1 Pt 5.7.
66. Cf. Is 53.4; Mt 8.17.
67. Using the variant reading, ἁγίου, instead of ἐν ἁγίοις; see SC 451, 674.

before the decree was given.[68] Moreover, the Canaanite woman renounced the secular people, the sorcerers, ventriloquists, and magicians, seeing that their art was both useless and demonic, and hastened to the Master, saying: "Have mercy on me, Son of David."[69] Indeed, the fact of her healing by the kind and loving Doctor was proclaimed to everyone from one end of the world to the other. I am omitting the rest in order to concentrate on these two women, so that I may someday reach the degree of their faith[70] and not fail to gain their beatitude. These two are sufficient for me as a rebuke of shame; so it is not necessary to introduce here the faith and humility of the centurion, who not only renounced doctors and others in order to come to the Master, but even deemed himself unworthy of bringing him into his house. He simply said with faith: "Only speak the word, and my servant shall be healed."[71] His faith was great, and it was praised by our Savior.

In saying these things, I shame myself; for I do not desire enough, or have enough zeal, or strive hard, or fall down to the ground, or even know when the hour of my judgment will arrive, wretched as I am. When shall I be called? When will the fearful and severe angel come in order to lead away my wretched soul with a reprimand? When will the door close, in order for me to stay and cry with the five virgins,[72] while no one will hear me? It is clear that these things sting me in the present moment; and it is no secret that slackness and reluctance have overcome me. What, then? Should I despair for myself? Surely not! For such a sin is unto death.[73] Nevertheless, I entreat you, brother, shed bitter tears for me, as if for a dead person, who has long been a stench in the tomb. We know the results of tears; for the experience of Peter's mourning has taught us.[74] Pray for me, who say these things but do nothing good, that the good Doctor may also be compassionate to me and heal the illnesses of my soul and body. To him be the glory to the ages. Amen.

68. Cf. Mt 9.20–22.
69. Mt 15.22.
70. Cf. Eph 4.13.
71. Mt 8.8.
72. Cf. Mt 25.11.
73. Cf. 1 Jn 5.16.
74. Cf. Mt 26.75.

LETTER 533

Question: "Behold, I surrender myself to God and to your hands. Therefore, compassionate father, take care of me for the Lord's sake." Response.

Brother, when you believe in this way, you will not be rejected by Christ, who said to the sinful woman: "Your faith has made you well."[75] Therefore, cast everything before God;[76] for he is the one who cares for us. To him be the glory to the ages. Amen.

LETTER 534

Question: A brother asked the same Old Man: "If someone has an illness that requires surgery, should he undergo surgery? Moreover, should that person seek the opinion of the fathers in this regard?" Response by John.

It is certainly necessary, child, for anyone who has any illness to ask one of the fathers about this and to do everything in accordance with his opinion. For there are times when the elder will have the gift of healing and may secretly work this healing; so it is not always necessary to seek doctors of the body.

LETTER 535

Question: "If something appears good to me, such as practicing abstinence, stillness, or almsgiving and the like, should I do this of my own accord, or should I do so with the advice of the fathers?" Response.

Not receiving the advice of the fathers, even in regard to something that is considered good, will in the final analysis lead to evil. For one is transgressing the commandment that says: "Son, do everything with consultation,"[77] as well as: "Ask your father, and he will teach you; ask your elders, and they will tell you."[78] Nowhere will you find Scripture permitting anyone to do anything on one's own accord. For not accepting advice is

75. Mt 9.22; Lk 8.48.   76. Cf. 1 Pt 5.7.
77. Cf. Prv 31.4.   78. Dt 32.7.

pride, and such a person becomes an enemy of God. "For God resists the proud, but to the humble he gives grace."[79] And who else is humble but the person who bows one's neck before the elders in order to receive their opinion in godly fear?

LETTER 536

Question: "If someone is suspected of being a heretic, but confesses the correct faith, should one believe that person or not?" Response.

The fathers sought nothing else but the correct faith and a verbal confession. Therefore, if someone is truly found to be blaspheming Christ[80] with the mouth and lives apart from Christ, then one should avoid and not approach such a person. For in terms of the heart, anyone who does not keep the commandments of Christ is a heretic; and if one does not believe in one's heart,[81] then that person's words are of no benefit to him.

LETTER 537

Question: "If someone's abba is found to proclaim heresy,[82] should that brother abandon him?" Response.

If it is determined accurately that the abba proclaims heresy, then the brother should indeed abandon him. If, however, there is only a suspicion about this, then the brother should neither abandon him nor examine what he believes. For what is concealed from people is revealed to God.[83]

LETTER 538

Question: "What happens if the abba has an orthodox belief, but some heresy is expected to move through that region and there is fear that the monks may be forced to violate the correct faith? If the abba does not wish to leave that place, but the brother,

79. Prv 3.34.   80. Cf. Mt 12.31.
81. Cf. Rom 10.9.
82. The various heresies prevailing at the time are also referred to, both implicitly and explicitly, in *Letters* 57–58, 547, 600–607, 694–702, 734–36.
83. Cf. Dt 29.29; Sir 11.4.

knowing his own weakness, wants to depart from that region for another, is this a good thing or not?" Response.

One should not leave before the heresy appears, which might force this departure. In this way, the words shall not be fulfilled: "The wicked flee when no one pursues."[84] If the heresy does indeed appear, then one should indeed flee, although always with the advice of spiritual fathers and with godly fear.

LETTER 539

Question: "Then, what happens if there are no fathers in that region who are assuredly able to discern this matter? Should one perhaps leave for the time being on account of the danger of heresy, and depart to another region where there are people able to discern, whom one might ask about this matter?" Response by John.

Yes, one should do precisely that and then fulfill whatever they tell him.

LETTER 540

Question: "If one of the fathers accompanies me on a journey and insists on carrying my baggage, and if this happens to be inappropriate or without edification for those present, since he is superior to me, then what should I do?" Response.

Make a prostration with humility, asking that you may carry the baggage. If, however, he does not accept even this, make a [second] prostration, saying: "Then, forgive me for the Lord, but we are unable to walk together; for this is creating a scandal for those who see us." If he continues to persist after the second prostration, then do not argue with him; for this belongs to the devil.

LETTER 541

Question: "So it is not beneficial to cut short the argument and allow him to carry the baggage, even if this creates a scandal for

84. Prv 28.1.

those present? For it appears that, in this case, the argument is worse than the alternative. Therefore, between two evils, one should choose the lesser evil." Response.

Argumentation after repentance reveals that something is according to the devil, and one should not pursue it. For the fathers say that anything excessive is from the demons.[85]

LETTER 542

A brother asked the Great Old Man whether it is beneficial for him to live in stillness. Response by Barsanuphius.

Those who want to walk in the way of God should not demand honor for themselves. For what else is the way of God but leaving behind one's own will in everything and regarding oneself as last and least of all? Such a person is able to walk in this way. For unless a person cuts off one's own will and places one's hope in the Lord,[86] then one is unable to walk in this way. In this person, then, the word of the holy Gospel is fulfilled: "Search, and you shall find; knock, and it shall be opened for you."[87] Life and salvation lie precisely in this; so strive to acquire these. There is no other way but this. Brother, do not be deceived.

LETTER 543

Question: "Father, what shall I do? For [spiritual] warfare afflicts and stifles me. Moreover, tell me, what is the sign that I have hope in God and the sign that my sins are forgiven? And how should I sit in my cell according to God?" Response.

Brother, the time of warfare is the time of labor. Do not slacken, but labor and struggle. When the warfare is stifling, you should stifle it in turn by crying out: "Lord Jesus Christ, you see my weakness and affliction; help me and deliver me from those who persecute me; for I have fled to you for refuge."[88] Pray also to receive strength to serve God with a pure heart.

85. *Sayings*, Poemen 129.
87. Mt 7.7.
86. Cf. Ps 145.5.
88. Cf. Ps 142.9.

The sign that a person has hope in God is shaking off from oneself every impurity of fleshly concern[89] and not thinking at all that one has anything to do with the present age; otherwise, one would have one's hope in it, and not in God. The sign that one's sins are forgiven is hating them and no longer committing them. If, however, one still thinks of these and still consents to them in one's heart, or even perhaps practices them, then this is a sign that they have not yet been forgiven and that one is still attached to them.

Sitting in one's cell according to God is to condemn oneself when the heart takes pleasure in the beauty of the cell or in some bodily comfort, by saying: "Woe to me, the sinner; for I am enjoying material things, which will condemn me and of which I am unworthy. Others, who are worthy [of these], are afflicted, spending their time without finding any bodily comfort. Lord Jesus Christ, forgive me for this, too, for the sake of your name, which is invoked upon us."[90] May the Lord strengthen and empower you,[91] child, so that you may progress and come to the measure of perfection.[92] Amen.

LETTER 544

A brother asked the Other Old Man, saying: "Father, pray for me for the Lord's sake, and tell me whether it is a good thing for us often to ask the fathers to pray for us, even when they have already assured us that they are doing so. Or does it perhaps seem as if we are tempting them?" Response by John.

Brother, I have often written to you about prayer,[93] that it is God's commandment that we should pray for one another, especially when we are asked by others to do so, since we are then obliged to do so. Therefore, we cannot but do our best. As for asking the fathers to pray for us, this is beneficial. For it is said: "Pray for one another."[94] And again: "Those who are well have

89. Cf. 2 Cor 7.1.   90. Cf. Jer 14.9.
91. Cf. Phil 4.13.   92. Cf. Eph 4.13.
93. A possible indication that this letter is addressed to Dorotheus of Gaza.
94. Jas 5.16.

no need of a physician, but those who are sick."[95] Nor should we be neglectful, remembering the boldness of the widow before the unjust ruler.[96]

Since, then, our heavenly Father knows what we need even before we ask him,[97] why did he not say: "Do not ask; for I know what you want even before you ask this of me"? Instead, he said: "Ask, and you shall receive,"[98] and so forth. Therefore, it is a good thing to ask that we might receive, in accordance with his promise. When you ask for prayers, you should say: "Abba, I am not well; I entreat you to pray for me in the manner that you know; for I need God's mercy." God will have mercy on you as he wills; for his is the loving-kindness and the glory to the ages. Amen.

LETTER 545

Question: "If one happens to be eating with other brothers and finishes the meal sooner than the others, is it a good thing to ask the abbot for a blessing to rise [from the table upon finishing], or should one wait until everyone has finished? Or should one perhaps measure out the way that one eats bread and take a smaller portion of the other cooked foods? Which is better?" Response.

When one is seated at the dining table, if one sees that one has finished eating and cannot stay there any longer without eating, then one should ask to leave the table. Staying there while not eating, however, is even better than this. As for dipping one's bread into a little of all the cooked foods, this is even better than the previous two options.

LETTER 546

Certain brothers, who wanted to keep abstinence, asked the abbot to allow them to leave the table before the other brothers because they could not control their stomachs if they remained at the table. When the abbot gave them permission to do so, some other brothers judged and criticized them, not understanding

95. Lk 5.31.   96. Cf. Lk 18.1–8.
97. Cf. Mt 6.8.   98. Jn 16.24.

the benefit that would result. So they sent a letter, asking the same Old Man about this. Response by John.

The first are like workers[99] who are vigilant over their souls, doing this in their struggle to maintain abstinence, lest by sitting at the table they become greedy and eat more of the food offered. For staying at the dining table and not being overcome by the stomach belongs to the perfect.[100] But you are idle; for you have not understood the words of the fathers, who say: "Do not say, 'What is this?' or, 'What is that?' or, 'Why is this?' but pay attention only to yourself." The same fathers again advise us not to criticize anyone, applying the prophetic word: "May my mouth not speak the deeds of [wicked] people."[101] Instead, you fell into the sentence that states: "The evil person brings evil things out of an evil treasure."[102] Why did you not rather remember good things about your brothers for your own edification, thinking: "We are neglectful, but our brothers keep abstinence"?

By the same token, your brothers, who rise from the table, think good things about you, saying: "Woe to us; for we rise out of weakness; whereas our brothers are not harmed, even if they eat more than we; for they do everything with discernment." In this way, they, too, avoid the threat against criticizing, namely: "Do not judge, so that you may not be judged,"[103] while you fall into this temptation by judging your brothers, who are superior to you, and by transgressing the word of the Apostle: "Those who eat must not despise those who abstain."[104] On the contrary, while you are eating, you should be more sorrowful than they, inasmuch as you are overcome by the stomach; and you should give thanks to God for the food, so that through your thanksgiving he might be able to liberate you from the [spiritual] warfare of the stomach and the condemnation of your brothers. If you wish to understand this better, these things are a matter of discernment; therefore, one must discern good from evil,[105] according to the Apostle: "Test everything; hold fast to what is

99. Cf. 2 Tm 2.15.
101. Cf. Ps 16.4.
103. Mt 7.1.
105. Cf. Heb 5.14.

100. Cf. Heb 5.14.
102. Mt 12.35.
104. Rom 14.3.

good."[106] Therefore, since the abbot has rendered judgment on this matter, then there is nothing to argue about.

LETTER 547

A brother asked the Great Old Man: "I have certain books on dogmatic issues;[107] when I read these, I feel that my intellect is transferred from passionate thoughts to the contemplation of dogmatic concepts. There are times, however, when my thought rebukes me, saying: 'You should not read such things; for you are wretched and impure.'" Response by Barsanuphius.

I would not like you to meditate on these because they raise the intellect upward; I would prefer you to meditate on the words of the Old Men because these humble the intellect downward. I am not saying this to shame you, but simply to advise you. For there is a distinction between instruction and indulgence.[108]

LETTER 548

A certain brother, who was a foreigner, fell ill and came to the monastic community in order to be healed; he was offered the cell of one of the brothers, who did not, however, take this very well. When the Old Man learned this, he declared the following to him.

Examine your thought, brother, and ask it: "If it were your own brother according to the flesh, would you not care for him as for your own eyes?" Therefore, your relationships according to the flesh are able to help you here; for you have rejected your spiritual brother. We are all one in Christ.[109] So pay attention to yourself, brother, in godly fear.

When the brother heard this, he was moved to great compunction. Having benefited, he announced to the Old Man: "Forgive

---

106. 1 Thes 5.21.

107. Other references to the availability of such books in the monastery of Seridos may be found in *Letters* 49, 228, 326, and 327.

108. The Greek text plays on the words *trophē* (τροφή, spiritual nourishment) and *tryphē* (τρυφή, sensual nourishment).

109. Cf. Gal 3.28.

me, lord abba, and pray for me; I shall receive my brother with
great joy."

A brother, who had been a disciple of the same Old Man before
the latter retired in stillness within the monastic community, left
for another place. Upon his return, however, he scorned another pious brother, calling him foolish and insignificant. So he sent
a letter, asking the Old Man to direct him as he had done previously, saying: "God has once again brought me to your holiness."
Response by Barsanuphius.

The Apostle says: "The kingdom of God does not depend on
talk."[110] Abba Macarius said: "Someone who believes correctly
and labors in piety will not be delivered by Jesus to the passions
and the hands of the demons."[111] The Lord said: "In the days of
Elijah, there were many widows in Israel; yet he was not sent to
any one of them except to the widow in Zarephath of Sidon,"
even though she was Greek.[112] Again, he said: "In the days of
Elisha, there were many lepers in Israel; yet none of these was
cleansed, except Naaman the Syrian."[113] Although he was a foreigner, nevertheless he believed.

I thought that, having traveled elsewhere, you would have
abandoned your pretense to rights and gained humility. As I
see from your thoughts, however, you remain the same, and are
perhaps even worse. If God has chosen the foolish and despised
things of this world, which are regarded as being nothing,[114] it is
clear that he has rejected those which are esteemed, which create pride among people. Therefore, that which pleases people
does not necessarily please God.[115] Rather, that which is dishonored among people for the sake of God is blessed by God. For
he says: "Blessed are you when people expel you, and when they
hate you, and when they reject your name as something evil on
account of my name. Rejoice in that day and leap for joy; for
that is what their ancestors did to the prophets."[116]

110. 1 Cor 4.20.   111. Unidentified saying.
112. That is, heathen. Lk 4.25–26; cf. 1 Kgs 17.8–24.
113. Lk 4.27; cf. 2 Kgs 5.1–19.   114. Cf. 1 Cor 1.27–28.
115. Cf. Gal 1.10.   116. Cf. Lk 6.22–23.

You spent quite a long time with us. Examine your heart to
see what word or what advice you received from us, which is
tearing you away from the way of God. As for the protection
that accompanied you, from where else could it come except
from the affliction you endured? For the Old Man asked you to
leave for your own benefit. Tell me, brother; is God interested
in one's beginning or in one's final steps and results? Therefore, you know what you have gained in the time of your absence abroad. You also know that, when you used to live with
me in the past, I told you if you obey me in one matter and argue against me in another, then your own will is manifest even
in the matter where you are obedient. Thus I cannot render a
judgment upon you, but your blood is upon your own head,[117]
for now you are mature enough to speak for yourself. If God
has brought you here, then he will also direct you; however, if
it was by your own will, then it is written: "I gave them over to
the counsels of their own hearts, and they will follow their own
counsels."[118] Therefore, pray for me and have nothing to do
with us. I, too, want to be carefree in the Lord in regard to everything.[119] Amen.

LETTER 550

Certain brothers left the monastic community and purchased
cells for themselves in a neighboring region, without the approval of their abbot. Since the abbot was disappointed with them for
violating the process, he was thinking of asking them to leave.
They endeavored to resist, and so the same Old Man was asked
whether the brothers had acted correctly. And what should be
done? Response by Barsanuphius.

We always find that argumentation destroyed many people,
like those around Dathan and Abiram, who resisted Moses.[120]
So this is a bad sign; for if they did not respect their abbot, then
whom will they respect? Not respecting someone is a sign of rebellious thinking. Such rebellion against an admonition comes
at the instigation of the devil; for the devil rebelled from the

117. Cf. Mt 27.25.
119. Cf. 1 Cor 7.32.
118. Ps 80.13.
120. Cf. Nm 16.16–35.

outset. Those, then, who do the same become his children.[121]
What happens to these people? Such people have exiled themselves from the land of humility, blocking their ears so as not to
hear the one who says: "When they persecute you in one town,
then flee to the next,"[122] and: "If anyone wants to sue you and
take your coat, give your cloak as well."[123] These brothers submitted to evil, and evil does not give rise to good. For it is said:
"A rotten tree cannot bear good fruit."[124]

By their disobedience, they trampled on the process recommended by the fathers; for the fathers say: "If you go and live
somewhere, ask whether anyone is hurt by your living there."[125]
Indeed, if the fathers prescribed this about others, how much
more so when this creates sorrow in the abbot of such a person.
This is how an end should be put to this matter. The brothers
who are at fault should take others with them and entreat their
abbot to forgive them and not to return evil for evil.[126] The abbot should forgive them; for it is written: "We who are stron-
ger must bear the failings of those who are weak."[127] In fact, the
Lord says: "If you do not forgive other people their transgressions, then neither will your Father who is in heaven forgive you
your own transgressions";[128] and again: "Be perfect, therefore,
just as your Father in heaven is perfect."[129] In this way, God is
glorified, and this matter will be for the edification of many.

LETTER 551

The abbot of this monastic community, where the holy Old Men
lived, ordered something to be done, but some of the brothers, retaining their own will, did not support this and grumbled.
When the same Great Old Man learned about this, he addressed
the following response to them.

Brothers, the Lord said: "My sheep hear my voice, and they
follow me,"[130] and so on. Therefore, if anyone is a true disciple,

121. Cf. 1 Jn 3.10.
123. Mt 5.40.
125. *Sayings*, Poemen 159.
127. Rom 15.1.
129. Mt 5.48.

122. Mt 10.23.
124. Mt 7.18.
126. Cf. Rom 12.17.
128. Cf. Mt 6.15.
130. Cf. Jn. 10.27.

that person will obey his abbot in everything until death.[131] Everything the abbot does is for our edification; so one should not dare to disagree with his words or to say: "What is this? Why is this?" Otherwise, one is not a disciple but a judge of one's abbot. All these things happen only as a result of a truly evil human will. Therefore, if someone's abbot asks for something to be done and the disciple resists, then it is clear that this disciple wants to impose his own opinion and invalidate the abbot's word. So the disciple can discern who is actually the abbot here: is it the one whose word was abolished, or the one whose word was applied? Whoever wants to impose his own will is a son of the devil; and whoever does the will of such a person is doing the will of the devil. Therefore, if anyone follows one's own will, that same person will not find rest in this way. What are the consequences of this? None other than disobedience, which is the destruction of the soul.[132]

Therefore, if someone notices that he is scandalized by his abbot, that person should depart from there in order not to lose his soul and bear the responsibility for the judgment against others, whom one leads astray in this way. This is especially so when one does not know whether or not the abbot has acted correctly; for one is scandalized inopportunely on account of one's own will. Indeed, even if one's own will was done, yet no one can be more justified than the abbot; in fact, if such a person knows better than the abbot what is of benefit [to the monastery], then why is that person still a disciple of that abbot? Let him go away and make disciples of others himself.

Do not be deceived by the devil, persisting in your own will to your own harm. In fact, your own will is never realized. For one evil does not abolish another evil; rather, it is only when you abandon your will to God that he does as he wills. Brothers, God knows that I have written to you because I am concerned about you.[133] If, then, anyone accepts my words, that person will be saved; if anyone does not accept them, it is up to him if he wants to spit upon what I have written, just as some have already

131. Cf. Phil. 2.8.   132. Cf. Mt 16.25.
133. Cf. 1 Cor 7.28.

done in their heart or still others have done by criticizing us with their mouth. Forgive me.

LETTER 552

Response by the same Great Old Man to one of the fathers, who asked whether he should punish his disciple severely for disobeying.

Beloved brother, recognize the times; for they are evil.[134] Indeed, discipline is good and admirable, and we have many witnesses about this. For it is said: "The Lord reproves the one he loves";[135] and again: "Blessed is the person whom you discipline, Lord,"[136] and so on. This brother is struggling against hardheartedness; so support him and labor with him. "Discipline, rebuke, and encourage" him,[137] in accordance with the words of the Apostle. If he accepts this discipline, then he is gained once again. Awaken him from the deepest sleep of hard-heartedness. For if his skin of thorns hardens, then he will suffer great and unbearable mourning. If, however, he labors to remove the thorns while they are still green, then he can quickly be delivered from this passion. Nevertheless, if the thorns are hardened, then they can only be removed with toil, labor, and pain.[138] Therefore, tell him to pay careful attention to himself.

LETTER 553

Response by the same Great Old Man to a brother who was a carpenter in the monastic community and who was troubled by various thoughts, saying to himself: "I am not benefiting at all here, and I have no one to assist me here."

Brother, it is we who do not want to be delivered from the evil days[139] and the terrible afflictions. For God gave people two gifts, through which they can be saved and redeemed from all the passions of the old self. These are humility and obedience.

---

134. Cf. Eph 5.16.
136. Cf. Ps 33.12.
138. Cf. 2 Cor 11.27.

135. Prv 3.12; Heb 12.6.
137. 2 Tm 4.2.
139. Cf. Eph 5.16.

Yet we do not seize these;[140] nor again do we want to practice them or exercise them in order to find assistance,[141] to be delivered from evils and to cling through these [gifts] to the great Physician Jesus, who is able to heal us of the inflammation [of the evils]. Why, then, do you store up all your evils in your treasury, being troubled and worried? Cease being angry, irritable, and envious. Know that these things are dishonorable and not honorable. Abandon all the crooked ways,[142] bowing your neck with humility and obedience, and you shall find mercy. If you do whatever you are told with humility and obedience, the Lord will not only guide the manual work that you are now doing, but also all of your works. For he guards the way of those who fear him and protects their journeys. Why do you complain? Why do you argue? The mercy of God will come to your assistance if you persevere with godly patience.

Wretched one, die to all people. Tell your thought: "Who am I? I am but earth and ashes,"[143] and a dog. Each day, say: "I have nothing of my own." Why do you predict your own destruction instead of fearing God? Are you not ashamed to say: "I have not received any assistance here"? Why does Satan blind your heart, leading you to ingratitude, as if you are not benefiting in this holy place? Imprudent man, had not the hand of God and the holy prayers of the saints here protected you, where would you now be? Nowhere else but in the outer darkness.[144] Where else would you have benefited in this way? Nowhere. Nevertheless, the devil wants to estrange you from the genuine [love] of the saints, from their protection and benefit, and therefore sows in you the seed of death for destruction, so that you may fall entirely into the hands of the enemies of truth, who will rend your lamb—I mean your soul—to pieces.

Do not pay attention to anyone who scorns or despises you; for such a person traps you in these things, troubles you, harms you, and exiles you from calmness and peace, as well as from stability, prudence, and every good thing. Leave these and follow my words; I shall bear your burden[145] and you will find assis-

---

140. Cf. Mt 11.12.
141. Cf. Heb 4.16.
142. Cf. Ps 124.5.
143. Cf. Gn 18.27; Jb 42.6.
144. Cf. Mt 8.12.
145. Cf. Gal 6.5.

tance, mercy, and salvation for your soul. Brother, we are saved only through labor. So you should by all means avoid saying: "What is this? Why is this? Why do I have the same as such-and-such?" Carefully perform your small manual labor with godly fear; for you shall not receive a small reward in return. And do not despair of yourself; for this is the joy of the devil. May God not grant him this joy; may he rather mourn over your salvation in Christ Jesus our Lord, to whom be the glory to the ages. Amen.

The same brother asked the Other Old Man: "My thought tells me that if I want to be saved, I should leave this monastic community and practice silence, as the fathers have said.[146] For I am not benefiting in this art of carpentry, because it brings me much turmoil and affliction." Response by John.

Brother, it has already been declared to you that it is not beneficial for you to leave the monastic community. Now, then, I am telling you that if you do leave, you will end up falling. Therefore, you know what you are doing. If you truly want to be saved, acquire humility, obedience, and submission, namely, the excision of one's own will, and you shall live in heaven as well as on earth.[147]

As for the silence, of which the fathers speak, you do not even know what this is; indeed, not many people know. For this silence is not a matter of shutting one's mouth. Someone may speak tens of thousands of useful words, and this is reckoned as silence; another may speak only one idle word, and this is reckoned as trampling the Savior's teachings.[148] For he said: "On the day of judgment, you will have to give an account for every careless word coming from your mouth."[149]

Since you also say that you do not benefit from the art of carpentry, believe me, brother; you do not know whether or not it is beneficial for you. These are tricks of the demons, who show your thought whatever they want, in order that you may estab-

146. Cf. *Sayings*, Nau 274.   147. Cf. Mt 6.10.
148. See *Sayings*, Poemen 27.   149. Mt 12.36.

lish your own will and disobey that of your fathers. For whoever wants to know the truth asks the fathers whether one is
benefiting or being harmed. And that person believes whatever they say, and practices that which is beneficial. Many people
have paid a price in order to be insulted and to learn patience.
Yet you are learning patience at no cost, since the Lord says:
"By your patience you shall gain your souls."[150] We should give
thanks to the person who afflicts us; for through such a person, we acquire patience. You do well to stay. May the devil not
tempt you. May the Lord assist you. Amen.

LETTER 555

A brother asked the same Old Man: "Since my abbot will give account on my behalf, how can I ask him about my manual work?
Should I ask him: 'Do you command me to do this?'" Response
by John.

In order that you may not have any will of your own in anything, say: "What do you command me to do?" For if someone
retains one's own will and asks about a particular thing, that
person will endure danger, even if permitted to do something,
because one is realizing one's own will.

LETTER 556

Question: "What happens, then, in the case where I retain my
own will in something but have not asked [the abbot] about it
specifically? If the abbot has already allowed me to do it of his
own accord, is this reckoned as being my own will?" Response.

Tell him: "I am retaining my own will in this; what do you command me to do?" If he tells you to do it, then you are obeying his
will. If he offers you another task to do, then accept this with joy.

LETTER 557

Question: "What happens if I do not retain my own will in this
matter, but I tell him so because I think it will be of service to the
abbot, and also because I know that it will be pleasing for me to

150. Lk 21.19.

do this. For example, if I have been permitted to do something, which was left unfinished, and the thought came to me to finish the task, is this improper, too?" Response.

It is better to wait until you hear from the abbot. If you see that he is not sure whom to ask, and you volunteer in order to be of service to him, this is not improper. If, however, you were asked to do something and it remains unfinished, remind him that it is unfinished, but do no more than this; then you will not be found to retain your own will in anything.

LETTER 558

Question: "Scripture says: 'If the thought of the ruler rises against you, do not leave your post.'[151] What does this mean?" Response.

Instead of allowing the ruler to rise against you, do not speak with him, but take refuge in God. For if you want to respond to him, you will find that you are wasting your time and will be prevented from reaching warmth in prayer.

LETTER 559

A brother asked the same Old Man: "If I hear that someone has spoken badly about me, what should I do?" Response by John.

Immediately arise and, first of all, offer a prayer for that person as well as for yourself, saying: "Lord Jesus Christ, have mercy on this my brother as well as on me, your worthless servant,[152] and protect us from the evil one, through the prayers of your saints. Amen."

LETTER 560

Question: "If one begins to criticize another person but then realizes what one is doing, what should one do then?" Response.

If someone begins to criticize, one should quickly stop, turning the word toward a beneficial conversation, without any de-

151. Eccl 10.4.
152. Cf. Lk 17.10.

lay, so that one may not again fall into criticism through loquacity.

Question: "If someone is not actually criticizing another person but is gladly listening to criticism, is that person condemned for this?" Response.

Even listening gladly to criticism is criticism and receives the same condemnation.

Question: "Whence comes despondency? And what should one do when it appears?" Response.

There is a natural despondency that comes from weakness, and there is a despondency that comes from a demon. If you want to test these, do so in the following way. Despondency that comes from the demon appears just before the moment when one requires rest. For when one begins a task, even before completing a third or a quarter of the work, despondency drives one to abandon the task and leave. Therefore, one should not tolerate it, instead praying, remaining seated for the task, and persisting. For when the enemy sees that one is praying for this reason, he ceases; for he does not want to give any opportunity for prayer. Natural despondency arises when one labors beyond one's strength and is obliged to refrain from doing any more. Therefore, natural despondency is caused by bodily weakness. In this case, one should test one's strength and give rest to the body in godly fear.

Question: "What happens, then, when the very place where demonic despondency appears is burning hot and contributes to natural despondency, which further burdens one so that one cannot resist either of the two? Should one not leave that place in time of [spiritual] warfare?" Response.

It is a good thing to struggle in order not to leave a particular place in time of [spiritual] warfare. If one sees that one is overcome by the burden of labor, then one should leave. In this way, relieved of one burden, one may struggle against despondency itself by invoking the name of God in order to obtain his help. For departing on account of despondency, when the place itself is not a burden, is a greater burden and actually increases the warfare, so that harm comes upon the soul. If this prevails over a person, it is averted only with much toil, even if prayers are offered for this person.

LETTER 564

Question: "If despondency causes drowsiness, preventing one from [accomplishing] the task at hand, should one stand or remain seated?" Response.

One should stand and not cease praying to God; for the Lord will only abolish drowsiness through prayer.

LETTER 565

Question: "Whenever a wicked thought comes to me, my heart is moved with anger toward this thought, to the point of even shouting. Sometimes this happens when others are also present. Is this evil or not?" Response.

It is not good to do this; do not let it become a habit and do not let it harm others or scandalize those present. Rather, one should calmly invoke the name of God, and it will be averted.

LETTER 566

A brother went out of the monastic community and slackened. He announced this to the same Old Man, saying: "Since I was at fault, being ridiculed by the demons and my own mother, and since I left your protection, my fathers, I entreat you to admit me among the beginners, who have not yet received the monastic habit." Response by John.

In regard to placing yourself in the least position,[153] this is not up to you to ask, but up to your abbot to judge. What is up to you is simply to prepare yourself for obedience.

LETTER 567

Request from one of the fathers living in stillness to the same Old Man: "Father, I entreat you to pray for me for the Lord's sake. Indeed, I am in great danger on account of both my laziness and the disturbance of the enemy. Unless God grants me strength through your prayers and bridles the enemy,[154] I do not even know whether my vessel will ever reach the harbor. Nevertheless, just as Moses urged God not to destroy completely so many people with his wrath,[155] you, too, holy father, should intercede for my wretched soul. For God is good and likes to be solicited by the saints for the salvation of souls. Therefore, it is appropriate for you to make such a request. Moreover, ask also the lord abba not to take so long to see us; for I love him very much, and I need his support." Response by John.

If your love has written about us, the least of all, that we do not desire the destruction of any,[156] then what would you say about him who swore to himself, saying: "As I live, says the Lord, I have no pleasure in the death of sinners, but rather desire that they should turn from their ways and live"?[157] In this regard, the Apostle bears witness, saying: "He desires that all people may be saved and come to the knowledge of the truth."[158] Brother, do not delay in approaching Jesus, saying: "Master, save us; for we are perishing."[159] You shall see what he does against his enemies. Tell him: "Lord, my God, show me your vengeance against them; for I have lifted up my soul to you."[160]

As for the fact that you will endure afflictions and temptations, there is no need to write to you because you know what the Apostle said about this[161] as well as about the result of patience. Let us not despair, my beloved brother, and the Lord

---

153. Cf. Lk 14.9–10.
155. Cf. Ex 32.11–12.
157. Cf. Ezek 33.11.
159. Lk 8.24; Mt 8.25.
161. Cf. Rom 5.3–4; 2 Cor 4.17.

154. Cf. Zec 3.2.
156. Cf. 2 Pt 3.9.
158. 1 Tm 2.4.
160. Cf. Ps 24.1.

who cares for us is great; he will support us. For it was in order to create courage within us that he said: "It is I; do not be
afraid."[162] And again: "But take courage; I have overcome the
world."[163] Therefore, let us not neglect to fall before him and entreat his goodness; for he will do "abundantly far more than we
can ask or imagine."[164] Remember that wherever there is labor,
there is reward, too; wherever there is testing through temptation, there also is the crown of victory; and wherever there is
love of God, there again [one is ready] to ascend the cross with
him in order to suffer with him and to be glorified with him,[165]
to die with him and to live with him.[166] Therefore, one who as-
cends the cross is lifted from the earth. Such a person has died
to the world.[167] So one should think of heavenly things, where
Christ is at the right hand of the Father.[168]

As for the abba, pray that the Lord may protect him; for [he
is encountering] many troubles. Nevertheless, we believe that
the Lord protects and assists him. I told him that he was taking too long, and he explained, as he has also assured you, that
circumstances have obliged him otherwise. As far as prayer is
concerned, I know that I am nothing; however, I cannot prevent love. Therefore, you also should pray for me for the Lord's
sake.

LETTER 568

Supplication from the abbot of the monastic community[169] to
the same Old Man [John]: "Since the times are distressing,[170]
pray, father, that the Lord may make them pass quickly and that
we, his servants, may be protected from all testing of our sins."
Response.

If we do good, then God will make the hard times pass. If,
however, we accumulate evils, then we are heaping up[171] our own

---

162. Mt 14.27; Jn 6.20.
164. Eph 3.20.
166. Cf. Gal 2.19–21; 2 Tm 2.11.
168. Cf. Col 3.1–2.
169. This supplication is a letter from Seridos.
170. Cf. 2 Tm 3.1.
171. Cf. Rom 12.20.

163. Jn 16.33.
165. Cf. Rom 8.17.
167. Cf. Col 2.20.

destruction in advance. Nevertheless, if you persevere in good, God will send his angel in order to seal you,[172] so that, through the prayers of the saints, the one who comes bearing the sword may be averted.[173] Amen.

LETTER 569

Supplication from the fathers living in stillness within the monastic community to the Great Old Man in regard to the world: "Since the world is in danger,[174] all of us entreat you, as your servants, to pray to God's goodness, so that he may lift his hand and return the sword to its sheath.[175] Stand upright among those who have fallen and who live with your holy incense, and put an end to this destruction.[176] Raise the holy altar on the holy threshing-floor[177] of Ornan, in order that God's wrath may cease.[178] We entreat you; indeed, we implore you, have compassion on the world that is perishing. Remember that all of us are your members.[179] Display your compassion and God's wonders[180] even in the present time. For his is the glory to the ages. Amen." Response by Barsanuphius.

Brothers, I am in mourning and desolation[181] in regard to the impending wrath. Indeed, we are doing things contrary [to God's will]. For he said: "Unless your righteousness exceeds that of the scribes and Pharisees, you will never enter the kingdom of heaven."[182] So our transgressions have surpassed those of other peoples. There are many people who entreat God's loving-kindness to remove his wrath from the world; and, of course, none is more kind and loving than God, who desires to have mercy and opposes the multitude of sins that occur in the world.

There are three men, perfect in God, who have exceeded the measure of humanity and received the authority to loose

172. Cf. Ezek 9.4.
173. Cf. Ex 12.13.
174. This letter possibly refers to the plague that occurred in Palestine between 542 and 543 during the reign of the Emperor Justinian.
175. Cf. 1 Chr 21.27.
176. Cf. Nm 16.35.
177. Cf. 2 Sm 24.18–24; 1 Chr 21.15–26.
178. Cf. Jb 14.13.   179. Cf. 2 Sm 5.1; Eph 5.30.
180. Cf. Dn 4.2–3.   181. Cf. 2 Mc 11.6.
182. Mt 5.20.

and bind, to forgive and hold sins.[183] These men stand before the shattered world,[184] keeping the whole world from complete and sudden annihilation. Through their prayers, God combines his chastisement with his mercy. Moreover, it has been told to them that God's wrath will last a little longer. Therefore, pray with them. For the prayers of these three are joined at the entrance to the spiritual altar of the Father of lights.[185] They share each other's joy and gladness in heaven.[186] And when they turn once again toward the earth, they share each other's mourning and weeping and lamenting for the evils that occur and arouse his wrath. These three are John in Rome and Elias in Corinth, as well as another in the region of Jerusalem.[187] I believe that they will achieve his great mercy.[188] Yes, they will undoubtedly achieve it. Amen.

May my God strengthen you to hear, believe, and bear these things; for they are indeed unbelievable to those who do not understand them.

LETTER 570

A brother sent a letter, asking the Other Old Man: "For the Lord's sake, if you need anything, tell me so that I may bring it to you." Response by John.

Brother, may God grant you a good reward for your intention. I have, however, never asked anyone when I needed something, saying: "Give me this." If God knows that I need something and suggests it to someone who brings it to me, then I accept it. For if I say anything, then it is no longer a need but a desire.

---

183. Cf. Mt 18.18; Jn 20.23.
184. Cf. Ps 105.23.
185. Cf. Jas 1.17.
186. Cf. Eph 1.3.
187. An indication that the cell of Barsanuphius lay within the jurisdictional region of the church of Jerusalem.
188. Cf. Ps 50.3.

ON ABBA JOHN,
THE OTHER OLD MAN (570B)

The abbot [Seridos] said about the same Old Man [John], that he never saw him smiling[1] or troubled; never did he take holy Communion without shedding tears after reciting the words: "Lord, may these holy things not be to me for condemnation." Once, it happened that the same Old Man asked the abbot to do something. When, however, the abbot left there, he forgot [what he had been asked]. On a return visit, when it was time to leave, he said to him: "If you remember, do what I have asked you." The abbot was sorry for forgetting and so asked for his forgiveness. But when he left, again he forgot. Some days later he returned to the Old Man. Once again, as it was time for him to leave, the Old Man gently reminded him about the matter. The abbot was deeply grieved. Yet the Old Man told him: "Do not grieve; but whenever you happen to remember, do it."

Now, since this occurred many times, the abbot reported this to the Great Old Man, asking to learn what it means. The Old Man said to him:

 HIS HAS HAPPENED with God's permission, in order that you may see the patience and long-suffering of the Old Man, so that you may imitate him."[2]

The benefit that ensued was great.

---

1. See the Latin version of Athanasius, *Life of Antony*, in PL 73.134, and *Sayings*, Pambo 13.
2. Cf. 1 Thes 1.6.

ON ABBOT SERIDOS (570c)

BOUT ABBOT SERIDOS, I have many things to tell you, which are great and admirable, as well as entirely worthy of relating; yet I shall omit most of them for the sake of brevity and shall only recall enough information to present the man's virtue. For he led a temperate life from his youth, more intensely abstinent than any other person. He suppressed the body so much that it was terribly wounded. Nevertheless, afterward, the holy Old Man[1] prayed to God and healed him, commanding him to control the body with discernment in order that he might carry out his spiritual ministry and persevere in his administration of the brothers. He acquired great obedience, submitting in everything to the same Great Old Man, even unto death. For in denying his own proper desires, as the same Old Man himself witnessed about him in the above responses, he also became perfectly obedient. Indeed, he suffered a great deal, being beaten and variously tested by him. Yet, through this severe and most onerous discipline, he was burned like gold in the fiery furnace,[2] becoming an honorable vessel, useful to the master.[3]

Furthermore, he never for any reason answered back in any way; nor did he regard himself as an abbot, but as a disciple of the [Great] Old Man, owing perfect obedience to him, a sign of his extreme humility. This is why the Old Man regarded him as his genuine child. So he entreated God to grant him the gift of discernment; once this was acquired, he was able to direct souls to life with the grace from above,[4] as well as to heal the afflicted, to bring the healing medicine of the word of the Spirit, and to negotiate a peace for those in conflict. For hav-

---

1. I.e., Barsanuphius.   2. Wis 3.6.
3. Cf. 2 Tm 2.20–21.   4. Cf. Rv 7.17.

ing first made peace with himself, he brought peace also to others as their mentor; in him was fulfilled the word: "Blessed are the peacemakers; for they shall be called sons of God."[5] He was long-suffering and free of turmoil, gracious to those who approached him. His word was joyful, seasoned with modesty and salt.[6] In accordance with Scripture, he possessed prudence and innocence.[7] He was deeply loved by the brothers, gladdening their souls with the spiritual word of counsel, and encouraging them in virtue through his good example of conduct and virtuous practice.

He would teach whatever he practiced and would mingle gentleness with godly fear. He would "discipline, rebuke, and encourage"[8] each person as needed and when needed, in accordance with the word of the Apostle. As he related to us for our benefit, when he was gravely ill, overwhelmed as he was with intense and continuous fever, he did not entreat God to bestow health upon him, nor again to relieve him of pain, but to grant him patience and thanksgiving.[9]

Once it so happened that a pious and highly valued brother was troubled by demonic action and wanted to leave the monastery. Although he counseled him a great deal, he could not persuade him to stay; so he stood in prayer and made several prostrations. When the brother saw this, he, too, arose and did the same. The abbot turned to him and sealed his heart,[10] saying: "Brother, what do you now want to do?" The latter calmly responded: "Whatever you want." So he said to him: "Well, then, go and continue your work." He went away and continued his work, as was his custom, living in peace and submitting in godly fear.

On another occasion, the same abbot urgently needed some land beside the monastic community in order to build a church and a guesthouse. He entreated the owner to sell the land for a certain price, but the latter did not accept. Since the brothers and the visiting Christ-loving laypersons bothered him about purchasing the land, being unable to endure the disturbance

5. Mt 5.9.   6. Cf. Col 4.6.
7. Cf. Mt 10.16.   8. 2 Tm 4.2.
9. See *Sayings*, John the Dwarf 13, Poemen 8, and Sarah 1.
10. I.e., with the sign of the cross.

and unsure of what to do, he announced this to the Other Old Man. The Old Man said to him: "The land must certainly be purchased, but it is not yet time. If your thought afflicts you, then say to it: 'Imagine that this is an imperial road and that you are unable to purchase it; then you will find rest.'" Therefore, whenever he was troubled by this thought, he would oppose it in this way and find rest. After some time, the owner was convinced to sell the property.

Now, there was a small monastery in that region, and a brother lived there from time to time. The abbot took the brother aside and asked him whether he was grieved by the sale, assuring him before God that, if he was indeed grieved, he would not go ahead and purchase the land. After the brother gladly consented, the purchase proceeded. When a Christ-loving layperson learned this, who was beloved according to God in the monastic community, he was not very edified by the abbot's conduct. So he asked him to go ahead with the purchase without any second thought, saying that the abbot had preferred caring for one man over caring for many brothers who were greatly afflicted at not having a [large] church, as well as the many visitors who were unable to receive care because they could find no [adequate] place of hospitality. Requesting forgiveness, he asked the abbot what his purpose was for doing this, at the same time confessing to him his own criticism. The abbot smiled and said: "Child, I did not wish to afflict the brother, and so I cast the matter before God, trying to judge God's will in this way. I believed that if God wanted us to purchase the land now, he would assure the brother that he did not need to be grieved. If he were grieved, however, then it would be clear that God did not want us to purchase the land at this time. Behold, then, God assured him and he consented joyfully, so that the matter occurred in peace." The layperson admired the faith of the abbot and his sure hope in God, as well as his love for his neighbor and his detachment from worldly things; for the necessity and urgency of the matter did not overwhelm him. He made a prostration before the abbot, asking forgiveness for his sin; and receiving great benefit, he glorified God for the virtue of the fathers and departed.

LETTERS TO ABBOT AELIANOS (571–598)

LETTER 571

A brother, who was a Christ-loving layperson[1] with much faith in the holy Old Men, Abba Barsanuphius and Abba John,[2] desiring that they direct him toward life,[3] sent a letter asking Abba John the following: "Father, with God's mercy I pray that I may renounce the world for the monastic life, but I hesitate, unsure as to whether I should renounce everything from now on and become a monk or whether I should first put my affairs in order and then leave[4] so that I might be carefree in my renunciation,[5] especially on account of my elderly wife, my children, and the sale of my properties. My thought tells me to leave her with her nephews, openly giving them sufficient property to sustain her and her whole household. Then I should stay and take care of the sale of the remaining properties. Therefore, tell me, father, which is better and what I should do; for God reveals to you everything that is beneficial." Response by John.

ORGIVE ME, lord brother, but I am a simple man,[6] unable to distinguish my right hand from my left. Sir, Scripture, however, says: "No one who puts a hand to the plow and looks back is leaving immediately for the kingdom of God";[7] remember also the wife of Lot.[8] Moreover, remember that a lion can be seized by a mere hair, and an eagle by the very edge of his claw. Therefore, hand over your elderly wife to her

---

1. This is Aelianos, who became a monk and later was both selected and elected abbot of the monastery. Other letters addressed to Aelianos as a layperson include *Letters* 463–482; letters addressed to him as abbot include *Letters* 574–598.

2. With the exception of *Letters* 572–573, the correspondence is between Aelianos and the Other Old Man, Abba John.

3. Cf. Rv 7.17.   4. *Sayings*, Arsenius 40.

5. Cf. 1 Cor 7.32.   6. Cf. 2 Cor 11.6.

7. Cf. Lk 9.62.   8. Cf. Gn 19.17, 26; Lk 17.32.

nephews, and she will always be carefree. Then count her expenses and those of your children, giving them the appropriate properties. In this way they will always grant her what she needs from the income of the properties, on the basis also of their hope to inherit something from these after the death of the elderly wife in return for offering her rest among them. Furthermore, ask the holy Old Man whether you should stay and sell the remaining properties, and do whatever he tells you. Thus you will be carefree in the Lord; for he is not far from us, but sees whether our heart is prepared and guides our progress according to our intention. After receiving, then, the Old Man's commandment, proceed resolutely with courage toward what he has told you [to do], and the Lord will guide and expedite your progress according to your faith.

LETTER 572

Question from the same person to the Great Old Man: "Holy father, I know that asking your holiness about my thoughts is beyond me. Nevertheless, having heard the divine voice saying: 'Those who are well have no need of a physician, but only those who are sick,'[9] I see myself being oppressed by the multitude of my evil actions and thoughts. Therefore, I cast myself into the ocean of your compassion, for the sake of the one who said: 'As I live,' says the Lord, 'I do not desire the death of sinners, but rather that they should turn from their ways and live,'[10] in order that, through you, I may hear him saying: 'Child, your many sins are forgiven.'[11] I know and I believe that God has granted you to know through his Holy Spirit, even before I ask you, what I want and about which thoughts I am asking. Nevertheless, since I have heard the prophet saying: 'Be the first to declare your sins, in order that you may be justified,'[12] this is why I am recording them in writing, entreating you not to overlook my wretchedness but to accept this supplication from me, a sinner. For you have been given authority from God to lead people out of darkness and the shadow of death[13] and to direct them toward the true light;[14] for he is good.

9. Lk 5.31.
11. Cf. Lk 7.47–48.
13. Cf. Ps 106.14.

10. Cf. Ezek 18.23 and 32; 33.11.
12. Cf. Is 43.26.
14. Cf. Jn 1.9.

"What, then, do you command me to do? Should I renounce everything at once and leave things without prior arrangements? Or should I first settle my affairs and then leave the world? Shall I find the concern for these things afflicting me in my renunciation, suggesting troubling thoughts that choke the good and spiritual fruits?[15] If you order me to settle my affairs first, then also indicate to me whether I should sell the smaller properties and ask God to assist me. I am asking you these things, not presuming that I am able to keep your commandments, but merely placing my hope in your prayers in regard to the orders and assistance. For if you ask God on my behalf, that he might render my request good and beneficial, granting me strength to keep your commandments, then he will not set aside your request. This, and this alone, gives additional courage to my weakness." Response by Barsanuphius.

Child, it is clear that "the days are evil,"[16] and whoever is able to escape will be saved like Lot from Sodom.[17] "For the world lies under the power of the evil one,"[18] according to what is written, and those who live in it are working in every way against it. Indeed, by becoming entangled in earthly things, they become earthly. Those, however, who have renounced these things have ascended from earth; therefore, they have clearly become heavenly. Yet we do not understand, wretched as we are, that even if we do not want to renounce these things for God's sake from now, yet we shall have to forsake them involuntarily at the time of our death.

Child, God's command is to cut [ourselves] off at once from everything. For to the man who approached him, asking and saying: "I will follow you, Lord, wherever you go; but let me first put my affairs in order at home," he said: "No one who puts a hand to the plow and turns back is fit for the kingdom of heaven."[19] Again, to another, he said: "Let the dead bury their own dead."[20] Moreover, he said: "Whoever loves father or mother more than me is not worthy of me,"[21] and so on. Also: "Whoever comes to me and does not hate father and mother,"[22] and so on.

---

15. Cf. Mt 13.7.
16. Eph 5.16.
17. Cf. Gn 19.15–29.
18. 1 Jn 5.19.
19. Cf. Lk 9.61–62.
20. Lk 9.60.
21. Mt 10.37.
22. Lk 14.26.

Why did he even say that one should hate one's own life?[23] How does one hate one's own life, except by cutting off one's own will in everything for the Lord, saying: "Not as I want, but as you want."[24] Now, if you say all this, behold, it is the will of God that we abandon everything and follow him. What then? Have we not abandoned everything? Nevertheless, since we have not reached this point, on account of our weakness, let us lower our neck, recognizing our weakness, and let us remain to place our affairs in order.

Let us not think arrogantly, believing that we are doing something good, but rather that we are still behaving like weak people. For those who completely renounce the world abandon everything once for all. You, then, child, being weak and not completely whole, should similarly arrange not to sell your property first, but to settle your elderly wife; otherwise, you will become entangled in these matters. Therefore, settle her in accordance with the response addressed to you by brother John.

In regard to the sale of your properties, the Lord will take care of you and arrange this, if only you cast your concern on him.[25] Therefore, each day and each night, remember to tell him: "My Master, open up the way for me in accordance with your will, for my own good and benefit." Indeed, he knows better than anyone else how to lead us easily out of the prison of darkness and from the congestion therein, namely, out of the affairs of this vain world. Therefore, do not let your heart slacken. For I hope in my God that, through standing on my feet in prayer, I shall see you bearing fruit for God.

LETTER 573

Request from the same person to the same Old Man: "Holy father, I give thanks to the kind and loving God that you have not turned your compassion away from me.[26] Therefore, fulfill your mercy with your servant,[27] entreating God our Master for the salvation of my soul, that I may be delivered from passions and wicked forgetfulness, that I may find mercy through your holy hands

23. Cf. Jn 12.25.
25. Cf. Ps 54.23; 1 Pt 5.7.
27. Cf. Ps 118.124.

24. Mt 26.39.
26. Cf. Ps 65.20.

in the present age and in the age to come,[28] that I may depart from the body under your protection, and—quite simply—that I may become your servant for all eternity, enjoying the grace that is unique to your good way of life." Response by Barsanuphius.

Child, you were correct to write about forgetfulness. For had you not forgotten what I had written to you, you would know from those letters that our Master and God, the merciful and foreknowing Lord, assured me that he considers you a genuine spiritual son. I have confided in you mysteries that I have not confided in many, as evidence of your adoption as a son. Indeed, in whom does a father confide, except in his son? This is, of course, done gradually, according to the son's progress, to the degree that he is able and endures and applies.

All of my supplication and prayer to God for you is that he may liberate you from all the passions of dishonor, among which forgetfulness is also reckoned, that he may send upon you the Spirit to teach you everything,[29] and that you may not be separated from us either in this age or in the age to come.[30] For it has been revealed to God how your memory is fixed in my heart; and I believe that it will never be effaced from there in all eternity. Believe me that God has already granted me salvation for your soul unto eternal life. Yet be very careful, and do not forget again to keep my words in mind constantly, and do not be negligent in applying them. Indeed, many people who gained and sealed their treasure lost everything they wanted out of neglect. Unless a person cultivates the land well, sowing the seed in expectation of rain, then all the rains, even if abundant, will be of no use for its fruition. Watch out that you do not grow lazy, observing another person holding your load, and see that you do not become soft. For he did not say: "The prayer of the righteous is powerful and active," but "very powerful,"[31] which means that it is powerful in many of the points I have presented to you.

Do your best. For many were with Christ but later were estranged from him. The Apostle says: "If the unbelieving part-

28. Cf. Mt 12.32.
30. Cf. Mt 12.32.
29. Cf. Jn 14.26.
31. Jas 5.16.

ner separates, let it be so."[32] Nevertheless, may God not permit this to be fulfilled in you; may you remain a genuine and most desired son of my pains in Christ, a sheep of Christ's flock,[33] a consecrated vessel,[34] an heir of his glory,[35] in order that, having lived according to the commandments of Christ, you may obtain eternal life.[36]

Do not put my old age to shame. For God knows how I do my best for your salvation, praying to him that he might assign you for eternity with his holy saints as a co-heir to their future goods,[37] "which no eye has seen nor any ear heard nor the human heart conceived, which God has prepared for them."[38] May you have a part and an inheritance with these to the ages of ages. Amen. Moreover, may the heavenly powers and the saints who are still in the body say: "Amen; amen; amen. Let it be; let it be; let it be!" And may the Father, Son, and Holy Spirit seal this.

LETTER 574

After some time, when Abba Seridos, the abbot of the monastic community, was about to depart, he prepared [a list of] his successors among the superior brothers, not in order for them to manage the monastery together—for this would be the cause of disorder—but in order that the first in line may be succeeded after his death by the second, and so on through the rest of them in order. At the end of the list, he also wrote down the name of this Christ-loving brother and layperson, Abba Aelianos, so that he, too, would be a co-heir after everyone else, if he became a monk. This brother, however, was unaware of it. Therefore, when, after formulating this arrangement, the abbot died in the Lord, the first among the brothers, called according to the list to administer the monastery, refused with much humility and modesty. The others followed suit, doing the same and imitating the first. In the meanwhile, this Christ-loving layperson and brother was overcome by sorrow from the devil in regard to the end of the world and other afflictions, which might supposedly seize

32. 1 Cor 7.15.
33. Cf. Zec 13.7.
34. Cf. 1 Thes 4.4.
35. Cf. Eph 1.18.
36. Cf. Mk 10.30; Lk 20.35.
37. Cf. Eph 3.6; Heb 10.1.
38. 1 Cor 2.9.

him in this life, as well as in regard to the eternal punishments.[39]
Pressed by these thoughts and in danger of falling into despair,
he sent a letter asking Abba John about this and requesting his
prayers as well as a word of consolation. The latter sent him the
following response, mostly about obedience. For he was about to
charge him with the administration of the monastic community,
as it later became clear. Response by John.

Beloved brother, faith in God means that one should give
oneself entirely to God, no longer being in control of oneself
but rather casting oneself under his authority until one's last
breath. Therefore, whatever happens to that person, he will accept it in thanksgiving as being from God. This is the meaning
of: "Give thanks in all circumstances."[40] For if a person refuses
whatever comes from God, then one is in fact disobeying God,
seeking to impose one's own will. It was in this way that the Jews
sought to impose their own will and were unable to submit to
the law of God.[41] For faith is humility: "Those whom he called
he also justified and glorified."[42] Therefore, cast away your sorrow, which brings about death, "while godly grief produces salvation."[43] Pray, then, for me and fear nothing. Otherwise, you
are irritating God by retaining your own will. May our Lord Jesus Christ grant you to fulfill his will and to find mercy before
him, to whom be the glory and the might to the ages. Amen.

LETTER 575

When he had received this response, the brother was immediately liberated from the thoughts that afflicted him. He did not,
however, understand the meaning of what had been written to
him and was surprised that, while he had asked certain questions, the Old Man had responded with quite different answers.
Then the Old Man openly told him what it was about, ordering
him to accept the care of the monastic community. Nevertheless,
the brother was surprised that anyone would think of him in this
regard, believing that he was incapable of doing this. Not daring
at all, however, to contradict the elder's order, he sent him a let-

39. Cf. Mt 25.46.   40. 1 Thes 5.18.
41. Cf. Rom 10.3.   42. Rom 8.30.
43. Cf. 2 Cor 7.10.

ter, saying: "Abba, I do not know myself better than the Spirit of God, which dwells in you, knows me,[44] and so I am fearful and terrified[45] at the risk that this entails. If you know that I am able in this matter to find mercy with your protection in Christ, then I do not resist; for you have authority over me, and I am in God's hands and yours." Therefore, the Old Man writes the following response to him.

Lord brother, God is my witness that I genuinely love you as my brother, and my prayer is that your soul may not be harmed at all. Trusting in your obedience and caring for your salvation, I have cooperated in this good.[46] For what is concealed from people is revealed to God. My brother, you also see that [this position embraces] many and immense responsibilities; yet you also should not doubt that everything in the monastic community, including the very sand on the ground, belongs to God. And he, who has united the earthly with the heavenly, has also sanctified everything through his presence.

Therefore, it is up to you to cooperate and suffer with him, so that you may be found to be a partaker of the souls of those who are saved. For the Apostle has said: "Bear one another's burdens, and in this way fulfill the law of Christ."[47] And again he said: "Associate with the lowly."[48] The Lord, too, said: "Whoever listens to you listens to me, and whoever rejects you rejects me."[49] Since, then, the entire matter belongs to God, you cannot refuse. For even if there is something that is [difficult] from a human viewpoint, you know that we are burdening you with godly concern, which means that it does not constitute any mere concern but in fact contributes to the salvation of your soul, as Scripture says: "Whoever brings back a sinner from wandering will save the sinner's soul from death and will cover a multitude of sins."[50]

Therefore, be brave in the Lord and believe in Jesus, and he shall protect us from the evil one, just as he asked his Father in regard to the apostles.[51] Do not hesitate, then, but pour out

---

44. Cf. Rom 8.11.
45. Cf. Heb 12.21.
46. Cf. Rom 8.28.
47. Gal 6.2.
48. Rom 12.16.
49. Lk 10.16.
50. Jas 5.20.
51. Cf. Jn 17.15.

your heart before God, the Lord Jesus Christ, and the Spirit of truth. Indeed, I believe that you will find mercy at the tribunal of God. May the grace of our Lord Jesus Christ and the communion of the Holy Spirit be with you.[52] Amen.

LETTER 575B

When the brother heard this, he declared the following to the Old Man: "Behold your servant, let it be with me according to your word,"[53] and, at the command of the fathers, he was deemed worthy of receiving the monastic habit. In fact, at the demand of all, the bishop even ordained him to the priesthood, and so he was formally installed as abbot of the monastery. After this, the first thing that he did was to seek to visit Abba John, who received him just as he used to receive the former abbot [Seridos] of blessed memory; for the Old Man was very humble. So he said to him: "Pray for me, abbot." Yet Aelianos stood there dumbfounded, not daring to pray over him. When he was asked a second time, he did pray in order not to refuse the Old Man. He was then invited to sit down, and the Old Man told him the following.

Brother, the holy [Great] Old Man predicted a very long time ago that you would become a monk and even abbot of the monastic community. Behold, then, his word has been fulfilled according to God's good pleasure. So pay attention to yourself, and may your heart be established in the Lord, who strengthens you.[54] Amen.

LETTER 576

The same person asked the Old Man, saying: "Father, forgive my rashness, but explain to me those matters about which I want to ask. Why did the superior brothers, who were first on the list as heirs, decline the administration of the monastery? And why did you allow them to do so, knowing both their virtue and their obedience, as well as the rank of their calling? At the same time, you ordered me to accept such an administration, when I am un-

52. Cf. 2 Cor 13.13.   53. Cf. Lk 1.38.
54. Cf. Phil 4.13.

worthy and have no experience in the monastic state, in which they are far more qualified." Response by John.

The brothers declined out of great humility. For although they had received the authority from God to administer the monastery in accordance with the contents of the will, yet they did not hurry toward it but instead preferred obedience. So they eagerly elected you, thereby providing rebuke to those who demand rights and gifts of inheritance, as well as to those who have a worldly mindset of avarice, preferring earthly things to the heavenly kingdom. Therefore, rejoicing in their humility, we allowed them to decline. As for you, we ordered you to accept for the sake of the calling from God, who disposes everything for the benefit of everyone, in accordance with his foresight.

Do not, then, think that this happened as a result of any disobedience on their part. For even Moses, entrusted by God with the administration of his people, said: "I am slow of speech and slow of tongue,"[55] and God forgave him, knowing that he said this not in a spirit of contradiction but out of great humility. Jeremiah the prophet did the very same thing, saying: "Master Lord, truly I do not know how to speak, for I am only a youth,"[56] and this was not reckoned as refusal. The centurion used the same words, when he said to the Savior: "I am not worthy to have you come under my roof,"[57] and his faith was admired, for it was mingled with humility. Do not ask, further, why it is that Joshua, son of Nun, did not decline the leadership[58] or why the apostles did not decline the proclamation.[59] Was this because they lacked humility? Indeed, whose humility was greater than theirs? Nevertheless, those who declined were obedient, and those who accepted were humble; for one cannot be separated from the other. Rather, everything occurs in order that God's judgments, which are beyond us, may be accomplished and in order that the virtues of the saints may be variously manifested. Therefore, you should believe that everything that happens

55. Ex 4.10.
56. Jer 1.6.
57. Mt 8.8.
58. Cf. Dt 31.7–8.
59. Cf. Mk 16.15.

from God will have a good end, and do not be anxious about anything else. May the Lord instruct you and illumine the eyes of your intellect through the prayers of the saints. Amen.

LETTER 577

When he heard this, he glorified God and said to the Old Man: "Father, since I am a beginner and know nothing, what do you command me to say to the brothers?" Response.

Tell them the following: "The Lord Jesus Christ, who cares for you, said: 'I shall not leave you as orphans; I am coming to you.'[60] Pay attention to yourselves with all humility and love toward God, and he shall bless you and become your protection and direction."

Also tell them the following: "Let no one conceal any thought, because the joy of the [evil] spirits is that we conceal our thoughts in order that they might destroy our soul."

If any of the brothers reveals his thoughts to you, say the following within yourself: "Lord, everything that you have for the salvation of the soul, grant it to me in order that I may speak to the brother, and in order that I may speak your word rather than my own." Then say whatever comes to you, believing within yourself that this is not your own word; for it is written: "Whoever speaks must do so as one speaking the very words of God."[61]

LETTER 578

Question: "When I bless the brothers, should I also give them my hand [to kiss] or not? For my thought tells me to kiss their heads affectionately. Is this a good thing?" Response.

When you are blessing them, give them your hand and tell them: "Know that God will do to you according to your faith[62] and consequently not according to how you please people." For the Lord himself has said: "Whoever welcomes a prophet in the name of a prophet will receive a prophet's reward; and whoever

---

60. Jn 14.18.   61. 1 Pt 4.11.
62. Cf. Mt 9.29.

welcomes a righteous person in the name of a righteous person will receive the reward of the righteous."[63] Therefore, if someone is a prophet or a righteous person, and another does not welcome that person as righteous or a prophet, then that person will not receive the reward. Whereas, if someone is neither a prophet nor righteous, and yet one welcomes that person as being a prophet and righteous, then one will receive the reward of a prophet and a righteous person. It is not necessary to kiss their heads affectionately; for this is a gesture of people-pleasing.

LETTER 579

Question: "How should I behave toward the brothers?" Response.

Consider yourself to be beneath them all and as servant of them all; for [the responsibility that you have assumed] demands compassion toward all, as the Apostle said: "Bear one another's burdens."[64] "Admonish the idlers, encourage the fainthearted."[65] Let no one return evil for evil, but only good.[66] If, however, someone does not submit, then bring that to his attention. The same Apostle will instruct you in everything else based on these few words.

LETTER 580

Question: "How should the canonarch[67] and the manager[68] behave toward the brothers?" Response.

They should be long-suffering, in order to bear those who are weak.

LETTER 581

Question: "If one of the brothers does something wrong, how should I rebuke him? Privately or in the presence of the other brothers?" Response by John.

---

63. Mt 10.41. 64. Gal 6.2.
65. 1 Thes 5.14. 66. Cf. Rom 12.17.
67. The canonarch (*kanonarchēs*, κανονάρχης) regulates the daily services in the church.
68. The manager (*oikonomos*, οἰκονόμος) organizes and supervises the daily commercial and material affairs of the monastery.

If the wrong is severe, then do so in the presence of the other brothers; however, you should also warn him in advance: "Unless you correct yourself, I shall speak in the presence of the other brothers." For this is how the Lord commanded: "Go and point out the fault when the two of you are alone. If he listens to you, you have [re]gained your brother. But if you are not listened to, then take one or two others along with you,"[69] and so on. If the wrong is slight, then rebuke him privately and give him the appropriate punishment.

LETTER 582

Question: "If one perseveres in the monastery, how is one saved? And how is it more advantageous for someone to live in a place where there are holy fathers?" Response.

If someone dies in the monastery with humility and obedience, then that person is saved through Christ. For the Lord Jesus will give account for that person. If, however, one retains one's own will and simply feigns obedience and humility, then this will be judged by God. As for the one who lives according to one's own will for bodily comfort and not for the soul's benefit, you should gradually counsel that person for the sake of him "who wants everyone to be saved and to come to the knowledge of the truth."[70]

Now if such a person persists in his own will, tolerate him until he feels ashamed or departs of his own accord. If he causes harm to the brothers, then solemnly address him, saying: "If you persist in this act, you cannot stay here with the other brothers." For it is naturally impossible for someone to tolerate the comfort of one brother at the cost of harming many others. Someone, however, who remains in the monastery in good faith and according to God receives protection from God and is edified. Someone who dies, after living in this way, will find rest.

The advantage for anyone living in a place where there are holy fathers is having faith in the good deeds and believing in the power of those fathers. For "the prayer of the righteous is

69. Mt 18.15–16.
70. 1 Tm 2.4.

very powerful and effective,"[71] which is something not found everywhere. Indeed, the Lord said about the apostles: "While I was with them, I protected them; but now I am coming to you; protect them in your name."[72] For yours is the glory to the ages. Amen.

LETTER 583

The same person asked the same Old Man: "Tell me what to declare to the brothers about patience and obedience; for they will accept your word." The Old Man announced the following to the brothers.

Brothers, you did not come here for comfort but for affliction. This is what the Lord prescribed for the apostles: "On the earth, you shall have affliction and sorrow; and the world shall rejoice."[73] If you follow the Lord Jesus, he, too, shall be with you. If you reject him, then he, too, shall reject you. Therefore, whoever wants to secure a blessing from God hears him who says: "Whoever keeps my word will never die to the age."[74] So whoever seeks eternal life seeks also to keep his word until the shedding of blood in the excision of one's own will. For no one who seeks [to retain] one's own will, which is displeasing to God, will have any part with Christ. Therefore, pay attention to yourselves in godly fear, and the Lord will protect you through the prayers of the saints. Amen.

LETTER 584

Question: "Father, tell me how I should meet with visitors, whether these happen to be laypersons or else certain fathers or other brothers." Response.

Walk in wisdom and welcome everyone without provocation, in accordance with the Apostle, who gave "no offense to Jews or to Greeks or to the church of God."[75] For the love of Christ, I remind my lord that the present time inclines toward bodily

71. Jas 5.16.
73. Cf. Jn 16.33.
75. 1 Cor 10.32.

72. Cf. Jn 17.11–13.
74. Jn 8.51.

comfort and filling the stomach, which give rise to all kinds of passions. Guard yourself, then, against those who come here for these false reasons, whether they be laypersons, brothers, or fathers. If such persons happen to come, then do not extend rich hospitality nor turn them away. If, of course, someone is only preoccupied with such things, then reject that person. In any case, you are not unaware of the abbot's [Seridos's] conduct and how he treated the visitors.

It is more beneficial for you to hear that you are stingy, when you are not, rather than hearing that you are luxurious. So welcome them with modesty,[76] always careful in your gestures, in order that you may be found to [do everything] a little less [than to full satisfaction]. And if someone forces you [otherwise], then tell that person: "I have been commanded this by the fathers and by the Apostle; for the Apostle says: 'Do not become drunk with wine; for that is debauchery.'"[77] The fathers say: 'We advise everyone who wants to show repentance unto God to refrain from drinking much wine, which gives rise to all kinds of passions.'"[78] Therefore, guard yourself against those who say: "Unless you drink, I shall not drink; unless you eat, I shall not eat." Advise them in all humility, repeating the words of the Apostle: "Those who eat must not despise those who do not eat; for it is to honor the Lord and to glorify God that they do not eat. Those who do not eat should not pass judgment on those who eat; for it is to honor the Lord and to glorify God that they eat."[79] Therefore, both of them are honorable before God; for each of them acts according to God's glory.

In brief, then, each should do what is necessary for the love of God, saying: "I am weak and unable [to do otherwise]; please be charitable with me." For the Apostle also said: "The kingdom of heaven is neither food nor drink, but love and purity of heart,"[80] and so forth.

Therefore, be prudent with your visitors, in order that you

76. Cf. 1 Tm 2.2.
77. Eph 5.18.
78. See Abba Isaiah, *Ascetic Discourse* 16.
79. Cf. Rom 14.3–6.
80. Rom 14.17; 1 Tm 1.5.

may prudently and wisely learn from everyone as to why and how they came here, and whether it was for God or for food. Do your best, furthermore, not to give yourself over to any fleshly teaching with your visitors, especially if someone happens not to request the word of God. Indeed, God will grant you prudence, but your conversation should always be from *The Lives of the Fathers*, the Gospel, the Apostle, and the Prophets. Do not submit to their invitation for you to speak about any worldly matters; for [such conversation can easily] turn to food and other fleshly matters. The texts I have just mentioned, however, are not fleshly teaching. Conversations about worldly matters should be interrupted, and these matters should not be discussed; for they refer to fleshly teachings. Tell that visitor: "Abba,[81] the Lord said: 'Give to Caesar the things that are Caesar's and to God the things that are God's.'[82] If, then, you have come here for God's sake, we are able to advise you in matters pertaining to God. The world loves its own,[83] and the mind of the world is not in harmony with the mind of God. Let us not be punished for talking to one another against the will of God. For the Apostle said: 'The mind that is set on the flesh is hostile to God; it does not submit to God's will; indeed, it cannot.'"[84]

LETTER 585

Question: "Father, tell me how a fleshly question is asked; and how does one respond in a godly manner to a person [asking such a question]?" Response.

Imagine that some people approach us in order to ask about a military expedition. We should respond that this matter is unjust; for God does not cooperate with injustice. If, however, someone asks you about fleshly matters, then offer a response that is true and stern, namely, a response that is according to God and not according to the flesh.

81. While the heading of this letter specifies that visitors may include lay persons, the title "Abba" here reflects an intimate address by monastics to all visitors, whom they respect as their peers.
82. Mt 22.21.
83. Cf. Jn 15.19.
84. Rom 8.7.

LETTER 586

Question: "Master, I entreat you for your compassion. Ask the holy Old Man that I may be delivered from arrogance in order that I may respond to each visitor with humble heart and godly fear, just as he asked [God] also for the sake of our holy father among the saints, the abbot of blessed memory [Seridos]."[85] Response by John.

Blessed be the Lord! May it be unto you according to your will! The kind and loving God, who abundantly provides[86] everything, will also grant you, through the prayers of the holy Old Man in the Holy Spirit, to speak in godly fear and to give a response to each person as needed, in all humility and unworthiness. Wherever you go, ask the holy Old Man in your mind, saying: "Abba, what should I say?" And do not be concerned about what you will say, in accordance with the commandment of the Lord, who says: "Do not worry about how you are to speak; for it is not you who speak, but the Spirit of your Father in heaven speaking through you."[87]

LETTER 587

Question: "How should we practice hospitality and the commandment about [charity to] the poor? Should we accept all of the visitors indiscriminately? And, since they disturb us for clothes, should we give them some, if we have any left over? Moreover, to whom [should we give clothes]?" Response.

Practice hospitality and the commandment [for charity] as much as you can; however, balance these also with your patience. Even if you have more than enough in your possession, you should still exercise balance, lest anyone develop a habit of asking continually on the pretext of poverty. Therefore, carefully examine the reasons for which each visitor approaches. If someone happens to be a thief, as the fathers have said, simply give that person a blessing and then ask him to leave. More-

85. See *Letter* 570c above.   86. Cf. 1 Tm 6.17.
87. Mt 10.19–20.

over, since some of them come here to exploit you, do not allow them any such boldness; for they are trying to exploit you with their greed, since they do not really need anything. And do not give a garment to anyone upon first encounter, unless it is a person who greatly fears God and is embarrassed to ask. So search out the truth, in order to see whether a person is genuinely poor and needy for God's sake rather than as a result of a prodigal life; and, afterward, show compassion to that person.

LETTER 588

Question: "Why should we not accept roaming monks in the monastic community?" Response.

Because, when they enter, they will cause you affliction. This is why you should simply give them a blessing and then ask them to leave.

LETTER 589

Question: "What happens when they insist on entering? Should we accept them or not?" Response.

The elders have told us that if any do not deserve to be accepted, then you should not accept them, even if they insist greatly. If necessary, however, give them a little more and then ask them to leave. For this is more beneficial.

LETTER 590

Question: "If someone is entirely unknown to us and we are not aware of who he is, should we accept him or not?" Response.

If you do not know someone, then you should accept him the first time at least, and you will learn what kind of person he is. Do not, however, allow anyone indiscriminately to stay in the monastery without first testing that person, so that you do not suffer temptation and affliction as a result of being unable to tolerate him.

LETTER 591

Question: "A monk, who is a priest, visits the monastic community from time to time and harms the brothers, by saying and doing scandalous things. He also wants to dwell nearby, some two miles from the monastery, in a place where the brothers pass by. What do you order me to do? Should I allow him to come to the monastic community in order to dwell nearby in the place I mentioned, or not?" Response.

Prevent him from entering the monastic community, saying: "Lord abba, you have scandalized the brothers and you should not come here, lest you create scandal for them again. Do not, however, think that we are rejecting you out of hatred. 'For whoever hates his brother is a murderer.'[88] It is simply because of the scandal. Moreover, it is also impossible for you to dwell nearby on account of the harm caused to the brothers." Tell him these things personally and immediately, in order not to shame him through another person; for he is also a clergyman.

LETTER 592

Question: "Another visitor to the monastic community did something deceitful and improper. For he took certain things in the name of the abbot of blessed memory [Seridos], without the knowledge of the latter. When that abbot learned this, he ordered that he should not be allowed to enter the monastic community. When the visitor heard this, however, he entered through a side door in the courtyard. The doorkeeper saw him and informed the abbot, saying: 'Cast him out.' He did indeed cast him out and completely cut him off from this place. Now, if he returns, should I allow him to enter or not?" Response.

You do not need to accept him; for this would not be beneficial to you. If, however, he still comes, then inform him by means of another person that he is not welcome here; for this is not spiritually beneficial.

88. 1 Jn 3.15.

LETTER 593

Question: "Another brother, who used to live in the monastic community but who was also not spiritually beneficial for the brothers, departed. After some time, he wanted to return, but the abbot did not accept him, saying: 'Even if I do want [to accept you], yet I cannot harm the conscience of the brothers. For they will be afflicted if I accept you; so this is simply impossible.' Since he has now arrived, desiring to be accepted, what do you order me to say to him?" Response.

Tell him: "You have spoken about this to the former abbot [Seridos] once or twice, and he informed you that this is simply not possible. Therefore, do not expect to dwell here either now or at a later time." Then ask him to leave. If he happens to visit once in a while, welcome him simply as a brother. If, however, he visits continually, then ask him: "Does your conscience not bother you?"

LETTER 594

Question: "If someone brings us something in the hope of re-ceiving more [in return], what should I do? Should I accept it or not? Sometimes I happen even to need that particular object." Response.

If you do not need it, then do not accept it. If you need it, then tell him: "If I take it, I shall pay you whatever it costs." And hasten to give him the equivalent value.

LETTER 595

Question: "There are times when faithful women visit us, or else mothers of our brothers, and we receive them in the outside cell. That cell has windows opening up to the monastery; should I converse with them through the window or not? Moreover, my elderly wife did not want to stay with her nephews, and so she gave me all of her belongings. Do you command me to speak with her whenever she comes and to meet her financial needs? Or what do you think that I should do? What should happen?" Response by John.

If there is any reason for these women to visit you for God's sake, not simply in order to see the place or for the sake of their own will, but specifically to hear the word of God or to bring something here, and if it is necessary to converse with them, then do so but force yourself to guard your eyes. For: "Everyone who looks at a woman with lust has already committed adultery with her in his heart,"[89] while everything that happens according to God will be protected by God. Do not do this in order to please people or to seek praise, but out of a pure heart,[90] extending your thought toward God. If it happens to be the mother of one of the brothers and she comes here for some necessity, then speak with her in accordance with the commandment that you have received. You should not see her, however, unless it is necessary. For her son is able to inform her, while you simply prepare whatever she needs, not giving to her wastefully, but again only what is necessary.

As for your elderly wife, for as long as she lives, you should speak to her from time to time and meet her needs, whether she wants to be in the city or in the nearby town. As for your children, however, you should not consent to fulfill their wishes until they are on a good course in their lives. Direct them with godly fear. Feed and dress them carefully in order to avoid both prodigality and scorn, so that they may not ask for more. Examine their needs and rebuke them, saying: "Give regard to yourselves; for you are no longer slaves but free people.[91] How carefree you are, and you enjoy more rest than even the rich!" And, when your elderly wife dies, give them their freedom as well as their share of property in a balanced way, whether here in the town or wherever else you want. For there is no law regarding this. If you threaten them, then they will become estranged from you, although the property will still be counted as yours.

LETTER 596

Question: "If it appears to me necessary to override one of the commandments that you have given me, should I do so or not?

---

89. Mt 5.28.   90. Cf. 1 Tm 1.5.
91. Cf. Gal 4.7.

If it is not necessary, but I am overcome as a human being, then what should I do?" Response.

If the matter truly demands that you override one of the commandments, then do not prevent yourself from doing so. If, however, it is not [necessary], and you are simply overcome as a human being, recognizing that there was really no great need in this matter, but your thought merely could not be controlled at all, then condescend to your thought but ask forgiveness from God and you shall receive it. It is not only in this matter, however, but in regard to every matter, that one should bear the blame. For it is said, even if you create a new heaven and a new earth,[92] nevertheless you are unable to be carefree.[93]

LETTER 597

Question: "If my conscience dictates that I change some of the regulations formulated by the abbot of blessed memory [Seridos], or even that I correct something in the monastery, do you command me to do so or not?" Response.

If it appears to you that anything needs to be changed in godly fear, then do not hesitate. And whatever needs to be corrected, you should correct it. Do not, however, do so excessively, but only as required; and even then, restrain yourself a little; for we are here temporarily.[94] The things of this age are like a tent.[95] Whenever you notice your thought wanting to do something, say to it: "Why do you want to do this?" And if it is a necessary requirement, then let it be done. If it is not necessary, tell your thought: "Of what benefit is this to you?" If it is a fleshly thought, then despise it; and if it greatly disturbs you, do not respond, but instead take refuge in God.

LETTER 598

Question: "Master, since you predicted your death to us, I am filled with fear and sorrow by the possibility of being abandoned by God for my unworthiness. Give me your word, I entreat you,

92. Cf. Rv 21.1.   93. *Sayings*, Poemen 48.
94. Cf. 1 Pt 1.17.   95. Cf. Heb 11.9.

that, just as we are assisted in your life, so also we may be assisted even after your departure to God, in order that God may cooperate with us[96] in all things according to his mercy." Response.

God said once for all: "I shall neither fail you nor forsake you";[97] and we trust in God, that he shall do with you even more than when we are with you. Therefore, whether you ask or whether you do not ask, he shall cooperate with you even more than you ask, as the Apostle said: "We do not know how to pray."[98] Our Lord Jesus Christ, who came down from his paternal throne for our salvation, will also save, restore, and protect us from the evil one, with our cooperation, through the prayers of the saints. Amen.

96. Cf. Mk 16.20.   97. Jos 1.5.
98. Rom 8.26.

LETTER TO THE MONKS OF
THE MONASTERY (599)

Some elders in the monastic community asked the same Old Man: "Master, we entreat you to tell us why, after promising us that you were imploring God the Master to leave the abbot of blessed memory [Seridos] with us, nevertheless he took him [away from us] even prior to you, although he always fulfills the desires of those who fear him.[1] Moreover, teach us this, father: How is it that God sometimes conceals something from the saints, as it happened with the prophet Elisha?[2] For what reason did the ulcers appear in the abbot when he was about to die?" Response by John.

 S IT WAS SAID TO ABBA ANTONY: "These are the judgments of God, and you cannot learn them."[3] That is how it is.

As for the ulcers and the change [in his health], once the abbot had received glory without measure from people and from God, [these occurred] in order that people might not deify him. For truly, he was deemed worthy of receiving the Holy Spirit and perfection; yet God extinguished the glory of people by means of this pretext, so that the glory of God might perfectly abound.[4] Indeed, having attained such a measure, he could no longer be concerned about earthly things; and, while still being among people, he could still not free himself from them. Therefore, God took him.

---

1. Ps 144.19.

2. Cf. 2 Kgs 4.27.

3. *Sayings*, Antony 2. While Antony is explicitly mentioned only once in the *Letters*, there are more implicit references to his *Sayings* and *Life*, such as in *Letters* 413 (*Saying* 12), 492 (*Saying* 4), 255 (*Saying* 7), 344 (*Saying* 37), 85 (*Saying* 1), and 508 (*Life* 7, PG 26.853).

4. Cf. Jn 5.41–44.

As for ourselves, what we expected is what happened, in accordance with the will of God, who excels in the providence of our salvation. It is not, then, for us to question the incomprehensible, but to cast our every thought and every good deed[5] before the one who has authority, in order that his will may be done. May the Lord Jesus Christ assure you and remove from you every doubt and wicked evil. I pray that you may be strong in the Lord. Amen. Pray for me, so that I, too, may find mercy and be saved from false knowledge and foolishness, in Christ Jesus the Lord, to whom be the glory to the ages. Amen.

5. Cf. 1 Pt 5.7.

ON THE DEATH OF THE OTHER
OLD MAN, JOHN (599B)

LETTER 599B

HE SAME Abba John inhabited the first cell of the Great Old Man, which was built for the latter outside of the monastery, and lived there in stillness for eighteen years until his death, which he predicted in the following way: "I shall die within seven days after Abba Seridos." When we entreated him not to leave us as orphans, he said: "Had Abba Seridos lived on, I would have stayed another five years; however, since God withheld this from me and took him, I shall stay no longer."

Then, Abba Aelianos, who had recently become a monk and at his recommendation [was elected] abbot of the monastic community, continually pestered Abba Barsanuphius with many supplications and tears to grant John to us; yet Abba Barsanuphius himself offered no response. Therefore, since Abba John realized this in his spirit, when we went down to see him the following day in order to entreat him, he initiated the conversation with Abba Aelianos, saying: "Why are you troubling the [Great] Old Man on my account? Do not torment yourself; I shall not remain." When we were filled with mourning and fell down before him, Abba Aelianos spoke on our behalf and said: "At least grant me two weeks, so that I may ask you questions about the monastery and its administration." The Old Man, moved to compassion by the Holy Spirit that dwelt in him, said: "Very well; you will have me for two weeks." So Abba Aelianos remained there and asked him about every detail in regard to the administration of the monastic community.[1] When the two weeks were over, he or-

---

1. See *Letters* 571–598 addressed to Aelianos on the administration of a monastery, as well as *Letters* 463–482 addressed to Aelianos before his election as abbot.

177

dered us not to reveal his death until the actual day. Then he invited all the brothers and those who happened to be in the monastic community, embracing each of them and blessing them. Afterward, he dismissed everyone and surrendered his spirit to God in peace.

LETTERS TO A MONK ABOUT
ORIGENISM (600–607)

LETTER 600

A brother asked the holy Old Man, Abba Barsanuphius, saying: "Father, I do not know how I came upon the books of Origen and Didymus, as well as the *Gnostic Chapters* of Evagrius and the writings of his disciples.[1] These books say that human souls were not created with the bodies but pre-existed them, being naked intellects or bodiless. Similarly, they say that both angels and demons were naked intellects. Human beings were condemned to the body because of their transgression, while angels became what they are by preserving their original condition. Demons, however, became what they are as a result of great evil.[2] In fact, they say many other things of this nature, such as that the future hell must have an end and that human beings, angels, and demons can return to the state they first enjoyed as naked intellects, something they call *apokatastasis*.[3]

"Therefore, my soul is afflicted, falling into doubt as to whether these things are true or not. Master, I entreat you to show me the truth so that I may hold to this and not perish. For nothing is said about these things in sacred Scripture. As Origen himself affirms in his *Commentary on the Letter to Titus*,[4] this is the tradition

---

1. *Letters* 600–607 deal with Origenism and other similar heresies of the time. *Letters* 601–602 belong to John; the rest are from Barsanuphius. They also appear in PG 86A.892–901 with the title: "Teaching of the Holy Barsanuphius in the Time of Aurelian, Bishop of Gaza, on the Concepts of Origen, Evagrius, and Didymus."

2. Cf. Rv 9.1–2 and 12.9.

3. Or, "restoration" of all things. Origen's notion of *apokatastasis* persists in a modified form in the theology of Gregory of Nyssa (see below, *Letter* 604) and Maximus the Confessor. For Gregory of Nyssa, see *On the Inscriptions of the Psalms* 2.6, PG 44.508, and *Commentary on the Song of Songs* 8.4 and 11.5, PG 44.948 and 1009. Nevertheless, the editor of our *Letters*, Nikodemus of Mount Athos, observes in a footnote that this notion is interpreted in an orthodox manner by the above writers.

4. Fragments in PG 14.1303–1306.

neither of the apostles nor of the church, namely, that the soul is an older creation than the body, as if he was characterizing any person saying this as being a heretic.

"Nevertheless, Evagrius, too, bears witness to this in his *Gnostic Chapters*,[5] that no one has spoken of these things, nor has the Spirit itself explained them. For in his sixty-fourth chapter of the second century of his *Gnostic Chapters*, he writes: 'On the former, no one has spoken to us; on the latter, only the one on Mt. Horeb has explained to us.' And again, in the sixty-ninth chapter of the same century, he likewise says: 'The Holy Spirit has not explained to us the first distinction between rational beings, nor the first essence of bodies.'[6] That there is no *apokatastasis* or end to hell, the Lord himself revealed to us in the Gospel, saying: 'These will go away into eternal punishment';[7] and again: 'Where their worm never dies and the fire is never quenched.'[8]

"Therefore, master, how could these people expound such teachings, when the apostles have not passed them down to us and the Holy Spirit has not explained them to us, as they themselves bear witness and as the Gospels contradict? Be merciful, then, with my weakness, since you are a father of compassion, and show me clearly what these doctrines are about." Response by Barsanuphius.

ROTHER, WOE upon and alas for our race! What have we left behind, and what are we searching for? What are we neglecting, and what are we striving for? How has our vigor been blunted? We have left behind the straight ways and want to walk in the crooked ways, with the result that the scriptural word may be fulfilled in us: "Woe to those who have abandoned the straight ways in order to travel in the crooked ways."[9] Truly, brother, I have left behind my own mourning, and I mourn over your fall; I have stopped weeping over my own sins, and I weep for you as if for my own child. The heavens tremble over the preoccupations of human beings. The

5. See A. and C. Guillaumont, in *Revue de l'histoire des religions* 142 (1952): 156–205. Cf. also A. Guillaumont, "Les Six Centuries des 'Kephalaia Gnostica' d'Evagre le Pontique," *Patrologia Orientalis* 28 (1958).

6. On the Evagrian interpretation of the pre-existence of souls, see *Gnostic Century* 3.28.

7. Mt 25.46.   8. Mk 9.48.
9. Cf. Sir 2.16.

earth shakes over how people want to scrutinize the incomprehensible. These are the doctrines of the Greeks;[10] they are the vain talk of people who claim to be something.[11] Such words belong to idle people and are created through deceit. For it is said: "Claiming to be wise, they became fools."[12]

Now, if you wish to learn about these things, pay attention. Our Lord Jesus Christ, our light and our king, says: "You shall know them by their fruits."[13] What fruits, then, do they have? Pride; scorn; slackness; neglect; scandal; estrangement from the law, or rather from the law-giver God;[14] a dwelling-place of the demons and of their chief, the devil.[15] These things do not lead those who believe in them to light but only to darkness. These things do not encourage one toward godly fear, but in fact toward hard-heartedness. These things do not lead to progress according to God, but rather to progress according to the devil. These things do not lift one out of the filth, but actually plunge one into that filth. These things are tares sown by the enemy in the field of the Master.[16] These things are thorns that grow in the soil that has been cursed by God the Master. They are entirely falsehood, entirely darkness, entirely deceit, entirely estrangement from God. Avoid these things, brother, so that their word may not be established in your heart. They dry tears, blind the heart, and quite simply destroy those who pay any attention to them. Do not dwell on them; do not study them; for they are filled with bitterness and produce fruit unto death.

As for knowledge about things to come, do not be deceived. Whatever you sow here, you shall reap there.[17] It is not possible for anyone to make progress after leaving this place. God will not labor to recreate the soul after one's death.

As for the heavenly orders, sacred Scripture silences everyone when it says: "He spoke, and they came into being. He commanded, and they were created. He established them forever and ever."[18] And what God has established never changes. For

---

10. That is, heathen.
11. Cf. Acts 5.36.
12. Rom 1.22.
13. Mt 7.16.
14. Cf. Ps 83.7.
15. Cf. Mt 9.34; Rv 18.2.
16. Cf. Mt 13.25.
17. Cf. Gal 6.7–8.
18. Ps 148.5–6.

there is no change in him,[19] according to Scripture. Where did you find it said that the zeal of a certain angel led him to progress?[20]

Brother, here is the place for labor; there is the place of reward. Here is the place of struggle; there is the place of crowns. Brother, if you want to be saved, do not preoccupy yourself with these things. For I bear witness before God that you have fallen into a pit of the devil and into ultimate death. Therefore, avoid these things and follow in the footsteps of the fathers. Acquire humility and obedience for yourself, as well as mourning, ascetic discipline, poverty, not reckoning yourself as anything, and other such virtues, which you will find in their *Sayings* and in the *Lives*. Bear "fruits worthy of repentance";[21] and do not pay any attention to me, who talk but do not practice. Rather, pray that I, too, may someday come to the knowledge of truth, to the glory of the holy, consubstantial, and life-creating Trinity, now and to the ages. Amen.

LETTER 601

The same brother asked the same question to the Other Old Man, Abba John. Response by John.

"Such wisdom does not come down from above, but is unspiritual and demonic."[22] This teaching is from the devil, leading to eternal hell those who pay attention to it. Anyone who is preoccupied with this teaching becomes a heretic; anyone who believes in it has deviated from truth; anyone who adheres to it is alienated from God's way. The workers of Christ, however, are not like this; the disciples of Christ have not taught this. Those who accept the word of truth do not accept such teachings. Brother, quickly detach yourself from these. Do not burn your heart with the fire of the devil. Do not sow thorns on your soil instead of grain; do not receive death instead of life. In

---

19. Cf. Mal 3.6; Jas 1.17.
20. Cf. Origen, *Commentary on Luke* 13.5–6, PG 13.1830–1832, and *Commentary on John* 13.8, PG 17.357–362.
21. Lk 3.8.
22. Cf. Jas 3.15.

short, do not receive the devil instead of Christ. Do not delay in these, and you will be saved like Lot from Sodom,[23] through the prayers of the saints. Amen.

LETTER 602

The same brother asked the same Old Man: "Should we not, then, read even the works of Evagrius?" Response by John.

Do not accept such doctrines from his works; but go ahead and read, if you like, those works that are beneficial for the soul, according to the parable about the net in the Gospel. For it has been written: "They placed the good into baskets, but threw out the bad."[24] You, too, should do the same.

LETTER 603

The same brother, who asked these questions, had doubts within himself, thinking and saying: "So how is it that some of the fathers in our time accept these teachings, and yet we regard them as being good monks and pay attention to their advice?" And some days later, it happened that this brother also asked the Great Old Man to pray for him. Then the Old Man revealed to him, of his own accord, what the brother was actually thinking in his heart, so that the latter was surprised and astounded.

Since you said and thought: "Why is it that some of the fathers accept the *Gnostic Chapters* of Evagrius?" it is true that certain brothers, who regard themselves as knowledgeable, accept these writings; but they have not asked God whether they are true. And God has left them to their own knowledge on this matter. Nevertheless, it is neither my role nor yours to pursue these matters; for our time is given us to examine our passions, as well as to weep and mourn for them.

LETTER 604

Question from the same person as well as from other brothers to the same Great Old Man: "Father, those who believe in the

23. Cf. Gn 19.15–29.
24. Mt 13.48.

pre-existence of souls do not hesitate to say that the holy Gregory of Nazianzus also develops the theory of pre-existence in his
works, especially in his writings on the Nativity of the Lord and
on the day of Pascha. They interpret certain words according to
their own heart, passing over what he clearly writes there about
the first creation of the human being, of the soul and the body,
according to the tradition of the church. For he writes as follows: 'Since the Creator, the Word, desired to show precisely this,
he created one being, the human person, from the unity of two,
namely, the invisible and the visible natures. And he took from
matter, which already existed, in order to make the body; then
he breathed into it his own life, which reason defines as the intel-
lectual soul or image of God.'[25]

"And then, in continuation, one discovers a great deal that is
clearly and unequivocally stated about the human being, made
from pre-existing matter and the soul given by God. Indeed,
Gregory greatly praises human nature, calling the salvation of
body and soul a worthy gift from God. He does not say what
these people claim, namely, that it is because of condemnation
that the soul was bound to the body, being chastised for the sake
of its former sins. Moreover, in various other writings, Gregory's
purpose is clearly revealed in safeguarding the doctrine entirely
pure. The same people also rejoice in regard to the holy Gregory, the brother of the holy Basil, because he, too, says the same
thing and speaks about pre-existence, and these people even mis-
interpret some of his words, too. Gregory, however, clearly writes
in the thirtieth chapter of his essay *On the Creation of Man*,[26] arguing strongly against this doctrine of pre-existence and refuting
it, just as did the blessed David, the followers of the holy John
and Athanasius, and all the other illuminators and teachers of
the church. In regard to the subject of the *apokatastasis*, the holy
Gregory of Nyssa himself clearly speaks about it, but not in the
manner in which they say he does, namely: 'When hell ceases,
humanity will return to its original condition, namely, that of
pure intellects'; rather, he does in fact say that hell will cease and
assume an end.[27] Therefore, father, tell us why such a person
does not speak correctly, as befits a holy person who has been

25. *Homily XLV On Easter* 7–8, PG 36.632–633. See also *Homily XXXVIII On
the Nativity*, PG 36.312–333.
26. Gregory of Nyssa, *On the Creation of Man* 27–28, PG 44.229.
27. Gregory of Nyssa, *On the Soul and on the Resurrection*, PG 46.108.

counted worthy of speaking for the Holy Spirit. For some of the fathers and teachers even disagree about paradise, saying that it is not material but spiritual. And on other chapters of Scripture, one again finds disagreements among some of them. So clarify this for us, master, we implore you, in order that we may be illumined by you and give glory to God, and so that we may not doubt our holy fathers." Response by Barsanuphius.

"Blessed is the God and Father of our Lord Jesus Christ, who blessed us in Christ with every spiritual blessing in heaven."[28] Amen. Brothers, it is opportune to say with the Apostle: "I have been a fool! You forced me to it."[29] For indeed, I am forced for your sake to examine matters that are beyond my strength and to speak of something that does not greatly benefit the soul and in fact may even harm it. We have ignored the Apostle Paul, who says: "Put away from you all anger and wrath and slander, together with all malice,"[30] and I would add gluttony, fornication, avarice, and the rest of the passions, for which we ought to mourn night and day, and to weep unceasingly, so that through the multitude of tears their filth may be entirely washed away, in order that, having been filthy, we may become pure; having been sinners, we may become righteous; and, having been dead, we may come alive. Let us not forget that we will give account for our every single word.[31] For it is written: "You will give back to each according to his works."[32] And again: "All of us must appear before the judgment seat of Christ, in order that each may receive recompense for what has been done in the body, whether good or evil."[33]

We should strive for these things, for which our fathers also strove, namely, those around Abba Poemen and the others who have struggled.[34] This struggle includes reckoning oneself as nothing, not measuring oneself at all, and regarding oneself as earth and ashes.[35] The struggle of these others, however, includes regarding oneself as being knowledgeable, puffing oneself up, reckoning oneself and measuring oneself in everything,

28. Eph 1.3.
29. 2 Cor 12.11.
30. Eph 4.31.
31. Cf. Mt 12.36.
32. Cf. Ps 61.13.
33. 2 Cor 5.10.
34. Cf. *Sayings*, Poemen 36 and 73.
35. Cf. Gn 18.27; Jb 42.6.

and keeping away from humility. Forgive me, but are you perhaps idle? Is this why you have come to ask such questions? If
this is the case, then you should go down into the market place
until the Master of the house comes and hires you for his vineyard.[36] If you had a thorn in your heart with regard to that fearful encounter, you would not have been thinking about these
things. The prophet "forgot to eat his bread,"[37] and if we, too,
did not waste our life with indifference, we would never have
fallen into such [preoccupations]. God does not demand these
things from us, but instead he demands sanctification, purification, silence, and humility.

Nevertheless, since I do not want to leave your thoughts un-
answered, and I have been afflicted in my prayers to God in order that he might assure me in this regard, I was constrained by
this dilemma, but chose rather to assume affliction for myself in
order to relieve you of your own affliction, remembering him
who says: "Bear one another's burdens."[38] So listen to the assurance, which I received from God three days prior to the time
that you actually submitted your question to me in writing.

May all of the fathers, who have pleased God, the saints and
the righteous and genuine servants of God, pray for me. Do not
think that, because they were saints, they were able actually to
comprehend all the depths of God. For the Apostle says: "We
know only in part, and we prophesy only in part."[39] And again:
"To one is given through the Spirit such and such, and not all
of these gifts to one and the same person; but to one person, it
was given in this way, to another in that way, and all of these gifts
are activated by one and the same Spirit."[40] Knowing, then, that
the [mysteries] of God are incomprehensible, the Apostle cried
out: "O the depth of the riches and wisdom and knowledge of
God! How unsearchable are his judgments, and how inscru-
table his ways! 'For who has known the mind of the Lord? Or
who has been his counselor?'"[41] and so forth. Applying themselves, therefore, to becoming teachers of their own accord, or

36. Cf. Mt 20.1–7.
38. Gal 6.2.
40. Cf. 1 Cor 12.4–11.
41. Rom 11.33–34, quoting Is 40.13.

37. Cf. Ps 101.5.
39. 1 Cor 13.9.

else obliged by others to come to this point, they achieved great progress, sometimes even surpassing their own teachers. Moreover, they were assured about the truth in developing new doctrines, while at the same time remaining faithful to the traditions of their own teachers.

In this way, there are also some [brothers] here who have received certain doctrines from their teachers, which are not, however, correct. For after achieving progress and themselves becoming spiritual teachers, nevertheless they did not pray to God about their teachers, in order to learn whether what they said was spoken through the Holy Spirit. Rather, trusting that their teachers possessed wisdom and knowledge, they did not in fact bother to discern their teachings. And so the teachings of their teachers became mingled with their own teachings, and they spoke sometimes from the doctrines learned from their masters, while at other times from the brilliance of their own intellect. Thus, even the words of their teachers were ascribed to their name. For while they received these words from others, they progressed and improved more than their teachers, and they spoke through the Holy Spirit; that is to say, they were assured by the Spirit and spoke from the doctrines of their teachers who preceded them, but they did not actually examine these words in order to discern whether they needed to be assured by God through supplication and prayer in regard to their truth. So the teachings [of the two] were mingled together. Thus, since it was they who spoke the words, it was to their names that they were ultimately ascribed. Therefore, when you hear that one of them received from the Holy Spirit whatever he speaks, then this is a clear assurance and we ought to trust him. When, however, this person speaks on those matters, it does not seem that he refers to the same kind of assurance, but rather to the teachings and tradition of those who preceded him. In this way, while paying attention to their knowledge and wisdom, nonetheless they did not ask God about these matters, as to whether or not they are true.

There, then! You have heard all my foolishness. So be calm, and commit yourselves to God, ceasing from such idle talk and paying attention to your passions, about which you will be asked to give account on the day of judgment. For you will not be asked about these matters, why you do not understand them or why you have not learned them. Therefore, weep and mourn. Follow in the footsteps of our fathers, of Poemen and all the others like him, and "run in such a way that you may win"[42] in Christ Jesus our Lord, to whom be the glory to the ages. Amen.

LETTER 605

Question from the same person to the same [Old Man]: "Father, you are truly guides for the blind and the light of Christ for those of us in darkness, and it is through you that the truth has been revealed to us. For indeed, we discover even in certain books of the elders that there was a certain great elder who, in his simplicity, used to say that the bread of which we partake is not by nature the body of Christ, but only a symbol; and had he not first prayed to God about this, he would not even have known the truth.[43] And someone else, again a great elder, thought that Christ was Melchizedek; but when he prayed to God, then God revealed [the truth] to him.[44] Nevertheless, for the Lord's sake, forgive me, father; for I dare to ask of matters that surpass me. Since, however, our God has illumined us in the straight way of truth through your holiness, I implore you to clarify this matter entirely for us, so that our intellect and weak heart may be cleansed from the pursuit of controversy concerning it. For whose sake did God allow these men to be deceived? Indeed, even if these did not at first ask for it, why was the truth not granted to them through grace in order to eliminate the harm that would come to people who would read their writings afterward? For even if they themselves were not hindered in regard to correct faith and virtue, nonetheless some slack and lazy people, such as myself, have received them in the faith that they deserved and have been easily harmed by them. For they were not aware of what you said, namely, that the saints were not able to understand all of God's mysteries and that they did not always pray to God for assurance in regard to the truth of these [teachings]. So clarify this, too, for me, compassionate father, condescending once again to my weakness." Response by Barsanuphius.

---

42. 1 Cor 9.24.   43. Cf. *Sayings*, Daniel 7.
44. Cf. *Sayings*, Daniel 8.

Child, God did not allow these men to be deceived. For allowing someone to be deceived is like being asked about the right
way and not telling the truth. They did not even ask God about
this, in order that they might receive the truth from him. Now,
you ask: "Why, then, did God not prevent them [from error] by
divine grace, for the benefit of those who would read [their writ-
ings] afterward?" Well, you could say the same thing also about
every sinner. For since God knows that when someone sins, that
person will be an example for many, why then does God not
prevent him [from sinning], so that many others would not be
harmed by him? In this way, however, there would be no freedom
in our life. For what prevents God in this way from saving every
person? After all, are there not also in Scripture certain words
that might be a stumbling block for the ignorant and for those
who do not know the spiritual meaning of Scripture? Therefore,
we should perhaps say: "Why, then, did God not make the spiritual meaning of Scripture clear to everyone, so that no one would
be harmed?" Instead, he left it up to the saints of each period to
toil over the interpretation of these issues. This is why there are
called "teachers and interpreters,"[45] as the Apostle says.

Do not be deceived, then, about the men about whom you
inquired. For if they had asked God, they would have received
from him [the truth]. As it is written: "Everyone who asks receives, and everyone who searches finds."[46] Just as God revealed
the way of life through the prophets and the apostles, so also
each of these spoke the truth partially. So the truth was not spoken through one person alone; but what one person left out,
another spoke according to God's will. God made the same
happen also in the case of the saints who followed after them.
Therefore, whatever ambiguous statements the previous ones
might have made with any doubt, the later ones would pro-
nounce in allegory, so that God may always be glorified through
his saints. For he is the God of the first as well as of the last. To
him be the glory to the ages. Amen.

45. Cf. 1 Cor 12.28.
46. Mt 7.8.

LETTER 606

Question from the same person to the same [Old Man]: "For the Lord's sake forgive me, sir, compassionate father, because I am greatly afflicted. Indeed, I have read a book of doctrines and see my heart being troubled. On the one hand, I am afraid to tell you about this; yet, on the other hand, I cannot keep silent on account of my thoughts. So what do you order me to do, holy father?" Response.

Since the devil wants to cast you into such useless preoccupations, tell me what you want to say, and may God not grant him any room.

LETTER 607

Question from the same person to the same [Old Man]: "On the subject of the resurrection of the saints' bodies, tell me whether they will rise in this body that we actually inhabit, namely, a body with bones and nerves, or else a body that is aerial and spherical. For some people also say that the Lord's body will resemble the latter kind in the future resurrection, denying the fact that he was risen from the dead in his human body, which he received for our salvation from the holy Theotokos and ever-virgin Mary. It will be, they say, as the Apostle says: 'He will transform the body of our humiliation that it may be conformed to the body of his glory.'[47] And again they say that the Apostle writes: 'Flesh and blood cannot inherit the kingdom of God,'[48] implying that this body cannot be eternalized, inasmuch as it is sustained by food, whereas in the future age there will be no eating or drinking. Again they say that the Apostle states about our Lord Jesus Christ: 'When all things are subjected to him, then the Son himself will also be subjected to the one who put all things in subjection under him, so that God may be all in all.'[49] Moreover, they quote the words of Ecclesiastes: 'It has already been, in the ages before us,'[50] and through this they construct their theory about pre-existence. And the words spoken in the Gospel: 'You will never get out, until you have paid the last penny'[51] assure us, they say, that there will be an end to the torments of hell.

47. Phil 3.21.
48. 1 Cor 15.50.
49. 1 Cor 15.28.
50. Eccl 1.10.
51. Mt 5.26.

"Therefore, for the Lord's sake, clarify these matters for me, master, so that the enemy may not deceive me and so that I may not fall into his evil snares out of ignorance; for I am sorely beset from every direction, as a result of my foolishness. This is because I have not adhered to your holy words, namely, that I should keep away from the pursuit of these matters from the outset, inasmuch as they contain great danger for the soul. Pray for me, good father, so that I may henceforth be vigilant and concerned about mourning for my sins. And forgive me for even daring to ask these questions; for although you know everything, you have still allowed me to speak." Response by Barsanuphius.

Brother, I have written to you before, that the devil has sown in you an inopportune preoccupation. For your time here is granted to weep and mourn for your sins. In order, however, not to abandon you to your thoughts, since you desire to learn about the resurrection, if you believe in the prophets, then God has shown us through Ezekiel the prophet how the resurrection will take place: how bone was gathered upon bone, and joint upon joint, and veins and flesh and nerves;[52] and thus people were resurrected. The Apostle also knew that we would rise in our bodies, and so he taught: "For this perishable body must put on imperishability, and this mortal body must put on immortality."[53] Do not be deceived; the bodies will rise with their bones, nerves, and hair. This is how they shall be in the age to come, although they shall be brighter and more glorious, according to the voice of the Lord: "Then the righteous will shine like the sun in the kingdom of heaven."[54]

The glory will be added to their bodies, much in the same way that a simple peasant enters the presence of the king; when the latter has made him a general, then that man leaves the palace in glory. Is he not the same person? Has his body changed? Or think of a deacon who is straightaway ordained to bishop, and is suddenly glorified. The same happens here. How is this so? While people are still in the body, do they not become God-bearers? Then how did Moses see the Lord? And, before him, there were Abraham, James, Stephen in the Book of Acts, and

52. Cf. Ezek 37.7–8. 53. 1 Cor 15.53.
54. Mt 13.43.

all the others. Were they bodiless? This is how it shall also be in
the resurrection; their bodies will be the same, but they shall
be incorruptible, immortal, and more glorious. This is why the
Apostle says about the human body: "It is sown in dishonor; it
is raised in glory. It is sown as an unspiritual body; it is raised as
a spiritual body."[55] He says this because many of the saints are
not even visible to us, but are rather seen as dishonored in our
eyes. And when they receive the glory there, as in the form of
ordination, then it is revealed to all that they are spiritual. This
is why it says: "It is sown as an unspiritual body" by people, but
"it is raised as a spiritual body,"[56] glorious, in order that all may
marvel. And so the Apostle says: "He will transform the body of
our humiliation, in order that it may be conformed to the body
of his glory";[57] because he renders the bodies light-like according to his own body, as the Apostle John writes: "When he is
revealed, then we shall be like him."[58] The Son of God is light;
they are the sons of God, according to the Apostle, and therefore they, too, are "the sons of light."[59] This is why it says that
they will be transformed.

As for the words: "When all things are subjected to him,
then the Son himself will also be subjected to the one who put
all things in subjection under him,"[60] first you should remember to whom Paul is writing. For Paul is writing to the Corinthians, and Hellenism still prevailed there. Indeed, it was customary for some of the Greeks to practice the following: when their
king's son grew to maturity, he would rise up and kill his own
father. Therefore, once they had received the preaching about
the Apostle's faith, in order to prevent them from also interpret-
ing the teaching about the Son of God according to this custom, he excluded them from making any connection between
the two. And so he said to them: "When all things are subjected
to him, then [the Son] himself will also be subjected to the one
who put all things in subjection under him."[61] When, however,
he says: "his enemies will be brought bound before his feet," he

55. Cf. 1 Cor 15.43–44.
57. Phil 3.21.
59. Cf. Eph 5.8.
61. Ibid.

56. Cf. 1 Cor 15.44.
58. 1 Jn 3.2.
60. 1 Cor 15.28.

means the devil, and his powers, and those who obey their wills. So this is why the Apostle said: "We do not yet see everything in subjection to him."[62] Until when is this so? Until the angels of God the Father arrive; for he said: "Sit at my right hand, until I make your enemies your footstool."[63] These are the enemies that he will lead to the judgment of the Son of God: "The Father," he says, "judges no one, but has given all judgment to the Son."[64]

Now listen and learn how the Son hands the kingdom over to God the Father. The incarnate Son of God came to call and to sanctify, through his holy blood, "a holy nation, a chosen people, zealous in good works, a royal priesthood."[65] Understand this well. After his enemies are subjected to him and he judges them, being himself an example of submission, he hands over the kingdom, which he has prepared as a holy people, to God the Father, saying: "Here am I and the children whom you have given me."[66] And so that you may learn the equality [that exists between the divine Persons],[67] the Father gave all the judgment to the Son, and the Son also gave to the Father those whom he had called. And so the word is fulfilled: "When all things are subjected to him, then the Son himself will also be subjected to the one who put all things in subjection under him."[68]

As for the ages spoken of in Ecclesiastes, you should know that one's entire life is called one's age. This is why it is not said that it happened in the ages that preceded this world, but in the ages of this world that preceded us. And if you want to learn how ignorant and superficial people distort the Scriptures by allegorizing according to the devil's teaching, the Apostle says: "Food is meant for the stomach, and the stomach for food, but God will destroy both the one and the other."[69] He is speaking of gluttony, indifference, and prodigality; so God did not abolish food and the stomach from the saints. For the Apostle who said this knew well that he was speaking about the passions, which

---

62. Heb 2.8.
63. Ps 109.1.
64. Jn 5.22.
65. Cf. 1 Pt 2.9; Ti 2.14.
66. Cf. Is 8.18; Heb 2.13.
67. A doctrinal affirmation already adopted and articulated at the Second Ecumenical Council in Constantinople (381).
68. 1 Cor 15.28.
69. 1 Cor 6.13.

the Lord abolished from himself and from those like him. So he began by saying: "We are no worse off if we do not eat, and no better off if we do."[70] Nevertheless, the meaning of these words is as follows. It is in the future age that God said that human beings would be equal to angels,[71] neither eating nor drinking, nor again desiring anything else.[72] And, of course, nothing is impossible with God.[73] For he demonstrated this through Moses, who lived like this for forty days and nights.[74] The one who did this [for Moses] is also able to do the same for anyone else, for all the years of eternity. And if someone should rave, saying that Moses nevertheless ate afterward, we were also given a partial example of what will happen in the future, as well as of the resurrection, through the Savior, who also resurrected other dead people, as well as through the apostles themselves. All of this shows us that there will be a resurrection. Even if [the apostles] died afterward, we should still not doubt the resurrection. Furthermore, it is said: "One does not live by bread alone, but by every word that comes from the mouth of God."[75] What can you object to this, unless you distort this, too, like the rest of the Scriptures?

And as for the statement: "Flesh and blood shall not inherit the kingdom of God, nor shall corruption inherit incorruption,"[76] flesh and blood imply impurity, fornication, and desires. Do you also want to learn how it is that, while still in the body, people nonetheless become spiritual? Then listen to the Lord, who says to Nicodemus: "You must be born from above";[77] and later he adds: "of water and the Spirit."[78] When they are born of the Spirit, then they become spiritual. Again it is said: "[They] were born, not of blood or of the will of the flesh or of the will of man, but of God,"[79] and: "God is Spirit."[80] So if they are now

---

70. 1 Cor 8.8.   71. Cf. Lk 20.36.

72. Cf. Mt 22.30.

73. Cf. Mk 10.27; Mt 19.26; Lk 1.37 and 17.27.

74. Cf. Ex 24.18.   75. Mt 4.4; Dt 8.3.

76. 1 Cor 15.50.

77. "From above": Greek, ἄνωθεν, sometimes translated in other contexts as "again."

78. Cf. Jn 3.3–5.   79. Jn 1.13.

80. Jn 4.24.

in the Spirit and have become spiritual, born of God, cannot
God also render them spiritual there?

Finally, let us look at the phrase: "He shall not leave there,
until he has paid the last penny."[81] Whence shall they pay? He
is referring to their eternal damnation. This is why it says: "He
shall not leave there." If a poor debtor is cast into prison, being
ordered by the magistrate not to leave there until he has paid
his debt, can you be certain that he will ever leave that place? I
do not think so. Do not be deceived like a foolish person. For
no one makes any [spiritual] progress there; whatever one has,
one has from here—whether this be something good, or bad,
or pleasant.

Therefore, relinquish your silly talk, and do not follow the
demons or their teaching. For they seize you once, and then
they bring you down heavily. So be humble before God, weeping for your sins and mourning over your passions. Remember
the Scripture that says: "Behold, now is the time, O Israel";[82] and
again: "Behold, I have made a beginning now."[83] Pay attention
to yourself. Then God will forgive you. Moreover, observe where
your heart inclines when you examine these doctrines.

---

81. Cf. Mt 5.26.   82. Cf. Dt 10.12.
83. Cf. Ps 76.11.

LETTERS TO VARIOUS BROTHERS (608–616)

LETTER 608

Another brother asked the same Great Old Man: "Tell me, father, what happens when I see someone doing something and I tell someone else, yet I say [to myself] that I am not condemning him, but that we are only holding a conversation? Am I condemning that person in my thought?" Response by Barsanuphius.

F THERE IS any passionate movement within you, then you are condemning that person. But if your thought is free from passion, then there is no condemnation. One is simply talking in order to prevent the evil from increasing.

LETTER 609

Question: "What do the words mean: 'With the crooked person, you shall turn away'?"[1] Response.

The Lord said: "If anyone strikes you on the right cheek, turn the other also."[2] This is how one should turn away from the crooked person.

LETTER 610

Question: "What does the following mean: 'Be wise as serpents, and innocent as doves'?"[3] Response.

Well, one who is able to combine the wisdom of the serpent in evil circumstances with the innocence of the dove in good circumstances will not allow either one's wisdom to become wicked or else one's innocence to become foolish.

1. Ps 17.27. 2. Mt 5.39.
3. Mt 10.16.

LETTER 611

Question: "Who are the ones who sin and do evil intentionally, and who are the ones who do so unintentionally?" Response.

Those who do evil intentionally are the ones who surrender their will to evil, who take pleasure in and make friends with it. These people are at peace with Satan and do not war against him in their thoughts.

Those who do evil unintentionally are the ones who, according to the Apostle, have a power that opposes them, at war in their members.[4] This is the misty power and the veil.[5] Yet in their thoughts, these people neither give their consent, nor take pleasure in, nor again obey, but rather contradict, oppose, reply, counterattack, and are angry at themselves [with regard to evil]. These people are considered as being much more beautiful and precious in God's eyes than those who choose to surrender their will to evil and take pleasure in it.

LETTER 612

Question: "What is the meaning of the words spoken by the Lord to the Samaritan woman: 'For you have had five husbands, and the one you now have is not your husband'?"[6] Response.

The meaning is quite clear. For according to the old law, any woman who was separated from her husband by death, being left without children, could in fact marry up to five times; however, after the fifth marriage, whether she had given birth or not, she could marry no more. So if someone married a sixth time, after the fifth, the sixth man was regarded not as her husband but in fact as an adulterer, since that union was actually against the law. This is exactly what happened to this woman.

If, however, one wants to give the text a more mystical meaning, then one could interpret the five lawful husbands as representing the [five] natural senses: sight, smell, hearing, taste, and touch. Through these, we come to know the nature of things.

4. Cf. Rom 7.23.
6. Jn 4.18.

5. Ex 34.33; 2 Cor 3.13–16.

The sixth sense, which is unlawful, is faithlessness, which is contrary to nature and by which the woman was possessed because of her ignorance. Therefore, Christ said to her: "You have spoken the truth, that you have five husbands,"[7] meaning: "You have had your five senses as husbands, submitting to them and living according to their desires," which also further means: "You have been sufficiently filled with desires that come from the five natural senses, which you have already lost on account of the decline that comes from bodily age; yet the one that you now have, namely, your faithlessness, is not in fact your husband," which implies that it does not dominate you according to nature, but rather has invaded you like an intruder.

LETTER 613

Exhortation by the holy and Great Old Man, Barsanuphius, to a novice who was ill and could not bear the affliction of his illness.

Brother, those workers who demanded their reward from their master had nothing else to be proud of but their claim: "We have endured the burning heat and the toil of the day."[8] Therefore, child, let us endure affliction gladly in order that God's mercy may richly come upon us; and let us not be discouraged and fall captive to despondency, since this brings us to the beginning of destruction.[9] Son, remember: "The one who endures to the end will be saved."[10] Child, the illness is also there to tempt us, and the temptation is there to test us: "For the untempted is also untested,"[11] since trial in danger proves a person, just "like gold in a fiery furnace."[12] Indeed, trial brings one to hope, and hope does not disappoint.[13]

So do not break down, nor allow the enemy to paralyze your intention according to God or shake your faith in the Holy Trinity. After all, what happened to you to make you break down? Tell me. Remember what the Apostle says: "In your struggle against sin you have not resisted to the point of shedding your

7. Jn 4.17–18.
9. Cf. *Sayings*, Poemen 149.
11. *Agraphon*, no. 90.
13. Cf. Rom 5.4–5.

8. Mt 20.12.
10. Mt 10.22.
12. Cf. Wis 3.6.

blood. And you have forgotten the exhortation that addresses you as sons: 'My son, do not regard lightly the discipline of the Lord, or lose heart when you are punished by him; for the Lord disciplines those whom he loves, and chastises every son whom he accepts.' Endure trials for the sake of discipline. God is treating you as his own sons; for what son is there whom a father does not discipline? If you do not have that discipline in which all share, then you are illegitimate and not in fact his sons."[14] If you bear the affliction gratefully, then you have become a son. If you break down, then you are an illegitimate child.

I implore you, child, as an elder to a novice, as one who has grown old in my monastic habit, even though I have been useful for nothing, to one who has just been tonsured. May this not be without reason; no, Lord Jesus Christ; nor let it be in vain! Be vigilant, awaken from the stupor of your heavy sleep, rise up with Peter and the rest of the apostles to cry out to the Savior of all, Christ, with a loud voice: "Master, save us, for we are perishing."[15] And he will surely come to you as well, rebuking the winds and the sea, calming the waves that surround your boat, namely, the storm of your soul. And he will lift you up from the blood-sucking lion, saving your dove from the belly of the beast,[16] and your seed from hail, and your olive tree from worms, and all your trees from frost, so that they may give forth fruits in their proper time [of harvest].[17] And the seed of your soil will yield ripe fruit according to the apostolic word: "One hundredfold, and sixty times, and thirty times."[18]

Brother, pay attention to why you are enduring this in God's name. The Apostle has enumerated the reasons: "Nothing will separate us from the love of Christ," and he says this: "Will hardship, or distress, or famine, or persecution, or nakedness, or peril, or sword?"[19] So can a small illness shake our intellect away from God? Let it not be so! But be strengthened, child, and you will see God's help. For this is but a first temptation, and if you should overcome it with the help of God, then it will no longer

14. Cf. Heb 12.4–8.   15. Lk 8.24.
16. Cf. Jon 2.2.   17. Cf. Mt 21.41.
18. Mk 4.8.   19. Cf. Rom 8.35.

dominate you; but if this overcomes you, it will lead you to a state of enslavement. Therefore, stand strong and endure. For you will certainly see, if you do indeed stay strong, what the Lord's mercy will bring you.

Let your love be reassured that I shall not cease praying to God for you, night and day, in order that he may save you and protect us all from the evil one. And I am striving hard, so that, with the saints, you may as their children inherit "what no eye has seen, nor ear heard, nor the human heart conceived, in regard to what God has prepared for those who love him."[20] Pursue these things, and you will be blessed in Christ. Amen.

LETTER 614

A brother committed a fault, and when the abbot asked him numerous times to say merely once: "Forgive me!" [his heart] was hardened, and he refused to do so. When the abbot said a prayer and knelt three times, he barely convinced him to say: "Forgive me!" So when the brother returned to his own cell, the abbot said to him: "Brother, when you are alone in your cell, examine your heart, and you will discover whence this hardness came to your heart." When he did this, the brother came and threw himself at the feet of the abbot, confessing his sin and entreating him to reveal this matter to the Great Old Man Barsanuphius, and to ask him to pray for him. The saint addressed the following words in response.

Brother, pay attention to yourself. It was you who asked me to sow seed on your soil; no one else obliged you to do this. See, then, that you do not allow the devil to sow any tares among your wheat, namely, the food of [eternal] fire. I am responding to you, since you asked me about your thoughts. The fathers say that, if someone asks about something, then that person should keep those answers until death; and if any are not kept, then they bring destruction. You have evil and terrible thoughts lurking in your heart. Why then do you consider those thoughts as being mortal, which in fact are not? The devil is the one who transforms for you the light into darkness and the darkness into

20. 1 Cor 2.9.

light, showing you the bitter as sweet, and the sweet as bitter. So now you regard life as death, and death as life.

Indeed, the enemy wanders about roaring, desiring to swallow you up alive.[21] Nevertheless, you do not understand that, were it not for the hand of God and the prayers of the saints protecting you, you would have fallen into his destruction and deceit. And so you reject the divine words spoken to you by your abbot, for the benefit and salvation of your soul, so that, as a result, you may never come to the knowledge of truth. You ignore the many labors that he performs for you as if for his own soul, imploring the saints also to pray for you, so that you may escape from the snares of the devil and of death, in order to be saved in the nest of the Lord. For this is how he toils for you. Should you, then, not keep his words as the apple of your eye[22] and regard him as being more valuable than your own life? Instead, however, you have become vulgar, feeling satiated by his continual presence, something of which you should never have felt satiated but rather prayed to be counted worthy. Indeed, in order that his continual presence with you may not be to your condemnation, you should have carried out his commands with zeal, great fear, and trembling, so that through him you may receive God's blessing and be delivered from the deceit of the enemy.

May the words not be fulfilled in your case: "Jacob ate his fill, and grew fat, and the beloved one kicked."[23] Let not also these words be fulfilled in you: "Woe to you, Chorazin! Woe to you, Bethsaida! For if the deeds of power done in you had been done in Tyre and Sidon, they would have repented long ago in sackcloth and ashes."[24] Do not be the one to hear: "You hate discipline, and you cast my words behind you."[25] Why do you place yourself in temptation so often, provoking others with your words and then being unable to bear what they say? Yet your heart is blinded by envy and jealousy, and so you bring turmoil upon yourself. Thus you have often fallen into sin, and smashed your face; and yet your copper forehead is not put to shame

21. Cf. 1 Pt 5.8.
23. Cf. Dt 32.15.
25. Ps 49.17.

22. Cf. Dt 32.10.
24. Mt 11.21.

and your iron neck is not bent, as [the Other Old Man] brother John had asked of you. Who has behaved like this and been saved? Cain behaved like this in the beginning, and he received a curse from the Lord's hand.[26] And after him the giants did, too, and they were drowned in the waters of the flood.[27] Ham and Esau did, too, and they were cast out of the holy blessings.[28] Pharaoh was hardened, and the water of the Red Sea swallowed him up and drowned him as well as those with him.[29] Those with Dathan opposed Moses, and the earth swallowed them up, together with their families.[30]

Moreover, if, as Scripture says, those who oppose the high priest are swallowed up by the earth, then how do you even dare to oppose the one who tells you simply to say: "Forgive me!" instead of saying it? And so you have alienated yourself from God's humility and the Fathers' *Discourses*, which say: "In every circumstance, we require humility, being prepared with every deed and with every word to say: 'Forgive me!'"[31] Nevertheless, although you heard the abbot say this so many times, yet you did not say anything. Even when you finally did speak, it was not a genuine response, because it was done by force and not spoken in repentance and compunction. How long will you be stiff-necked and uncircumcised in heart?[32] Look, and you will see that no one else is that hard. So why do you give the devil a hand and the strength to destroy your soul?

Therefore, be vigilant, my brother, and be alert; awaken from the deep sleep and the drunkenness that is without wine, but which possesses you. Where is your humility? Where is your obedience? Where is the excision of your will in everything? For if you cut off your will in one matter but do not do the same in another, it is clear that even in the one where you did cut it off, you still have another desire. Indeed, a submissive person submits in everything; and such a person is carefree about salvation, since someone else will give account for him, namely, the

---

26. Cf. Gn 4.
27. Cf. Gn 6–7.
28. Cf. Gn 9 and 27.
29. Cf. Ex 14.16–28.
30. Cf. Nm 16.
31. Abba Isaiah of Scetis, *Ascetic Discourse* 3.
32. Cf. Acts 7.51.

one to whom one has submitted and to whom one has confided oneself. So if you want to be saved and live in heaven as well as on earth, then keep these things, and I shall give account for you to God, brother. But if you are neglectful, then you are on your own.

Do not cut off your hope; for this is the joy of the devil. I have persuaded the abbot to receive you in his embrace, as before. Indeed, he was stunned by your disobedience and inattentiveness; yet I have convinced him to accept you in godly fear as a genuine son, not as an illegitimate child.[33] You, too, however, should entrust yourself to him in everything, according to godly fear. The Father, Son, and Holy Spirit bear witness to me, that I am bearing all of your concern before God; and he will seek your blood from me, if you do not disobey my words. So make a new beginning from today, assisted by the hand of God. Behold, you are young; guard yourself, and do not give yourself over to foolish talk or useless acquaintances. May the Lord grant you prudence and strength to hear and practice these things. And if there is anything that you may want to ask me from time to time, I shall not delay in responding with whatever God grants to my mouth, in order to reassure your heart and tell you whatever is necessary for the salvation of your soul, in Christ Jesus. Amen.

LETTER 615

The same brother was again disobedient to the abbot, and asked the Great Old Man whether it is beneficial for someone to keep any promises made under oath at a time of anger, or else better to retract one's words and not act on the promises made under oath. The Old Man responded with these words.

The Lord said to Moses: "Go down at once! Your people, whom you brought up out of the land of Egypt, have acted perversely; they have turned aside from the way that I commanded them; they have cast for themselves an image of a calf, and have worshiped it."[34] Wretched one, how were you deceived so quickly, [led astray] again from obedience, from which the devil wants to alienate you and because of which he rages against

---

33. Cf. Heb 12.8.   34. Ex 32.7–8.

you? Is this not what I spoke to you about, namely, that you are foolish and uncircumcised in heart?[35] Where did you cast my words? Why are you hurrying to fall into the pit of the devil? Why does the enemy blind you in matters about which you have already heard? Were you not ordered to commit yourself to the hands of God and to the hands of your abbot? Did you not hear me saying that he desires the salvation of your soul as if it were the benefit of his own soul? You should not have disobeyed him, even if he had told you to commit murder,[36] especially in matters that are for the benefit of your brothers.

Nevertheless, Satan removed [this opportunity] from you on the pretense of your rights, so that neither you could benefit nor anyone else through you. So you shall hear the "Woe!" addressed to the Pharisees and the threat to the watchman whom Ezekiel describes in relation to the coming of the sword.[37] So be it! If you cannot be useful to anyone, then why do you not speak to someone who can indeed be useful? Why do you rapidly become like a dog "that returns to its own vomit,"[38] and like a swine wallowing in garbage,[39] remaining thus unbent in your hard-heartedness? He ordered you to tell him everything that happened, and he would assume your sin; yet you frustrate him as the Israelites did to Moses.[40] So be ashamed of yourself and return to your former habit; repent, and God will receive you; for he is merciful. Moreover, do not seek to please people; otherwise, you will be destroyed and will not become a servant of God.[41]

Pay attention to yourself, wretched one, and fear God. Indeed, it is not beneficial for you to keep your promises made under oath at a time of anger or wrath, and then to transgress the commandment of God "not to kill."[42] For it is better to repent unto God rather than to do whatever you swore to do or not to do; otherwise, you will fall into the condemnation of Herod, who, in order to keep his sinful oath, cut off the head of John the Forerunner[43] and fell from eternal life, committing

---

35. Cf. Acts 7.51.
36. On obedience to the point of the absurd, see also *Letter* 288.
37. Cf. Ezek 33.1–6.   38. Prv 26.11; 2 Pt 2.22.
39. Cf. 2 Pt 2.22.   40. Cf. Ex 32.9 and 19.
41. Cf. Gal 1.10.   42. Ex 20.13.
43. Cf. Mt 14.7–10.

himself to the bitter and endless torments [of hell]. Instead, you should repent and ask for forgiveness from God, who [alone] is able to grant this. Herod, too, would have been blessed, had he done this. Since, however, he did not do this, he became three times wretched and completely accursed to the [end of the] age. Even Peter, the chief of the apostles, swore three times and took an oath that he did not know the Savior; afterward, however, he recognized his mistake with very bitter mourning and sincere repentance, thereby wiping away his sin;[44] and he was received by the kind and loving Master, Christ the Savior. Indeed, not only was he counted worthy of the joy of the angel who said to the women: "Tell his disciples and Peter . . . ,"[45] but the Lord himself asked Peter three times, in place of the three denials: "Do you love me, Peter?"[46] revealing to him that through his good repentance, the sin of his three denials was healed. Therefore, no longer swear,[47] when at the same time you are transgressing God's commandment. If, however, you happen to fall into this sin, then do not hesitate to repent. For had even Peter stayed with his oath that he did not know his own Master, he would have been estranged from him and his glory.

LETTER 616

The brother was reassured with these words and therefore asked the same Great Old Man: "Your love for God told me that sinners are able to wipe away their own sins through repentance. What does this mean? Does such a person not also require the prayer of the saints? Can that person do this alone? And if such a person does not show sincere repentance, if the saints pray for him, are his sins not wiped away on their account?" Response by Barsanuphius.

If a person does not do whatever he can, also joining this effort with the prayer of the saints, then the prayer of the saints is of no benefit to him. If they lead an ascetic life and pray for him, while he leads a life of waste and wantonness, then to what avail is their prayer for him? For the saying is fulfilled: "When one builds

---

44. Cf. Mt 26.69–75.
46. Jn 21.15–17.

45. Mk 16.7.
47. Cf. Mt 5.34.

and another tears down, what do they gain but hard work?[48] Indeed, if it were possible for such a thing to happen, namely, for the saints to pray for someone and he would be saved, while the latter was not even a little careful, then nothing would prevent them from doing this for all the sins of the world.

On the other hand, however, if a sinner labors even a little, he certainly also requires the prayer of the righteous. For the Apostle says: "The prayer of the righteous is very powerful and effective."[49] Therefore, when a saintly and righteous person prays for someone, the sinner should also contribute all that is possible through repentance, again through the prayer of the saints; for sinners are entirely incapable of repaying their debts alone. Indeed, the sinner contributes little, while the prayer of the saints contributes much. Just like someone who needs to carry ten measures of wheat, but is unable to carry even two, that person finds another God-fearing person to carry the other nine, in order that he may let him carry only the one, and rescue him. In this way, he will be preserved; for he will reach the city without being attacked by thieves on the way. The same may be applied here.

Or again, a sinner is like someone who owes one hundred coins and is reminded by the lender about the deposit of his debt. Then, going to another pious person, who is also wealthy, he entreats that person to give him as much as possible, according to love. And that kind and loving benefactor sees his affliction and shows compassion, saying: "Brother, whatever I have available at hand, I shall give for your sake; however, see that you also offer at least ten coins from your own pocket; for I have ninety coins, and I will give them to you in order to relieve you of your debt." So it is up to the debtor to strive to give a little in order to be freed from much. For if that compassionate benefactor sees that the debtor has not brought forward even those ten coins, then he hesitates to give the ninety, knowing that the original lender will not wipe away the debt unless he receives the full hundred coins that are owed.

48. Sir 34.28.
49. Jas 5.16.

LETTERS TO LAYPERSONS OF VARIOUS PROFESSIONS (617–787)

LETTER 617

A Christ-loving layperson asked the Other Old Man, John: "I implore you, father, clarify this for me, too, so that I may depart joyfully. Since my thought tells me to offer some alms from my possessions, what is more beneficial for me to do? Should I give things away gradually, or should I give them away all at once?" Response by John.

ROTHER, EVEN IF I am not capable of responding to you as I should, yet you heed the counsel of Scripture: "Do not say: 'Go, and come back again tomorrow, I will give it,' when you can give it now. For you do not know what the morrow will bring."[1] Moreover, there are particular measures, and each person acts according to his own measure. For one person is able to give away only some of his income, while another person will tithe his fruits or else give away one quarter, or a third, or even half; each one gives according to his own measure. If anyone wants to come to the measure of perfection,[2] then that person should not ask me, the least of all, but rather should ask the teacher and healer of souls, Jesus the Lord, who said to that rich man: "If you wish to be perfect, sell your possessions, and give the money to the poor, and you will have treasure in heaven; then come, follow me."[3]

The advent of death also strengthens your thought; for it is concealed from all people. Therefore, let us strive to do what is good before we are seized at the hour of death—for we do not know on what day we shall be called—lest we be found unprepared and be shut out with the five foolish virgins, who did not

---

1. Cf. Prv 3.28.   2. Cf. Eph 4.13.
3. Mt 19.21.

take oil in their flasks with their lamps.[4] Let us do our best according to our weakness, and the Master of all is good; he shall lead us with the wise virgins into his wedding-chamber and into the ineffable joy[5] that is with Christ. Amen.

LETTER 618

A brother asked the same Old Man whether he should receive money from others in order to give to the poor; for some people were actually requesting this. Response by John.

Since we are on the subject of almsgiving, not everyone can bear the application of this virtue, but only those who have reached stillness and mourning for their own sins. For there are some who commit themselves to such a service, and God knows what to do with them in this regard. Those who mourn [i.e., the monks], however, are not preoccupied with this. Indeed, how is it possible, when they have renounced their own possessions, for them also to manage the possessions of others? This is what the holy Hilarion did. For when someone entreated him to accept a large amount of money and distribute this [to the poor], he said to that person: "You should be distributing your own money; for you are the one traveling from city to city, and so you are more familiar with the towns. Whereas I, who have left behind even my own property, cannot possibly accept the property of someone else to distribute it. After all, this can give rise to an excuse for vainglory or avarice."[6]

LETTER 619

Question: "If the one who is proposing this insists by saying: 'If you do not accept the money and distribute it [to the poor], then I will offer nothing,' should I allow the poor to suffer hunger?" Response.

As I told your love, there are some who have committed themselves to this kind of service. If, however, you want to mourn for

4. Cf. Mt 25.1–13.
5. Cf. 1 Pt 1.8.
6. See Jerome, *Life of Hilarion* 18, PL 23.36.

your sins, do not pay any attention to this matter, even if you see someone dying in front of your very cell. Do not take part in the distribution of another person's possessions and be distracted from your mourning. Nevertheless, the owner of the property should distribute the goods himself, if he cannot find someone else to perform this service for him, so that in this way the work is not hindered.

LETTER 620

A Christ-loving layperson asked the same Old Man: "If someone is asked to give alms but has nothing to give, is that person obliged to borrow in order to give?" Response.

If one is asked to give something that one does not have, then there is no need to borrow in order to give. For even the Apostle Peter was asked to give alms and responded: "I have no silver or gold";[7] and he did not borrow any money in order to give some. Indeed, even if one only has the bare necessities, then again there is no need to spend it all, so that he may not later miss it or be afflicted by its absence. Moreover, if the person from whom alms are demanded says to the person making the request: "Forgive me, but I have nothing to give you," then this is not a lie. For someone who has nothing beyond what is necessary does not have anything to give to another person. He should simply say to the person who is asking: "Forgive me, but I only have what I need myself." Remember the five bridesmaids who asked the others to give them oil for their lamps; the latter replied: "There will not be enough for us and for you."[8] And the Apostle Paul writes in his letter to the Corinthians: "May your abundance be for their need,"[9] as well as: "I do not intend that there should be relief for others and pressure on you."[10]

LETTER 621

Question from the same person to the same [Old Man]: "Father, tell me what you meant when you said: 'If someone only has the

7. Acts 3.6.   8. Cf. Mt 25.9.
9. Cf. 2 Cor 8.14.   10. 2 Cor 8.13.

bare necessities, then there is no need to spend it all, in order not to be afflicted.' How is it possible for someone to be afflicted when one does something voluntarily?" Response by John.

One should always do everything with discernment. To know one's limits is discernment as well as security of thought, in order not to be troubled later. Doing anything beyond one's measure, whether this be almsgiving or anything else, is lack of discernment. For later this brings one to turmoil, despondency, and murmuring. So it is a good thing, indeed a very good thing, to give like the widow to anyone who asks;[11] there is nothing wrong with this. But as for a person giving more than one can possibly bear, even God only asks for what one can give.

LETTER 622

Question: "So are you saying that someone who is wealthy and has more than the bare necessities does not require this discernment? After all, that person is also acting according to his ability." Response.

No, such a person, too, requires discernment, in order not to be found to act beyond the ability of his thought and then regret what he has done. This is why Paul also said: "Do not give out of reluctance or necessity; for God loves a joyful giver."[12] Indeed, the perfect measures are for the perfect, and the lesser measures are for the lesser. The perfect person bears even poverty with courage, scorning wealth and bearing everything calmly, according to the Apostle: "I can do all things through Christ who strengthens me,"[13] and: "For me, the world has been crucified,"[14] and so on.

LETTER 623

Question: "What should someone do in order to become accustomed to giving alms, if from the outset one does not actually enjoy giving at all?" Response.

---

11. Cf. 1 Kgs 17.10–12.   12. 2 Cor 9.7.
13. Phil 4.13.   14. Gal 6.14.

That person should remind himself how God will reward those who give,[15] and should begin with small things, always advising himself that one who gives little will receive little, whereas one who gives much will also receive much, according to the words: "The one who sows sparingly will also reap sparingly; and the one who sows bountifully will also reap bountifully."[16] And, from the little, the thought is gradually moved to desire the bountiful reward, thus always progressing toward perfection. Such a person can reach perfect measures, in order to render oneself naked of all earthly things and to become one in spirit with the heavenly things.

LETTER 624

Question from the same person to the same [Old Man]: "If someone is solicited on all sides to spend all of one's possessions in almsgiving, and then the same person regrets doing so, how can one be consoled in order not to be consumed by such demonic sorrow?"[17] Response.

First, that person should blame himself for lack of discernment, and recall his thought from sorrow, saying: "Since I have spent all my belongings on a good thing, the kind and loving God is able to have mercy on me and arrange my affairs, too, according to his will."

LETTER 625

Question: "If there happen to be two poor persons, and I do not have enough money for both, which of the two should I prefer?" Response.

You should prefer the more vulnerable one.

LETTER 626

Question: "If I would like to give alms, but my thought has doubts about giving, what should I do?" Response.

15. Cf. Sir 32.9–12.   16. 2 Cor 9.6.
17. Cf. 2 Cor 2.7.

Examine yourself, and if you find that you are doing this out of stinginess, then give something even a little beyond what you should have given, such as an additional small amount, and you will receive God's mercy.

LETTER 627

Question: "Abba sir, clarify this for me as well. How is it possible for someone who has nothing to give to become a partaker of the blessing[18] expressed by the Savior to those on his right: 'Come, you that are blessed by my Father, inherit the kingdom prepared for you from the foundation of the world; for I was hungry and you gave me food to eat,'[19] and so forth?" Response by John.

Brother, is it possible that the apostles, who did not have any possessions, are not in fact partakers of this blessing? For there are various ranks of people, and God has spoken to each person according to his own rank. He demonstrated through the Beatitudes how those who are saved are distinguished among various ranks.[20]

So from material examples, one may grasp spiritual meanings. Suppose, for instance, that one person has fresh vegetables and sells them for a small coin of gold. Someone else, who owns wilted vegetables, will sell those for the same gold coin. Yet another person has different goods and sells them for the same gold coin. The same occurs with various professions; one person is a carpenter and earns a small amount of gold each day, while another is a builder and earns a similar amount each day. Someone else has yet a different profession and again earns the same salary each day. Now the various professions may be different, and the results of each also differ; but the cost and salary are the same. Now let us turn this to understand what occurs in the salvation of the soul. It is to those who have money, giving to the poor without vainglory, that these words are addressed: "Come, you that are blessed by my Father, inherit the kingdom prepared for you from the foundation of the world; for I was hungry and you gave me food to eat,"[21] and so on.

---

18. Cf. Eph 3.6.
20. Cf. Mt 5.3–12.

19. Mt 25.34–35.
21. Mt 25.34–35.

Nevertheless, pay attention to the rest of the Beatitudes, and you will discover a great difference among them; for one speaks of salvation of the soul, and another of the heavenly kingdom. Therefore, he said: "Blessed are the poor in spirit; for theirs is the kingdom of heaven."[22] And again: "Blessed are those who are persecuted for righteousness' sake; for theirs is the kingdom of heaven."[23] The other Beatitudes, too, are different from these, but they do not differ greatly in regard to [the reward, which always remains] the kingdom of heaven. So if you have nothing to offer in terms of giving alms, then become poor in spirit in order that you may inherit, with the saints, the kingdom of heaven.[24] Mourn over your sins in this world, in order that you may be comforted with those whose names are written in the Gospel. Acquire gentleness in order that you may inherit the earth. Hunger and thirst after righteousness in order that you may be filled with the same. Be pure in heart in order that you may see God in his glory. Become a peacemaker in your heart in order that you may be called a son of God.[25] Be prepared through your good deeds to be persecuted for the sake of righteousness, from town to town,[26] namely, from the evil thought of the devil to the good thought of God, in order that you may rejoice in the inheritance of the heavenly kingdom.[27] Endure reproach, persecution, and slander for the sake of the Lord in order that you may rejoice jubilantly; for you will find that the reward is great in heaven.[28]

LETTER 628

Question from the same person to the same [Old Man]: "Since each of the Beatitudes contains a single virtue, is this one virtue sufficient, father, for salvation, if a person should acquire it?" Response.

Just as the body is one but has many members,[29] and if one member is missing, then the body is incomplete, you should un-

---

22. Mt 5.3.
23. Mt 5.10.
24. Cf. Eph 1.18; Col 1.12.
25. Cf. Mt 5.5–9.
26. Cf. Mt 5.10–23 and 34.
27. Cf. Ps 105.5.
28. Cf. Rom 7.22.
29. Cf. 1 Cor 12.12.

derstand the inner self[30] in the same way, too. For the inner self has many members, namely, the virtues, and if one of these is missing, then a person cannot be perfected.[31] This resembles a craftsman who knows his profession well and who may also be able to handle other crafts on account of his skills; nevertheless, he is not called a craftsman except in his own profession. Likewise, one needs to have all the virtues, but will only be recognized by and renowned for one particular virtue, through which the grace of the Spirit especially shines.

LETTER 629

Another Christ-loving layperson gave a particular [monetary] blessing to someone else in order to distribute alms to the poor, entrusting him with this and saying: "Take [this money], and give account to God alone." Nevertheless, he did not realize that he was placing a great burden on him, and thought that, since he had agreed entirely to distribute the money, he would give account to God in any case, even if he had not said so. When asked about this, the same Old Man said the following.

The one who received the money was deceived, because he was entirely confident that he could give account to God about any matter. Yet who can be confident that he has a pure heart?[32] For this belongs only to the perfect fathers. He should have responded to the donor: "I am not capable of receiving this and of giving account to God alone; for I am a sinful person.[33] Therefore, I shall do my very utmost to cooperate in this matter, but it is up to God to cooperate with me, according to his will." Had he spoken thus, it would have been reckoned to him as humility, and God would not have condemned him for accepting something beyond his ability.

When, however, one agrees to give account so confidently, one is also required by God to give a very accurate account. At the same time, of course, the one who gave the money should also not have demanded such an account from the brother. For

30. Cf. Rom 7.22.
31. Cf. 1 Cor 4.2 and 15.15.
32. Cf. Prv 20.9.
33. Cf. Lk 5.8.

although he seemed to trust him, in his ignorance he actually considered him untrustworthy. Instead, once he trusted him, he should have left the matter entirely up to God and not have doubted the person. For one who doubts should not also entrust.

LETTER 630

Question: "Since there are some who openly and publicly receive alms, while others, because of their sense of dignity, are embarrassed to receive them openly, and yet others are ill in bed in their homes, should one discriminate between them or give the alms to everyone in the same manner?" Response.

You should regard all those who openly receive alms as being in one category, unless there is one among them who is vulnerable and afflicted; for you should give a little more to that person. Those who are embarrassed about receiving openly and publicly, as well as those who are ill, should be regarded as being in a different category; and you should give these people more than they require, according to whatever you are carrying at the time or can find.

LETTER 631

Question from the same person: "If someone gives another person some money to distribute, whether to the fathers or to the poor, conveying this to him in an open place where there are also certain poor people around, is it inappropriate to offer these poor people some of the money as well?" Response by John.

It is not inappropriate to give them some as well, if these are indeed very poor. For it happens that the person giving the money may not have known that there were poor people around, and this is perhaps why he did not say that they should receive some, too. If, however, that person specifies that the money is not to be given elsewhere, but only to some particular place, then one should not transgress that command. Therefore, it is necessary first to ask him about this and then do whatever he says; in this way, one will remain carefree.

LETTER 632

Question: "Since such a matter as almsgiving also requires assistants, if I am to choose some people whom I trust, father, should I also doubt as to whether I can fully entrust them with such a matter?" Response.

If you have reached the point of trusting them, then do not doubt this confidence. For everything is revealed to God and he knows the depths of our hearts, granting to each according to their deeds.[34] Therefore, if they happen to mishandle the money, then it is they who are responsible for themselves.[35]

LETTER 633

Question: "If I understand that one of them has mishandled the money, what should I do? Should I rebuke that person and confiscate the money from him, or not?" Response.

If you discover with certainty that he has mishandled the money, then examine first whether his thought can tolerate rebuke. And afterward, tell him about the matter with gentleness and counsel, according to God, and confiscate the money from him. If, however, he does not tolerate such rebuke, then do not harm his conscience, lest out of shame he come to something worse.[36] Instead, allow him to stay with whatever he has received. For he received the goods that belong to God; God himself knows better than anyone else whether he needs what he received, and he also knows how to judge this matter.

LETTER 634

Question: "So should I no longer trust that person?" Response.

If you learn that he has also done this previously and is trying to cover up the matter, then trust him no longer. If, however, he was always good before, and was seized by the devil on this occa-

---

34. Cf. Ps 61.13.   35. Cf. Mt 5.26.
36. Cf. Mk 5.26.

sion,[37] or else if he took the money because he needed it, then it is not inappropriate to trust him again. For he will surely correct himself. Simply do not scandalize him.

LETTER 635

Question: "What should I give to the poor who go from house to house?" Response.

Give them whatever comes to hand,[38] whether a little piece of bread, or else some undiluted wine, or two small coins,[39] or perhaps a little more money. Simply offer whatever you do without affliction, according to godly fear; for the kind and loving God is glorified in this.

LETTER 636

Question: "It happens that I have something very important to me, while something else happens to be of less significance, such as some additional wine or bread. Therefore, my thought tells me to give to the poor from that which is very important, but I hesitate to do this, namely, to give away the important things and to retain the less significant ones. When the fathers visit me, however, I consider that I prefer these to the poor, and so I do whatever I can to make them feel at home. Am I thinking properly or not?" Response.

As far as the poor are concerned, until we reach the point of regarding them as our equals and of loving our neighbor as ourselves,[40] then just do your best, being conscious of your weakness and giving them what is of less significance to you. As far as the fathers are concerned, you should indeed honor them more than the poor, because they are servants of God;[41] and it is written: "Pay respect to whom respect is due";[42] for even the Lord honored them.

37. Cf. Lk 8.29.
38. Cf. Eccl 9.10.
39. Cf. Mk 12.42.
40. Cf. Lv 19.18; Mt 19.19.
41. Cf. Acts 16.17.
42. Rom 13.7.

LETTER 637

Another Christ-loving layperson was ill and asked the same Old Man, John, whether he was going to live or die. And he responded as follows.

If I tell you that you will die, then your salvation will be the result of the fact that you are constrained by circumstance. For if you see that you are at the jaws of death, then you will necessarily abandon everything that you have. If, however, you expect to live many years, and your thought tells you that you must be saved, you will apply your thought to that which is good. Then, even if you happen to die immediately, your salvation will be the result of free will and not constraint.

LETTER 638

Question: "What then? If someone does something good for fear of death, is this not counted for one's salvation?" Response.

Salvation as the result of necessity is not the same as that which results from free will, although it is definitely better than doing nothing at all. For doing nothing at all brings destruction to the soul, since we are not interested in controlling ourselves. Therefore, now that you know both, apply what you will to yourself; but do so prudently, unlike the foolish virgins who were shut out of the wedding-chamber for not having the fruits of almsgiving and good deeds.[43]

LETTER 639

Question: "If one reminds one's own soul about death, and as a result strives to do what is good, is this not counted as a reward gained by free will?" Response.

It is a good thing to remember death,[44] in order that one may recognize one's mortality and know that a mortal is not eter-

---

43. Cf. Mt 25.1–12.
44. Cf. Sir 28.6 and 41.1. On remembrance of death, see also *Letters* 92, 94, 98–99, 123, 232, 242, 256, 259, 346, and 637.

nal; for someone who is not eternal will surely leave this age, even if involuntarily. Therefore, from continual remembrance of death, one also learns to do what is good according to one's free will. So, then, when one sees death before one's eyes and does [what is good], this is not the same as one who freely practices continual meditation of death. For the former is saved by necessity, for the sake of the fear of impending death.

LETTER 640

Question: "Father, tell me. How is it that [both] salvation according to free will and salvation out of necessity benefit the soul?" Response.

Salvation according to free will entirely delivers the soul from death; on the other hand, salvation out of necessity receives lesser grace and is inferior.

LETTER 641

Question: "If someone leads a negligent life and is about to die, but promises God that, should he live longer, he would strive to please him, will God grant this person more years?" Response.

God knows our hearts[45] and pays attention to the directness of our heart. Therefore, if he sees that such a person will in all truth and with all his heart repent,[46] then he will grant additional years. Indeed, it is said: "May God grant you according to your heart's desire;"[47] for God's will is the salvation of all, as he has said: "I swear that I do not desire the death of sinners, but rather that they should turn from their ways and live."[48] Therefore, let us direct our heart toward him and "cast our every concern upon him,"[49] and he shall direct our interests toward salvation.[50]

LETTER 642

Question: "Father, tell me if there is a set limit to the end of the world." Response.

45. Cf. Acts 1.24.
46. Cf. Mk 12.30.
47. Ps 19.5.
48. Cf. Ezek 18.23 and 32; 33.11.
49. Cf. Ps 54.23; 1 Pt 5.7.
50. Cf. Ps 67.20.

There is certainly an end to the world, but if God finds that we are pleasing to him,[51] then he may add more time. For it is said: "Righteousness adds days, but the years of the wicked will be short."[52] Whatever God commands is also the set limit for people's lives. Even when the apostles asked him about this, however, he said: "It is not for you to know the times or periods that the Father has set by his own authority."[53]

LETTER 643

Another Christ-loving layperson was taken ill and greatly consumed by fever. So he asked the Great Old Man to pray for him in order that he might be relieved of pain. He also sent him some water, so that the Old Man may bless it for him to drink; for he could not tolerate the burning fever. When the Old Man prayed for him, he drank, and the fever immediately subsided, and the pain ceased. The brother was astonished and glorified God for this,[54] also telling others about the power of God and the benefit received through the holy Old Man. On the next day, however, the fever once again attacked him vigorously. So he sent off to the Old Man, asking him to have mercy on him. The Old Man declared the following.

This happened to you in order that you may not be a chatterbox.

And he was relieved completely through the prayer of the holy Old Man. Therefore, from that time onward, he was afraid to report to anyone about the prayer of the holy Old Man, as well as about other benefits that he experienced from the holy Old Man.

LETTER 644

When the same brother noticed that the abbot was telling visiting brothers all about the wonders performed by the holy Old Man, he asked the Other Old Man, John, about this matter. When John explained the purpose of this, he no longer questioned him about it. He also, however, asked this of the same Old Man: "Father John, why is it that, from time to time, I see the abbot

51. Cf. 2 Cor 5.9.   52. Prv 10.27.
53. Acts 1.7.   54. Cf. Mt 15.31.

speaking of the virtues of the elders, and I rejoice in his words, believing that they are edifying. Yet on other occasions, I think that they are not edifying, but rather scandalous, although he is praising our own fathers; and so I am grieved. The same occurs to me in regard to other fathers, when I think that they are speaking too easily. Therefore, I entreat you, father, to tell me why this happens, and to pray that I may be delivered from this evil thought." Response by John.

Brother, may God grant you to hear, understand,[55] and put into practice whatever you are told. This is happening to you as a result of your pretense to rights and the condemnation of others. Pretense to rights, because you reckon yourself as being worthy of telling similar stories. Condemnation, because you say: "Why is he telling stories?" Instead, you should remember that: "The Spirit blows where it wills."[56] Are you able to tell me why it is that the Lord healed some people and then commanded them not to tell anyone what had happened, while to another person he said: "Go, show yourself to the priest, and offer the gift for your purification,"[57] immediately adding: "as testimony to them,"[58] and again: "Declare all the wonders that God has done for you"?[59]

Therefore, the words of the abbot are for the benefit of those who listen with fear, but for the condemnation of those who do not accept them with faith. Yet, for the time being, you are unable to discern these things, because your heart is still in the process of being transformed. For the Apostle says: "We are the aroma of Christ to God, among those who are being saved and among those who are perishing; to the one a fragrance from death to death, to the other a fragrance from life to life. Who is sufficient in these things? For we are not peddlers of God's words like so many."[60] So if you have doubts about the Old Man, as to why he should have rebuked you for speaking and yet not rebuked the abbot when he spoke, you should instead try to understand what it is that distinguishes you from him; and then you will be humble in your heart, saying: "The Old Man re-

55. Cf. Song 6.1.
56. Jn 3.8.
57. Mt 8.4; Mk 1.44; Lk 5.14.
58. Ibid.
59. Lk 8.39.
60. 2 Cor 2.15–17.

buked me because I am unworthy; however, he did not rebuke the abbot because he is worthy, allowing him instead to speak for the benefit of those listening."

We should try to understand that the Old Man is leading us in every way to humility, so that we may blame ourselves and consider ourselves as being unworthy. Nevertheless, it is we who do not want to lower our heads. Therefore, let us come to humility, and God will reveal to us his mysteries[61] in order that we may always speak where necessary and again always keep silent where it is not necessary to speak. In this way, both of these will occur for our benefit and for the benefit of those listening. Let us, then, not condemn or scorn those who listen, so that we may not be condemned but rather be edified. For if we question our thought that says: "We know how that person is speaking, and whether he is speaking from the Spirit," then we shall discover that we do not really know. So let us think good things and not evil things; for an evil person will think evil things, while a good person will think good things. In Christ Jesus our Lord, to whom be the glory to the ages. Amen.

LETTER 645

Another Christ-loving layperson was afflicted in the body, and sent a request to the same Old Man, John, in order that he might pray for him to receive healing. And the Old Man said: "God will quickly heal you." It took a long time, however, for him to be healed. Having faith in the Old Man, he was surprised, saying: "What is happening? The Old Man cannot be lying; for God speaks through him;[62] yet I have not been healed." So he came and asked the Great Old Man about this. Response by Barsanuphius.

If we believe that God does not lie,[63] and that everything is possible for the one who believes,[64] then how is it that you have not achieved that which you desire? Is it perhaps because, without your knowledge, there is some faithlessness lurking in your heart? I truly believe that whatever God has spoken to you through

---

61. Cf. Eph 3.3.
63. Cf. Ti 1.2.

62. Cf. Ps 59.8.
64. Cf. Mk 9.22.

brother John will happen to you. But I entreat your Christ-loving love not to drag me any longer to the hippodrome; for I am in old age. By this, I am referring to the single-mindedness that you claimed to have with us. After all, no one divides one's soul into two parts, giving rest to one part and work to the other. I have told you these things so that you may learn that I shall not cease praying to God[65] for you until he brings you, together with me, "to his gates with thanksgiving and to his courts with praise."[66]

> On hearing these things, he was astonished at how the Old Man revealed to him about the matter of the hippodrome, and he glorified God.[67] Thenceforth, he refrained from such wicked spectacles.

LETTER 646

Question from the same person to the same Great Old Man: "I had a beloved friend and soul-mate who lived elsewhere. In this way, we used to live as brothers, sharing everything. Now I have moved on, married, and settled, but we have retained the same friendship. Nevertheless, my thought tempts me, saying that the marriage might have created doubts in his heart about our friendship, and that perhaps he does not retain the same disposition." Response by Barsanuphius.

If you want to learn how his heart is disposed, you may do so in the following manner. Examine your heart carefully to see whether you retain the same disposition toward him after being married. If you have not retained the same disposition, then neither has he. If your disposition has remained the same, then you can be sure that his has, too. So, then, always have this as your criterion: according to your own heart, you will always discern his heart, with God's guidance.

LETTER 647

Another Christ-loving layperson sent asking the same Great Old Man to pray for him, that the Lord may remember him in his kingdom.[68] Response.

65. Cf. Col 1.29.
67. Cf. Mt 15.31.
66. Ps 99.4.
68. Cf. Lk 23.42.

Behold, the Lord Jesus Christ has not put my person to shame,[69] but rather has granted me the salvation of your soul and given me grace to remember you in his kingdom.[70] Therefore, having received such grace, let us guard it with gratitude; and let us not become like swine, which cannot discern precious pearls.[71] For you know that, if someone is honored by another, then one should not dishonor that person. Having been honored, then, by God, in spite of our unworthiness, let us make ourselves worthy. Let us honor him by keeping the commandments of his saints. For he said: "If then I am a father, where is the honor due me? And if I am a master, where is the respect due me?"[72] May he, the almighty God, assist you, child, to hear and to keep what is beneficial.

LETTER 648

Question: "There is a garden that belongs to my nephews, who live at some distance, and some people have decided to purchase it as a place of prayer. My nephews have charged me to deal with these people in regard to the price of the garden. I am seized, however, by two thoughts: one thought tells me that I should give it to them at no cost, since it will be used as a sacred place; another thought tells me to keep the charge entrusted to me by those who asked me to negotiate a price. So I do not know on which side to lean. For I fear God; but I also think that it would be a sin to harm my nephews. What, then, should I do, father?" Response.

Declare to these people the fair price of the garden, entreating them and saying: "You know that we are all indebted to our masters, the saints. So whatever the Lord assures you that you should contribute to them, perhaps lowering the price a little, it is up to you." Put this in writing. It is then up to them to accept this or not, but you cannot be blamed about it. For it is not an onerous sin to demand a fair price, even if it happens to be for a house of the Lord. It is, however, beneficial also for the one who owns and controls the garden, if that person does not

---

69. Cf. 2 Sm 19.5; Ps 33.6.

70. Cf. Lk 23.42.

71. Cf. Mt 7.6.

72. Mal 1.6.

happen to be poor, to lower the price as much as possible, since it is for a house of God; for that person will certainly receive abundance in fruits as a result of this. If, however, the owner is unable to lower the price, God will not demand anything more than a good intention.

When he heard these things, he left rejoicing and glorifying God.[73]

LETTER 649

Question: "Father, since I want to buy some slaves, but doubt whether they will actually be useful to me, tell me whether I should in fact procure them. What should I do?" Response.

Let us learn that we, too, have a Master. If we submit ourselves to our Master, then he will make our slaves also submit to us.[74] So, then, you have heard my response. Go and procure them[75] in the name of the Lord.

LETTER 650

Question: "If the law of God decrees something, while the law of the world prescribes the opposite, what should one do? For my thought tells me that society is regulated by the laws of the world, and someone who transgresses these is in fact doing wrong." Response.

The law of God is more precious; for it speaks of the soul's salvation. The law of the world is fleshly, and deals with fleshly matters.

LETTER 651

Question: "What does it mean when it says: 'You shall not be partial to the poor in a lawsuit'?"[76] Response.

This is said in order that the one who is passing judgment may judge something fairly and not on the pretext of being

---

73. Cf. Lk 5.25; Acts 8.39.
75. Cf. Rv 10.8.

74. Cf. Ti 2.9.
76. Ex 23.3.

compassionate to a poor person; otherwise, a judge is violating justice. For a judge, however, to entreat the adversary of a poor person to be compassionate[77] is not wrong.

LETTER 652

Question: "If one of the holy fathers, about whom I have a great sense of assurance, tells me to impose my authority in some matter in a way that appears to me to be wrong, what should I do, in order not to transgress his spoken command?" Response.

The spiritual fathers say nothing idly, but they say everything for the sake of the salvation of the soul. Therefore, inform him about this matter, and do whatever he tells you; and do not transgress his command. For things that are pleasing to God are both just and beneficial.

LETTER 653

Another Christ-loving layperson had a servant[78] who was not useful, who ran away at one point but then returned again after a while. He asked the Old Man, John, whether he should keep this slave. And after the Old Man had declared to him that in fact he should be released, the servant began to show good conduct, and the master was grieved about releasing him. So he sent off again asking about this matter, namely, whether he should still release him. Response by John.

Keep your servant for the time being, testing both him as well as yourself through him. And if he should be corrected, then all is well and good. If, however, he persists in the same conduct, and you keep him for God's sake, this, too, is fine; for you will receive the reward of patience. If, however, you see that you cannot tolerate him, but that you are coming to be harmed on his account, then release him so that he may leave, remembering one of the saints who said: "If you see someone drowning in the river, do not reach out your hand to him, in case he drags you, too, into the water; instead, stretch out your staff to

77. Literally: "to make mercy with." This copticism is also found elsewhere, such as in *Letters* 55, 232, 264, and 494.
78. Lit., "slave" (δοῦλον).

him. If you are able to save him by using your staff, then well and good. But if you cannot save him, you should let go of your staff, so that you also are not drowned with him."[79]

LETTER 654

Some days later, the servant tried to tempt his master by stealing something, but the Lord protected the master by the prayers of the saints, and the servant ended up leaving. So his master came to thank the Old Man for this protection, blaming himself because, after the first response, he nevertheless still delayed in releasing the servant. The Old Man declared the following to him.

It was not with the purpose of expelling him that I told you to release the servant, but on account of the weakness of your thought. For you could not endure being tempted by him. After all, we are sinners, and it is not up to us to expel anyone. Had you been able to keep him in spite of his laziness, you would have received your reward on his account. For indeed, some of the fathers used to say about Abba Poemen, regarding a certain elder, that he kept his disciple in spite of his laziness. And Abba Poemen said: "If I could, I would place a pillow under his head." And they said to him: "Then, what would you say to God?" And he replied: "I would say to God: 'You are the one who said, Hypocrite, first remove the log from your own eye, and then you will see clearly to take the speck out of your brother's eye.'"[80]

LETTER 655

Question: "So did that abba do the right thing in not correcting his brother?" Response.

Brother, it is not by chance that the abba did not stop counseling him; instead, he advised him on many occasions, but the latter did not accept the advice. Therefore, on seeing that the brother was not responding to correction, he left the matter to God's judgment, saying: "God knows what is beneficial; for my brother is much better than I." This is what the perfect used to

---

79. *Sayings*, Poemen 92 and Nau 472. See also *Letter* 733.
80. Cf. Mt 7.5. See *Sayings*, Poemen 117 and 131.

do; for they did not dare judge anyone, putting to shame those who are nothing[81] and yet continue to judge everyone.

LETTER 656

Question: "When my servant makes a mistake and I want to discipline him, with what purpose should I do this?" Response.

With the purpose of love, that is, according to God, so that by being corrected through your discipline, he may cease to sin, and so that this may occur for the salvation of his soul. Yet you should not do this with anger; for nothing good comes out of evil.[82] Therefore, if your thought is troubled, wait until it calms down. And, in this way, discipline him with compassion and with godly fear.

LETTER 657

Question: "But when I want to discipline him, my thought tells me: 'Your sins are worse than his; so why are you disciplining him when you do not correct yourself?' So I refrain from discipline." Response.

This thought comes from the devil, in order that the brother may remain uncorrected and in order that you might give account for him. Tell your thought: "It is true that I commit greater sins—that is evident, and I acknowledge it—but I am unable to give account both for me as well as for him; for God will demand of me his correction." And, after you have disciplined him carefully and with godly fear, repeat to yourself the words of the Apostle: "You then that teach another, you do not teach yourself."[83] In this way, you will be found to correct him with humility.

LETTER 658

Question: "When I see someone insulting religion and blaspheming the holy faith, I am aroused to anger against this person, supposedly out of zeal. What does this mean?" Response.

81. Cf. Gal 6.3.   82. Cf. Rom 3.8–12 and 17.
83. Rom 2.21.

You have certainly heard that no one can come to correction through evil, but rather only through good. Therefore, speak to this person with gentleness and long-suffering, advising the insulting one with fear of God. If, however, you see that you are aroused to anger, it is not necessary to say anything to him.

LETTER 659

Question: "It happens that, when I meet someone, I look at that person passionately and am afflicted in my soul. And, should it become necessary to be in that person's company, I am unable to look him in the eyes, and then this sometimes gives him the impression that I am arrogant. Indeed, this happens to me so intensely that I even have to shut my eyes, being unable to bear his sight. So I am grieved, not knowing what to do about this. But pray for me, master, and send me a word of life[84] and a medicinal dose of your loving-kindness." Response by John.

Since your love has asked about looking passionately at someone in your presence, and admittedly this comes from attacks of the devil, you should know that even looking at that person in your mind also comes from the devil. Therefore, in addition to this, you should remember the corruption and stench of our nature, as well as what we will become once we enter the grave. Nevertheless, why am I speaking to you about corruptible things? Why do you not rather bear in mind that you should keep before your eyes the future fearful judgment of God, which will [certainly] come?[85] Then, where is to be found the inheritance of those who do these things? And how can you ever bear that great shame when our actions will be revealed before the angels and archangels and all people, in the presence of the righteous judge?[86] How will the mouth of those who practice these be shut firm?[87] Let us fear the one who says: "Do not be deceived! Fornicators, adulterers, indulgent persons, and male prostitutes will not inherit the kingdom of God."[88] Also: "One who even looks

84. Cf. Jn 6.63–68.
85. Cf. Heb 10.27.
86. Cf. 2 Tm 4.8.
87. Cf. Ps 62.12.
88. 1 Cor 6.9–10.

at a woman with lustful desire,"[89] and so on. And: "If your eye causes you to sin, then cut it away."[90]

So you should always have these things in your memory, without spending too much time with other people with whom you find that you are tempted. At the same time, however, you should not show them why you are staying away from them, so that you do not lead them into other thoughts as well. Yet, even if you are required to speak with them, invoke the holy name of God for your assistance, saying: "Master Jesus, protect me and help me in my weakness." And be confident that he will crush the arrow of the enemies.[91] For it is in his name that one avoids doing evil deeds. Furthermore, instead of saying much, say little, and do not submit your ears and eyes to them; but remain constrained, modestly and calmly, so that no one may understand what is happening to you. Moreover, if you happen to receive confidence from them, you should still not be bold before your enemies; for they are shameless. Even if conquered thousands of times, they will rise up again and attack you. Nonetheless, the God who grants victory also assists us in our humility. Indeed, this is why he desired to become incarnate. Amen.

LETTER 660

Question: "What does it mean when it says: 'Watch out, that the thought of fornication does not seize you'?" Response.

This happens not only with fornication, but also with other matters, when the intellect is afflicted by distraction. One should, therefore, recall the intellect, saying: "Lord, forgive me for the sake of your holy name; for this has happened to me through my negligence. Deliver me from distraction and from every snare of the enemy; for yours is the glory to the ages. Amen." The reason for which the intellect has been seized is the following. If one is speaking, and the intellect is distracted, then it happens that while one is speaking about a certain matter, the intellect is being seized by another. This is precisely what "being seized" means. Just as when one is working and is distracted from one's

---

89. Mt 5.28.   90. Mt 5.29.
91. Cf. Hos 1.5.

work, or is not paying careful attention to it, then it is forgotten or ruined or else overdone. This, too, is what it means to be "seized."

The same occurs with the thought of fornication. For it happens that while one is talking to someone, if the enemy arrives in order to attract the intellect from vigilance before God, then the intellect is found to be distracted toward the enemy and the desire of fornication; then the intellect is seized. So it does not happen through planning or pondering, but rather through inattentiveness. Such a person resembles someone who is traveling but, out of a sense of faintheartedness, leaves the straight path[92] and finds oneself on another path.

Therefore, one should vigilantly recall the intellect, according to what we have said, and run toward the mercy of God. For he is compassionate and awaits us like that prodigal son. We are of course not unaware of how kindly he received him.[93] And when this war is sown in the intellect without distraction, it is necessary to be vigilant, neither taking pleasure in it nor prolonging it, but swiftly escaping toward God the Master.

LETTER 661

Question: "If necessity dictates that I speak with a woman, what should I do? Or how should I handle myself during the encounter? Tell me also whether I should be involved in any issues pertaining to women, pretending to do so out of piety or compassion." Response.

We find in every way that those who do not have an understanding of the works of God are harmed by the company of women. Therefore, as much as you can, keep away and do not engage yourself in the company of women. For this is not beneficial for you, even if they are women with good morals. Since, however, we have not entirely renounced the world, and necessity does sometimes dictate that we be in their company for some exchange or another, we should first firmly establish in our intellect the following example. Just as a person who approaches

92. Cf. 2 Pt 2.15.
93. Cf. Lk 15.20–24.

fire to do his chores surely takes precautions in order that he may not be burned by the fire, so, too, should we use the same precautions in all things. It is as if we are approaching fire, and we need to protect ourselves in every way with godly fear. Otherwise, we may think that we shall benefit from them; whereas our supposed benefit shall prove to be of great harm. Now if we want to lead our lives entirely for God, then we should try and do the same thing for every other person, if possible. Let us not tolerate looking at them in the eyes; nor again should we submit our sight to them. Furthermore, let us not prolong our encounter with them; for this brings forth the fire of desire. Instead, let us strive to depart from them quickly, praying to God that he might save us in that hour of necessity from the snare of the devil that lies stretched out before us;[94] and let us remember God unceasingly.[95] For his strength is great, and he is able to protect our weakness, in Christ Jesus our Lord, to whom be the glory to the ages. Amen.

LETTER 662

Another Christ-loving layperson asked the Great Old Man whether he should leave his wife for the purpose of becoming a monk. Response by Barsanuphius.

Child, do not assume the responsibility of leaving her, because you are transgressing the commandment of the Apostle, who says: "Are you bound to a wife? Then, do not seek to be free."[96] For if she sins and becomes a sinful woman, the responsibility for the sin lies with you, unless the decision is taken by mutual agreement[97] or with counsel. Simply leave the matter to God, and his loving-kindness will do as he wills.

LETTER 663

Another Christ-loving layperson asked the same Great Old Man: "What should I do? For I fall into passions very quickly." And the Old Man responded as follows.

---

94. Cf. 1 Tm 3.7.
96. 1 Cor 7.27.

95. Cf. 1 Thes 5.17.
97. Cf. 1 Cor 7.5.

Do not make any agreement with them;[98] "turn your eyes away in order not to look at vanities,"[99] keep your hands away from greed, and God will free you from these. Therefore, lead a modest life, and do not eat or drink to the point of satiation. Then you will subjugate the passions, and you shall find rest.

LETTER 664

Another Christ-loving layperson, who was a professor of secular wisdom, asked the Great Old Man whether he would do well in accepting a promotion. He said the following.

Do not feel arrogant,[100] and you shall find grace from God[101] and among people, as well as enjoy great success wherever you happen to be.

LETTER 665

The same person asked the Other Old Man about this. Response by John.

God has always chosen the humble. Have humility, and God will assist you quickly.

LETTER 666

The same person again entreated the same Old Man John to pray for someone who suffered [from demonic possession]. Response.

Let him struggle as much as possible, and they will be heard who pray for him. "For the prayer of the righteous is very powerful and effective."[102] The Lord also said: "This kind can only come out through fasting and prayer."[103]

LETTER 667

Another Christ-loving layperson asked the same Old Man, saying: "Since the thieves who broke into my house on account of

98. Cf. 1 Mc 11.9.
100. Cf. 1 Tm 6.17.
102. Jas 5.16.
99. Cf. Ps 118.37.
101. Cf. Lk 1.30.
103. Mk 9.29; Mt 17.21.

my sins took nothing from the house, should I chase after them, or should I pretend that nothing has happened?" Response by John.

If we truly believe that it is because of our sins that the thieves broke into the house, then God did not allow anything evil to occur on account of his loving-kindness. So why is it that we want to take revenge instead of leaving everything to God, who said: "Vengeance is mine! I will repay!"[104] If we feared God, then if we noticed that they left something behind, we would even assist them as much as we could.[105] Yet, since we have not reached this point, lest we want to fall into vainglory, let us do nothing either good or evil to the thieves, but let us instead thank him who did not do unto us according to our sins.[106]

LETTER 668

Question: "If they happened to steal something from us, what should we have done?" Response.

It belongs to the perfect[107] to scorn everything. Those who are on the lower level, however, seek to recuperate what they have lost, even if the damage is little; for they look at the strain and need that they suffer without their goods. This brings some people to turn to the courts, especially when the thieves are ungrateful. Nonetheless, we should learn that this action is actually caused by avarice, giving rise to harm in our soul; for we are transgressing the spoken commandment: "If anyone wants to sue you and take your coat, give your cloak as well."[108]

LETTER 669

Question: "Father, what happens if someone comes with the intention to take my cloak? Should I give it to him immediately? For how many such evil and wicked people exist, who would gladly do this, to the point of even leaving someone naked if they could?" Response.

104. Heb 10.30; Dt 32.35.
105. See Abba Zosimas, *Reflections* 12.
106. Cf. Ps 102.10.   107. Cf. Heb 5.14.
108. Mt 5.40.

This is not said in order that whoever simply wants to take something from you may receive it from you; rather, it is said for the one who wants to sue you, which signifies inhumanness, as well as for the courts, which bring harm to the soul. Therefore, in that case, one should scorn fleshly things in light of the salvation of the soul. For it is said: "What will it profit them, if they gain the whole world but forfeit their life?"[109]

LETTER 670

Question: "Since there are some who are familiar with the court system, and they are not harmed as much as those who are unfamiliar, is it good to handle such legal matters through them?" Response.

Even if they are familiar with the courts, yet it is we who would be responsible[110] for adding harm to them. Nevertheless, in comparing the [two] evils, the latter is no less harmful; for when we instigate this procedure, we are brought to the destruction of our soul. If, however, they, too, are being harmed as we are, then we are responsible for their harm; that sin will weigh down on us, and we shall bear the harm. For it is written: "Evil is bound to come, but woe to anyone by whom it comes."[111] Now, if someone is not satisfied with the conclusion [of the court], striving to make his adversaries suffer great evils, then this is worst of all and angers God still more. For he said: "Do not repay evil for evil,"[112] and: "Forgive, that you may be forgiven."[113]

LETTER 671

Question: "If it is necessary for someone to bear witness about a murder that really happened, should one lie in order that the murderer may avoid death?" Response.

If you never lie, then you should not lie in this either. For it is written: "Do not be partial to the poor in a lawsuit."[114] If it is not the will of God, then that person will simply not die. If, however,

109. Mt 16.26.
111. Lk 17.1.
113. Cf. Mt 6.14.

110. Cf. Gal 2.17.
112. 1 Pt 3.9.
114. Ex 23.3.

you happen to lie in other circumstances and wish to lie in this case as well, then do as you usually do. For it is written: "Everyone who commits sin is also guilty of lawlessness."[115]

As for me, I have nothing to say about this. If, however, it is not necessary for you to bear witness, then you need not say anything at all. For there is a useful proverb here: "Saying: 'I do not know' places no one in prison!"

LETTER 672

Question: "If one has debtors who happen to be wealthy, should one demand interest as well from these people? And if they happen to be poor, should one perhaps even demand all the capital?" Response by John.

It is written of the righteous: "They do not lend their money with interest."[116] This means that we may receive the capital. Now, if some of them are unable to repay this, it has also been written about them: "When your friends[117] are in poverty, do not distress them by imposing demands on them."[118]

LETTER 673

Question: "What happens if both he [the debtor] and I [the lender] happen to be poor? Am I committing any sin by demanding what I need?" Response.

No, you are not committing any sin. It is good, however, not to distress one's brother, at least as much as this is possible, if he happens to be too poor to repay us.

LETTER 674

Question: "When I am harmed in some way and my heart is not grieved, my thought suggests to me that this is the result of harshness, and that I should feel sorrow on the one hand but gladly endure everything on the other. Are these good thoughts?" Response.

115. 1 Jn 3.4.
116. Ps 15.5.
117. Lit., "your brother" (ὁ ἀδελφός σου).
118. Cf. Sir 31.31.

One should not feel sorrow about anything in this world at all, except about sin.

LETTER 675

Question: "How should one apply the phrase: 'Rejoice with those who rejoice, and weep with those who weep'?"[119] Response.

Rejoicing with those who rejoice means sharing the joy of those who achieve virtue according to God and who delight in the hope of the good things that are to come.[120] Weeping with those who weep means sharing in the suffering of sinners who repent for their sins.

LETTER 676

Question: "If someone whom I love loses a child or something else, and is sorrowful as a result of this, how should I share in this sorrow, when the person is so close to me?" Response.

You should share in his sorrow for the following reason: lest he bring some harm to his own soul through being possessed by great sorrow and not bearing the matter with thanksgiving.

LETTER 677

Question: "Since it is written: 'Blessed are the peacemakers,'[121] is it therefore good to strive to make peace with everyone?" Response.

It is better to bring peace to one's own heart; this is what is fitting for every person to achieve; and blessed is the one who does so. As for making peace with one's enemies, this does not belong to everyone, but only to those who are able to fulfill this calmly. Whereas the weak person should rejoice at the peace of all people, but should not present himself for the purpose of mediation of peace with everyone, but only with those whom he loves in a godly way, and only when this brings no harm to his soul.

119. Rom 12.15.   120. Cf. Heb 10.1.
121. Mt 5.9.

LETTER 678

Question: "When I do something that is according to God but am scorned for this by other people, then I feel sorry for scandalizing them." Response by John.

If you are scorned unjustly, then do not feel any sorrow; for the devil envies good and incites such things in order to cut it off. Afterward, however, the devil is abolished,[122] and God brings the matter to glory. Nevertheless, if you are scorned justly, because you are truly sinful, then you should bear the shame yourself; and if you repent, this is turned into joy.

LETTER 679

Another Christ-loving layperson was greatly mistreated by someone, and informed the same Old Man about this. And the Old Man said the following.

Do good to him.

LETTER 680

After doing this, he was still greatly mistreated by him; so once again he declared this to the Old Man, saying: "Behold, I am doing good to him, but he does not stop doing evil to me." And the Old Man said the following.

You are not actually doing anything good to him, but only to yourself; for the Lord said: "Do good to your enemies, and pray for those who abuse you."[123] So each person will receive according to his own work.[124]

LETTER 681

Another Christ-loving layperson, who was hosting certain fathers, asked the same Old Man, saying: "What should I do? For I am always grieved that one of the fathers visits me but I can never find the necessary things to offer to him." Response by John.

122. Cf. 2 Thes 2.8.   123. Cf. Lk 6.27–28.
124. Cf. Ps 61.13.

This thought is diabolical. For it is sufficient for you to offer the fathers what is at hand, according to the words: "Be content with what you have";[125] and God will assure them. For if someone worries about such things, that person cannot be hospitable, but will always pray that no one visits him.

Now, if something is in fact available to be offered, and one is sparing with it out of stinginess, then even if one happens to receive them into hospitality ten thousand times, their hearts will not be assured, unless of course you happen to need something that is required for some more pressing circumstance or else is reserved for other people who are ill or more noteworthy.

So one must do everything with discernment and godly fear. Moreover, if you need to travel somewhere, do not expect to receive any hospitality, and then you will always be calm. For if you expect to receive hospitality and do not, then you will slander your host; and slander is the soul's death. Rather, give thanks in all circumstances[126] for this is truly spiritual and beneficial nourishment as well as rest for the soul.

LETTER 682

Question: "What happens if I did not receive any hospitality at all, but simply happened to be extremely tired from the journey[127] and in need of food?" Response.

Then remember who is the one that truly cares for all and nourishes everyone; for that is God. Therefore, if God in fact wanted you to be fed, he would have assured them in regard to receiving you. Since they did not offer you any hospitality, it is clear that God does not actually want them to do this; and so they are not responsible for it. For everything happens to us for our testing and salvation, in order that we may endure[128] and blame ourselves in all things as being unworthy.

LETTER 683

Another Christ-loving layperson asked the same Old Man: "My thought sows cowardice within me, telling me that the devil can

125. Heb 13.5.   126. Cf. 1 Thes 5.18.
127. Cf. Jn 4.6.   128. Cf. Rom 5.3.

force me to sin, even if I do not want to, and that, supposedly, I
have become indebted to him. So I am greatly grieved at this."
Response by John.

Do not believe that the devil has any authority over anyone.
Otherwise, the responsibility for sin would not lie in our free
will but only in the constraint of the one who has snatched this
authority. In that case, one would have no need either of salvation or of sin. Did the devil deceive Eve by means of authority or
by means of advice? Authority appears nowhere; otherwise, no
one would dare to escape the one with authority. Therefore, we
resemble a free person who was enslaved to someone out of his
own free will. Then, in time, that person came to himself[129] and
repented. Yet, had he not taken refuge in someone more powerful than he,[130] then surely no one would be able to liberate
him. If, however, he did take refuge, then the devil would realize that he is not really his slave and would not dare to do anything to him on account of that more powerful one.

Therefore, it is clear that the devil has no authority over us.
You should say to your thought: "I am a debtor, but a debtor
who has taken refuge in him who can liberate and call me,[131]
who says: 'Come to me, all you that are weary and are carrying
heavy burdens, and I will give you rest,'[132] and so I must always
be vigilant in order not to fall again into the hands of the devil." And if your thought again tells you: "Well, since the devil
cannot force you into sin, then you must be sinless," and as a
result the devil continues to oppress you with such thoughts,
then respond to him: "If you are telling me that I shall sin no
more, then I will not believe you until I reach that city." For if
someone travels an entire journey, but still has one mile that
remains in that journey, and then that person falls down, then
of what use is it when one is just outside the city? Therefore,
let us cast our weakness before God, and he will abolish all the
machinations of the devil, through the prayers of all his saints.
Amen.

129. Cf. Lk 15.17.   130. Cf. Lk 11.22.
131. Cf. 1 Pt 1.15.   132. Mt 11.28.

LETTER 684

Question: "My fields are being damaged by locusts. If, however, I chase them away, my neighbors become angry with me; and if I leave them alone, I am harmed by the locusts. What should I do?" Response.

Take some holy water and sprinkle it through your fields. And if you can [handle your neighbors] peacefully and without turmoil, then chase the locusts away or destroy them; for this is not a sin. But if they are angry with you about this, then, for the benefit of your soul, leave the matter in the hands of God; and whatever happens shall be by the will of God.

LETTER 685

Question: "Tell me, master, should we completely chase away the anger of God, or are we provoking God's anger by doing so?" Response.

The perfect do not chase it away; for they place all their hope in God. We, however, who are fleshly and have need of earthly things,[133] should condemn ourselves as being sinful and seek to reach this stage through prayer and psalmody, imploring God to forgive us and striving henceforth to be thankful to him. For even if one particular evil passes, nevertheless our sins will bring upon us even worse evils; and we shall be unable to cease from these without repentance and mercy. For it is said: "Blessed are the merciful; for they shall receive mercy."[134]

Moreover, do not say: "Then why does God, who sends his anger for our discipline, endure those who are unrepentant and who chase away his anger?" For God brings anger as a form of threat, in order that we may repent; and he endures us when we chase it away, in his long-suffering awaiting our return to him. Thus, if we persist in the same, even after chasing [God's anger] away, we shall fall into worse sins; and then the words of

133. Cf. Jn 3.12.
134. Mt 5.7.

the prophet are fulfilled in us: "We have healed Babylon, but it was not healed."[135] Then there is nothing else to expect, except the eternal torments and the outer darkness and the poisonous worm and the gnashing of teeth.[136]

LETTER 686

Another Christ-loving layperson asked the same Old Man: "I want to press some Jewish wine in my winepress. Is this a sin?" Response by John.

If, when God sends rain, it rains in your field but not in that of the Jew, then do not press his wine. If, however, God is kind and loving to all and sends rain upon the just as well as upon the unjust,[137] then why do you prefer to be inhumane rather than compassionate; for he says: "Be merciful, even as your Father in heaven is merciful."[138]

LETTER 687

Question: "If someone confides in me about something, ordering me not to tell anyone else, but another person puts me under an oath to talk about this, what should I do? For if I tell, then I am actually grieving the one who entrusted me with the matter; and if I do not tell, then I am in fact grieving the one who asked me [to do so]; in any case, I am also afraid of the oath itself." Response.

The one who has put you under an oath is the one who actually bears the responsibility for this sin. Therefore, it is not necessary to reveal the secret of your brother on the pretext of the oath. Tell him: "Had you entrusted me with some word, would you have been happy for me to reveal it to anyone else? If, in that case, you would not have been happy, then do not ask me in turn to tell you what my brother told me." For it is said: "Whatever you hate to be done to you, do not do it to your neighbor."[139] And again: "Do to others as you would have them do to you."[140]

135. Cf. Jer 28.9 LXX.
136. Cf. Mt 8.12; Mk 9.48.
137. Cf. Mt 5.45.
138. Cf. Lk 6.36.
139. Tb 4.15.
140. Lk 6.31.

LETTER 688

Question: "What should be my perspective? Should I think that every person is righteous, or rather that I am in fact more sinful than everyone else? For my thought has difficulty believing that every person is righteous." Response.

Always regard yourself as being more sinful and as being the least of all, and you will find rest.

LETTER 689

Question: "When I am talking to someone about the *Lives of the Fathers* or their *Sayings*, my heart conceives great things. So tell me how I may speak with humility, as well as to whom I should speak, and with what purpose." Response.

When you are speaking about the *Lives of the Fathers* or their *Sayings*, you should condemn yourself, saying: "Woe to me! How can I speak about the virtues of the fathers, when I have not acquired any of them? I have not even begun to make progress; yet I am sitting down and speaking with others for the sake of their benefit! If only the words of the Apostle had not been fulfilled in me: 'You then that teach others, you do not teach yourself.'"[141] And when you say this, your heart will burn, and you will find a way to speak with humility.

You should also be careful in the matter of whom you actually speak to. If you observe that this person wants to benefit, then speak; but if not, then there is no need to speak. For it is written: "Blessed is the one who speaks to the ears of those who listen."[142] May you never be found to offer holy things to dogs or cast pearls before swine.[143] May the Lord grant you prudence, brother, so that you do not deviate from the way of humility.

LETTER 690

Two Christ-loving laypersons sincerely loved one another in the Lord and were being guided by the fathers in the spiritual life.[144]

141. Rom 2.21.
143. Cf. Mt 7.6.
142. Cf. Sir 25.9; Mt 13.16.
144. Cf. Ps 15.11.

Once, however, one of them happened to say something in conversation to the other about a third person. Now the other, seized by the devil, thought that he was actually speaking about him, and so was greatly troubled. Even when assured by the brother that he was in fact referring to a third person, he did not believe it. As a result, they had a little argument. Then both of them came to the fathers, and declared to the same Old Man, John, what had happened. He told them the following.

I am telling you, since you are of the same soul as I, the whole truth before God. Both of you are obliged to make a prostration before God—indeed, not negligently but with all your heart[145]— so that he may forgive you through the prayers of your fathers. As for one of you, it is because you were slandered but were unable to endure the blame. Therefore, say: "I have sinned and am entirely at fault, since my brother was troubled on my account." And as for the other one of you, it is because you did not discern the words before speaking, in order to find out that it was not actually said about you. Therefore, you should say nothing against him until your death. Furthermore, like you, he, too, was not found to be patient.

Nevertheless, it is not you who are responsible, but rather it is we who are responsible for the evils; for we did not pray for you. Had we prayed, you would have been protected from the evil one who sows tares among you[146] in order to tempt you. This is our prayer: that you be protected. Are you not afraid of God's judgment,[147] that people may not be scandalized through you, saying: "Look at the children of these fathers; they have no patience, but instead rise up against one another"? Therefore, if you are ashamed about this and make a prostration before one another with all your heart, then we, too, shall make a prostration for your sakes; for the primary shame belongs to us. May the Lord forgive you and guard you from the evil one,[148] swiftly crushing him beneath your feet. Be of one soul with one another in the Lord, as well as of one mind and one faith. May

145. Cf. Mk 12.30–33.　　146. Cf. Mt 13.25.
147. Cf. Lk 23.40.
148. Cf. Ps 120.7; 2 Thes 3.3; Mt 6.13.

the Lord strengthen you and preserve you unshaken[149] in his fear. Amen.

Another Christ-loving layperson was offering hospitality to the fathers and sent letters asking the same Old Man whether he should abandon the world entirely and enter the monastic life. And when the Old Man wrote in response that the monastic life is more perfect, he took his word as a decree. So, as a result, he was deeply grieved and thought that he should never again ask the fathers about anything. Knowing this in his spirit, the Old Man said that the following response should be addressed to him.

Before all else, we embrace your love in the Lord, entreating you to reject every thought of sorrow and to live henceforth with joy and godly fear,[150] as well as to understand what I previously wrote to you in an earlier letter. For we wrote nothing to you in the form of an order, having learned from the Apostle, who says: "I am not putting any restraint upon you."[151] Instead, however, we are drawing here a distinction for you between two different matters in order that you may see the difference in benefit that derives from each. In the same way, we have all heard the Savior declaring in the Gospels what was written in the law: "Do not commit adultery; do not kill,"[152] and so on. Nevertheless, when that inquirer proceeded to ask: "I have kept all of these, what else do I lack?"[153] he spoke to him about perfection, saying: "If you want to be perfect, [go and] sell all of your belongings,"[154] and the rest which you know.

Nevertheless, that hater of good is always searching for ways to prevent every good deed. For when he saw the benefit about which I wrote to you, even before you understood the actual meaning of our words, he slightly confused your thought. In fact, it is truly amazing how he covers up our intellect, seizing our thought in order that we may not benefit at all. Indeed, he

149. Cf. 2 Thes 2.17.
151. 1 Cor 7.35.
153. Mt 19.20.

150. Cf. Mt 28.8.
152. Cf. Mt 5.21 and 27.
154. Mt 19.21.

does not allow us even to ask ourselves why we are troubled at all, or to say: "Why are you cast down, my soul, and why are you disquieted within me? Hope in God; for I shall again praise him,"[155] and so on. The devil does this in order to show us that, had these words come from holy people, then they should have brought us some assistance rather than causing turmoil and temptation.

A vigilant person, however, understands that the apostles, too, were troubled on account of their faithlessness when they saw their Lord and Savior Christ. For he made this clear to them, saying: "Why are you troubled, and why do doubts arise in your hearts?"[156] And then calm immediately followed his words.[157] The same applies now to us also. Had we read with peaceful heart the words addressed in the letter, we, too, would have discovered that we cannot reach that measure about which it is written: "To some people one hundredfold, to others sixtyfold; and if this is not possible, then to the third group, namely, thirtyfold."[158] In order, then, that we may learn that everything written was entirely beneficial, even if we cannot reach that perfect measure, we are in fact slapped[159] in the present work of hospitality in order not to feel arrogant, and not to believe that we are doing something important, but to discover that we cannot reach perfection in our work.

Therefore, what we wrote in the previous letter was not supposed to undermine what you are presently doing, but its contents was aimed at making you rise to that which is superior; or else, if you happen to remain in the same state, then it was to make you perform your work with humble thought. So do not be surprised by these temptations. For we have been commanded: "Whenever you face trials of any kind, rejoice."[160]

Once a brother asked one of the holy fathers: "What is happening, Abba? For when I am about to sleep and labor in prayer, making the sign of the cross, on that very night I dream about fornication. And if I do not say my prayers or make the sign of the cross, then I do not in fact dream of such things." And

155. Ps 41.12.
157. Cf. Mt 8.26.
159. Cf. 1 Cor 4.11.

156. Lk 24.38.
158. Cf. Mk 4.8.
160. Jas 1.2.

the elder responded, telling him: "The demons do this as part of their strategy in order to stop you from praying and making the sign of the cross. For they know that we receive assistance through these." The same may be said in your case. If you ask the fathers about something, and the demons trouble your thoughts for a while through their words, you should nonetheless never refrain from asking the fathers. For they never decree anything that is harmful or heavy. They are, after all, the disciples of the one who said: "My yoke is easy and my burden is light."[161] Then we shall discover the fruit of their benefit and cry out with the psalmist: "You have turned my mourning into joy,"[162] and so forth.

LETTER 692

Another Christ-loving layperson asked the same Old Man: "Sometimes I happen to be in conversation with someone, and suddenly my thought is distracted, so that I feel that I am alone and ultimately even forget what that person has just said. Not because my intellect is transferred to something else, but because it is simply beside itself. What does this mean, father, and what should I do? For I am greatly grieved." Response.

This is diabolical temptation that wants to put us to shame in regard to the present things. If, however, one freely reveals this matter to the other person in conversation, saying: "Forgive me; for I was distracted by the devil," then the devil is put to shame and the temptation ceases. After that, you may continue the conversation with vigilance. It appears as if this means nothing, but to such a person as thinks that it means nothing, it brings much shame. Moreover, remembrance of the name of God completely abolishes all evil and strengthens our weakness. Amen.

LETTER 693

A Christ-loving layman, who practiced great ascetic abstinence and cared for his soul, sent a letter asking the same Old Man: "What is beneficial for someone to do? That which appears to

161. Mt 11.30.
162. Ps 29.12.

one as being good? Or [what one hears as being good] after asking the fathers?" Response by John.

If someone meditates on what good one should actually do
but does not in fact ask the fathers, then that person is unlawful and has done nothing according to the law. If, however,
someone does something after asking the fathers, then such a
person is in fact fulfilling the Law and the Prophets.[163] Indeed,
asking is a sign of humility. Such a person is, therefore, an imitator of Christ, who humbled himself to the point of becoming a
slave.[164] For they say that a man who is without counsel is an enemy unto himself. And again: "Everything that you do, do with
counsel."[165] Moreover, John the Dwarf says: "If you see a young-
er monk rising up to heaven through his own will, hold his foot
and pull him back down."[166] Therefore, it is more beneficial to
ask humbly rather than to journey in accordance with one's
own will. For it is God who places the response in the mouth of
the one being asked, as a result of the humility and directness
of heart in the one actually asking.

LETTER 694

Question: "If I am sitting in the company of certain fathers, and
they are discussing the faith of one of them, that perhaps he is
not thinking correctly, should I participate in the conversation
as well or not? For my thought tells me that if I am silent, I am
betraying the faith. And if they are having a simple conversation
about doctrinal matters, should I say what I happen to know, or
should I keep silent? Moreover, if I am asked [to say something],
what should I do?" Response.

Never take part in conversations about the faith; for God will
not demand this of you, but only whether you believe correctly
what you have received from the holy church at the time of your
baptism, and whether you keep his commandments. So maintain these things, and you shall be saved.

163. Cf. Mt 7.12–26.   164. Cf. 1 Thes 1.6; Phil 2.9.
165. Cf. Prv 24.72.
166. *Sayings*, Nau 111. Some manuscripts attribute this saying to John Clima-
cus (or *Klimakos*), but it clearly belongs to John the Dwarf (or *Kolovos*).

Furthermore, it is not necessary to talk about doctrines; for this is beyond you. Instead, pray to God for all your sins, and let your intellect spend time on these matters. See, however, that you do not condemn within your heart those who do talk about doctrines; for you do not know whether they are speaking correctly or not; nor do you know how God will judge the matter. So, if you are asked, simply say: "These things are beyond me; forgive me, holy fathers."

LETTER 695

Question: "If the heretic happens to be arguing better than the orthodox brother during this discussion, is it then good perhaps for me to support the latter as much as I can, lest he be harmed in the orthodox faith by losing the debate?" Response.

If you enter into any conversation, speaking publicly before God and people, then you are considered to be the one teaching. Moreover, if one teaches without having authority to do so, then one's words are not in fact assured by God but remain fruitless. So, if there is no benefit in your speaking, why is it necessary for you to speak at all? If, however, you truly want to be of assistance, then speak within your heart to God, who knows our secrets[167] and is able to accomplish far more than we could ask for.[168] He will deal with those who are debating, in accordance with his will, while you will find humility through this.

This situation resembles someone who imprisons another person by force and without just reason. When a third person sees what has happened, although he cannot do or say anything in opposition, yet he may go secretly to a more powerful person, who will send for the first person's release on his own authority. Meanwhile, the one who imprisoned that man is troubled because he does not actually know who reported it. The same also applies here. Let us approach God in the prayer of our hearts for our faith and for our brothers; then he who swore unto himself:[169] "that he desires everyone to be saved and to come to the

---

167. Cf. Rom 2.16.   168. Cf. Eph 3.20.
169. Cf. Gn 22.16.

knowledge of the truth"[170] and life will do with them according to his will.

Question: "Should I first ask to learn what they are discussing in order to be sure?" Response.

Ask for nothing that God will not demand of you. Nor contribute any dangerous words. Instead, be satisfied, as I have already told you, with the confession of the correct faith, and do not meddle in anything else beyond this.

Question: "If, however, the discussion concerns the Scriptures, should I still keep silent, or may I then speak? And if they happen to be unsure of something about which I do know, is it perhaps good for me to speak then or not?" Response by John.

Silence is always better. If, however, they are unsure about something, and you happen to know about this, then in order to solve their doubt, you should say what you know with humility. But if you do not know, then do not say anything at all from your own thought; for this is foolishness.

Question: "If the conversation concerns various matters that are not harmful to the soul, should I keep silent or speak?" Response.

It is never good to speak before being asked.[171] If you are asked to say something, then say what you know with humility and fear of God. Neither feel arrogant if your words are accepted, nor feel grieved if your words are not accepted. For this is the way of God.[172] Moreover, in order that you may not be considered as being silent, say something from what you know, but be brief and avoid too many words or inopportune glory.

---

170. 1 Tm 2.4.
171. *Sayings*, Euprepios 7, Poemen 45, and Nau 468.
172. Cf. Mt 22.16.

LETTER 699

Question: "If someone asks me to anathematize Nestorius and the heretics with him, should I do this or not?" Response.

The fact that Nestorius and those heretics who follow him are under anathema[173] is clear. But you should never hasten to anathematize anyone at all. For one who regards himself as sinful should rather mourn over his sins, and do nothing else. Neither, however, should you judge those who anathematize someone; for one should always test oneself.[174]

LETTER 700

Question: "But if someone happens to think, as a result of this, that I believe the same as Nestorius, what should I tell him?" Response by John.

Tell him: "Although it is clear that those people were worthy of their anathema, nevertheless I am more sinful than every other person, and I fear that, in judging anyone else, I may actually condemn myself.[175] Indeed, even if I anathematize Satan himself but happen to be doing his works,[176] then I am in fact anathematizing myself. For the Lord said: 'If you love me, you will keep my commandments.'[177] And the Apostle says: 'Let anyone be accursed[178] who has no love for the Lord.'[179] Therefore, one who does not keep his commandments does not love him; and whoever does not love him is under anathema. So, then, how can such a person [who is already under anathema] anathematize others?" Say these things in response; and if that person still persists in this, then for the sake of his conscience, anathematize the heretic.

173. This refers to the decree known as the *Three Chapters*, promulgated by Justinian in 543–544 and condemning the forerunner of Nestorius, Theodore of Mopsuestia, together with Theodoret and Ibas.
174. Cf. 1 Cor 11.28.
175. Cf. Rom 2.1.
176. Cf. Jn 5.36.
177. Jn 14.15.
178. Or "anathema" (ἀνάθεμα).
179. 1 Cor 16.22.

LETTER 701

Question: "If I am actually unaware of whether the one he is asking me to anathematize is truly a heretic, then what should I do?" Response.

Tell him: "Brother, I do not know what this person believes, about whom you are speaking to me. Therefore, to anathematize someone I do not know appears to me to resemble condemnation. I can, however, tell you this: Beyond the faith of the holy 318 Fathers,[180] I know no other faith; and one who believes contrary to this casts oneself under anathema."

LETTER 702

Question: "If there is a persecution [of believers], what should I do? Should I stay, or should I leave?" Response.

Ask your spiritual fathers, and do whatever they tell you. But do not follow your own judgment, lest through lack of knowledge you fall into danger.

LETTER 703

Question: "And if I cannot find any fathers in whom I can confide at a time of need, in order to ask them about this, then what should I do? Should I stay, in order that I may not appear to betray the faith, or should I leave for fear of being overcome?" Response.

Stand in prayer, and ask the kind and loving God with all your heart, saying: "Master, have mercy on me for the sake of your goodness, and do not allow me to deviate from your will, nor deliver me to the present temptation for my destruction." Repeat this prayer up to three times, in the manner of the Savior at the time when he was handed over.[181] And afterward, if you still observe within yourself an unwavering eagerness to stay

---

180. On the Fathers of the First Ecumenical Council (Nicaea, 325), see also *Letters* 58 and 694.

181. Cf. Mt 26.39–44.

and endure by the grace of God all the horrors that will come upon you, even to the point of your own death, then stay. But if you observe any cowardice in your heart, then depart.

And do not think that you are betraying the faith by doing this; for God does not demand anything beyond your strength.[182] Indeed, if you stay, in spite of your cowardice, and it happens that you can no longer bear the impending afflictions and torments, then you may come to betray the truth, thus bringing upon yourself eternal damnation.[183]

LETTER 704

Question: "If I fall into [this last] temptation without knowing it, what should I do?" Response.

Cast all your care on the kind and loving God,[184] saying: "Master, for the sake of your goodness and the prayers of all your saints, since I have not put myself in this situation, as if I were able to do so, but have encountered it without desiring it, do not allow me to betray the holy faith."

LETTER 705

Question: "How should I ask the fathers for forgiveness of my sins? Should I say: 'Forgive me'? Or should I tell them: 'Ask for [divine] forgiveness for me'?" Response by John.

When we are asking those who have already gone to the Lord, we should say: "Forgive me." When, however, we are asking those who are still among us, then we should say: "Pray for us, that we may receive forgiveness."

LETTER 706

Question: "And when I am asking the Master himself, how should I ask?" Response.

You should say: "Master, have mercy on me, for the sake of your holy martyrs and the holy fathers; forgive my sins through

---

182. Cf. 1 Cor 10.13.   183. Cf. Mt 25.46.
184. Cf. 1 Pt 5.7.

their intercessions." For the prophet also said: "Through Abraham, your servant,"[185] and the Lord himself said: "I shall defend this city for my sake and for the sake of my servant, David."[186]

LETTER 707

Question: "If I am sitting in the company of certain secular people and they begin to engage in idle talk, should I stay or depart? Moreover, if it is necessary for me to stay, then what should I do?" Response.

If it is not necessary for you to stay, depart; if, however, it is indeed necessary for you to stay, then transfer your intellect to prayer, without condemning the others, but realizing your own weakness.

LETTER 708

Question: "And if they happen to be my beloved ones, do you decree that I perhaps transfer this conversation to another topic that is more useful?" Response.

If you know that they would gladly receive the word of God, then speak from the *Lives of the Fathers*, and transfer the conversation to the salvation of the soul.

LETTER 709

Question: "So is it good to invoke the name of God[187] when in conversation with someone?" Response.

It is always necessary to invoke the name of God both during conversation with someone and before such conversation, as well as after the conversation, and indeed at every time and in every place. For it is written: "Pray without ceasing."[188] This is how every temptation is in fact abolished.

---

185. Cf. Dn 3.35.
186. Cf. 2 Kgs 19.34; Ps 131.10.
187. Cf. Acts 2.21.
188. 1 Thes 5.17.

LETTER 710

Question: "And how is it possible for someone to pray without ceasing?"[189] Response.

When one is alone, one should recite the Psalms as well as pray with one's mouth and one's heart. When, however, one is in the marketplace, or in the company of other people, then it is not necessary to recite the Psalms with one's mouth but only with one's mind. It is also necessary to guard one's eyes and lower them on account of the distraction and snares of the enemies.

LETTER 711

Question: "When I pray or recite Psalms, I do not always understand the meaning of the words on account of the hardness of my heart. Of what benefit, then, are they to me?" Response.

Even if you do not understand the meaning of the words, yet the demons understand it;[190] they hear and tremble at the meaning. Therefore, do not cease reciting Psalms and praying; for gradually God will soften the hardness.[191]

LETTER 712

Question: "If I happen to be close to a church where they are chanting the *Trisagion*,[192] and am sitting among some fathers or with secular people, should I stand up and recite the prayers while they remain seated, or not?" Response by John.

If you are with some fathers, then do whatever they are doing. If the secular people are superior to you, and you know that they may be scandalized, then it is good to protect their con-

189. Ibid.   190. Cf. *Sayings,* Nau 626.
191. Cf. *Sayings,* Poemen 183.
192. A fifth-century Eastern hymn to the Holy Trinity, the title of which is derived from the Greek meaning "thrice holy," and which has been expanded from Isaiah 6.3 and Revelation 4.8. The full text is as follows: "Holy God, Holy Mighty, Holy Immortal, have mercy on us."

science and do as they are doing. For you can always recite the prayers in your heart while sitting with them. If this, too, bothers you, then the mere remembrance is sufficient. If, however, they are not your superiors, then stand up and say your prayers. In fact, this may encourage them also to stand up; for this is not inappropriate. Nevertheless, let them do as they please.

Question: "If I am alone, but happen to be holding something in my hands that prevents me from standing up, then what should I do?" Response.

If you cannot stand up, you should not be grieved at not being able to do so. It is all a matter of [good] thoughts and discernment.

Question: "If I happen to visit the fathers, and they insist on my staying with them, what should I do if I have something pressing to which I must attend?" Response.

If they are capable of discerning matters according to God, then tell them in all humility: "Forgive me, but I have a pressing matter to attend to." And do whatever you hear from them, without worrying, but believing that it will certainly be to your benefit.[193] If, however, they are not discerning, and your matter is indeed very important, then interrupt their insistence and make a prostration before them so that you may leave. If, even after you have made a prostration, they still continue to insist, then tell them: "Forgive me, but I simply cannot stay."

Question: "If I am sharing a meal with some fathers, and one of them blesses the food on the table, should I first say: 'Bless me!' before eating, and wait for him to bless me again, or should I be satisfied with the first blessing? For sometimes his intellect happens to be elsewhere and he delays in responding, and I

193. Cf. 1 Cor 12.7.

am always grieved. Or is it perhaps good enough for me simply to make the sign of the cross over the food [that I am about to eat]?" Response.

If he has blessed the food once, then this is more than enough. In regard to making the sign of the cross, this, too, is not necessary. For the blessing is a seal in itself. In fact, you would be providing occasion for the one who blessed the food, or indeed for any other person present, to think that you do not trust his blessing; and this may cause scandal.

LETTER 716

Question: "If the fathers whom I am visiting demand that I bless the food on the table, should I consent to this or not?" Response.

Do not consent, saying: "I am neither a clergyman, nor do I have the monastic habit, but I am merely a sinful layman; therefore, this is beyond me. Please forgive me, for the Lord's sake."

LETTER 717

Question: "If all of us around the table happen to be laypersons, then what should we do when we do not have anyone else to bless the food?" Response by John.

It is still a good thing for laypersons to bless God when they are about to eat. For the food is always blessed through remembrance of God.[194] Of course, this blessing is unlike that of clergy, but is still doxology and remembrance of God. It is fitting that everyone remembers God and glorifies him. So it is good for laypersons to do this as well, when they have no one else able to bless the food.

LETTER 718

Question: "If, nevertheless, these laypersons hesitate as to who should bless the food first, since each of them defers to the other, what should be done?" Response.

194. Cf. 1 Tm 4.5.

The one who invited them should also ask whom he wants to bless the table, and that person should bless. If no one accepts, then in order to avoid any argument, the host himself should consent to do this, simply saying: "Through the prayers of the holy fathers, may the Lord be with us. Amen."

LETTER 719

Question: "Since you said that it is good for laypersons also to remember God at their meals in order that, through remembrance of him, the food may be sanctified, is it a good thing perhaps to say the aforementioned verse or to recite the usual prayer of blessing before the bread has actually been placed on the table?" Response.

It is indeed possible to say these things, but because the prayer in fact says: "Bless that which is at hand," it is also good to wait for the bread to be placed at the table before saying the prayer.

LETTER 720

Question: "If the fathers ask me to offer my judgment on a particular matter, but I do not feel very confident in myself, then what should I do? Should I avoid or accept? And should I say whatever I think is correct, or should I ask others who know better, before actually offering my opinion?" Response.

For the sake of the command of the fathers, accept and tell those receiving the judgment: "I shall judge only according to what I think is right." Moreover, see that your thought is accurate, and do not incline your heart[195] toward someone for the sake of passion or favor; simply say what you think is right. God judges our intention; for he alone knows what is truly right. If, however, you are also able to ask someone who knows better than you, this, too, is not inappropriate.

LETTER 721

Question: "If the matter demands taking an oath, should I require this or not?" Response.

195. Cf. Ps 140.4.

Never require someone to take an oath; for God forbade us to take oaths.[196] Simply say: "This matter requires an oath; if you want to take an oath, it is up to you." Now, if you have been asked by someone with superior authority to pass judgment, and you are obliged to require an oath, then first examine the interests of both parties,[197] and then require the oath without any discrimination.[198]

LETTER 722

Question: "If I am sitting beside an elderly man or someone else important who is reading, and if that person happens to err on some accent or word, and if I know the proper way of reading, should I correct him, or not?" Response.

If you know that this person will gladly listen to you, then correct him; if not, then say nothing. Be careful also not to accept vainglory through your thought. Indeed, it is more beneficial for you to keep silent than to say anything with vainglory.

LETTER 723

Question: Another Christ-loving layperson asked the same Old Man, saying: "If a monk asks me to assist him in some task, but this does not appear to me to be according to God, what should I do?" Response by John.

If it is indeed not according to God, then do not assist him but refuse, simply speaking the truth to him, namely: "From what I can see, I am not being asked to do the right thing." On the other hand, if it is according to God and will not bring harm to your soul, then help him as much as you can; for you will have a reward. If, however, it is harmful to you, do not apply yourself to this task; for God does not demand of you anything harmful for your soul.

196. Cf. Mt 5.34.
197. Cf. Phil 1.10.
198. Cf. Jas 1.6.

LETTER 724

Question: "Whenever I see a monk insulting someone else or doing wrong, I am troubled. Is this good or bad perhaps?" Response.

Nothing that occurs with turmoil is good, but always comes from the power of the devil through our pretense to rights. Therefore, if you are troubled, do not say anything; otherwise, you will also further trouble that monk. For evil does not uproot evil.[199] If, however, you are not troubled, then gently say to him: "Do you not fear sin, unjustly insulting the abbot? Do you not know that the monastic habit which he wears is from God, and that God is angered in this way?" In speaking thus, you will be speaking according to God; and God has the strength to calm him as he wills.

LETTER 725

Another Christ-loving layperson asked the same Old Man, saying: "I have an outstanding legal matter with someone. What do you order me to do? Should I claim strict justice with that person, or should I ignore strict justice for the sake of a quicker reconciliation?" Response by John.

Strive, to the best of your ability, to be reconciled quickly; for it is a sign of the perfect not to be troubled by temptations that come upon them. The weak person, however, if he postpones reconciliation, later arrives at it and ends up regretting the matter; then, instead of blaming himself, he turns to blaspheme against God and loses his soul. Thus the following words are fulfilled in that person: "For what does it profit one to gain the whole world and forfeit one's life?"[200]

LETTER 726

Question: "Someone owes me money, but unless I ignore this a little, we shall never come to have peace. What do you order me to do?" Response.

---

199. Cf. Rom 12.21.   200. Mt 16.26; Mk 8.36.

Whoever seeks peace[201] is not deprived of God's peace. "Whoever is faithful in very little is faithful also in much";[202] and: "Mercy triumphs over judgment."[203] Therefore, unless a person despises the needs of the world, that person does not attain to the peace of Christ.[204] "The one who began a good work among you will bring it to completion by the day of our Lord Jesus Christ."[205] For this is our prayer: that God may grant us peace, so that we may complete the work of God, as borne witness by the most holy Guest-Master of the entire church.[206]

LETTER 727

Question: "Should I welcome any foreign monk that visits me, without asking who he is? If I hasten to welcome him, when should I ask him to leave? Moreover, should I offer him something on his departure? For some people demand this sort of thing, too." Response.

It is written in Proverbs: "Do not invite everyone into your home."[207] Therefore, when a foreigner approaches you, first pray to God and then ask him about his particulars, whence he comes and where he goes. And if it appears that you should welcome him, then accept him but ask him to leave after the meal, without giving him anything else. For if you want to deal with matters beyond your measure, you will not be able to endure them later.

LETTER 728

Question: "What happens if I am assured about him and decide to keep him for a few days? What if I want to go somewhere but am embarrassed to ask him to leave, in order that he may not be scandalized? Or, again, if I want to ask him to leave without any reason, then what should I do?" Response.

201. Cf. Ps 33.15.
202. Lk 16.10.
203. Jas 2.13.
204. Cf. Col 3.15.
205. Phil 1.6.
206. Reference to St. Marcian, formerly a Roman soldier, who was martyred during the reign of Emperor Diocletian (284-305).
207. Sir 11.29.

Tell him joyfully: "Abba, have you decided to go anywhere now?" If he replies: "Yes," then tell him: "I, too, have a need that I want to attend to and must leave." If he replies: "No," then say: "What do you think should happen? For I need to go somewhere, and there is none here who can attend to you." In this way, he, too, will leave in peace.

LETTER 729

Question: "Is it a good thing to tidy the contents of one's cell, in order not to lose anything? Or should one leave this matter to God?" Response.

It is a good thing to be tidy, not only in regard to those things that belong to hospitality but also those which are necessary for one's own service, after one has finished whatever one needs to do. One should never give any excuse to the devil for temptation.

If something happens to be lost out of forgetfulness or indifference, then do not be afflicted, but only blame yourself for this indolence, asking forgiveness from God. Do not let this divert you from the good task of hospitality, but persist as much as you can and not beyond your strength, doing so with discernment and careful henceforth not to give occasion to temptation.

LETTER 730

Question: "The Lord said: 'Blessed are those who mourn';[208] and the Apostle speaks of 'being cheerful and friendly.'[209] Should one act in such a way as to appear mournful or cheerful? And how can the two be practiced together, namely, both mournfulness and cheerfulness?" Response by John.

Mourning is godly sorrow,[210] which is produced by repentance. The characteristics of repentance are fasting, psalmody, prayer, and the study of God's words. Cheerfulness is godly joyfulness, which appears in the words and on the faces of those who possess it with modesty. Therefore, let the heart have mourning,

208. Mt 5.4.   209. Rom 12.8.
210. Cf. 2 Cor 7.10.

while the face and the words should have modest joyfulness. In this way, both can be held together.

Question: "If a friend asks me to be his guarantor, should I accept or not?" Response.

Providing someone with guarantee always brings temptation. Therefore, if you want to avoid temptation, do not become a guarantor. Rather, confidently tell him the truth, saying; "You know the love that I have for you; however, I have been ordered by the fathers not to become a guarantor for anyone. For they know my weakness; indeed, they know it even before I do. So I am afraid of transgressing their commandment and sinning before God." Say these things; and if he grieves, do not worry.

Now if you are able to avoid this through some reasonable excuse, this is a good thing. It may, of course, happen that he will refuse to accept you as a guarantor, whether out of honor or some other reason, without your having caused this situation for yourself; then, the sorrow does not occur at all. If, however, you are caught by surprise and accept to become a guarantor, then do not bring yourself to greater indifference; instead, tell your thought: "Whatever has happened has happened. May the Lord redeem me and protect me in the consequences." Do not cease praying to God about this; and he is able[211] to show his great mercy.[212]

Question: "I have a close friend, who is in danger of losing the salvation of his soul as well as losing his property. Do you order me to support him?" Response.

If he is a close friend according to God, and is in danger of losing the salvation of his soul as well as losing his property, then try to support him as much as you can, but not to the degree that your own soul is harmed. If, however, your soul will be harmed, then refrain from helping him, instead leaving the

---

211. Cf. Rom 4.21.   212. Cf. Ps 50.3.

matter to God and praying to him that he might assist your neighbor. And God is able to do that which is beneficial for him and which we lack the ability to do.

LETTER 733

Question: "I have a close friend, who has proved to be a heretic. Should I counsel him in the correct doctrine or not?" Response.

Counsel him to know the correct faith. Do not, however, argue with him; nor seek to learn what he believes, in order that he may not instill in you his poison. Instead, if he wants to benefit entirely and to hear the truth about faith in God, take him to the holy fathers, who are able to provide benefit for him in Christ. In this way, he shall have your godly assistance without this bringing you any harm.

If, however, after the first and second exhortation, he refuses to accept correction, then in accordance with the Apostle,[213] have nothing to do with him.[214] For God does not want one to do more than one can, as the fathers say: "For if you see—it is said—someone drowning in a river, do not give him your hand lest he drag you with him and you die with him. Rather, give him your staff, and if you are able to drag him out, all is well and good; otherwise, you should let go of your staff and save yourself."[215]

LETTER 734

One of the fathers had a friend in Christ, whom he thought to be a correct believer but who proved to be heretical in belief. So those who were his friends left him. Afterward, on hearing that he openly wanted to be separated from the church, they thought of going to make a prostration before him, lest he was doing so out of sorrow and lest the judgment be ascribed to them. They came to ask the Old Man about this. Response by John.

A passion is a passion; do not, therefore, pretend otherwise. For you are not showing repentance because you have sinned against him, but only lest he be separated from the church.

---

213. Cf. Ti 3.10.   214. Cf. ibid.
215. *Sayings*, Nau 472. See also *Letter* 653.

LETTER 735

The same people again asked: "If he has been separated from the church and we happen to meet him, should we greet him or not?" Response.

You should behave toward him in the same way as you behave towards all such persons, placing him in the same category as them.

LETTER 736

Question: "If one enters the church during the time of liturgy and leaves before the end, is this a sin?" Response.

What is perfect and pleasing to God is for a person entering the church to hear the Scriptures and remain in the liturgy until the very end. Indeed, unless there is good reason, one should not leave before the end; for this is scornful. Now if some need happens to present itself, then that person has permission [to leave]. Even then, however, such people should not justify themselves, but only ask forgiveness from God, saying: "Master, forgive me; for I was not able to stay."

LETTER 737

Question: "Should one speak in church or not?" Response.

One should not speak at all in the house of God during the divine liturgy, but rather spend time in prayer, listening attentively to the sacred Scriptures; for they speak of things necessary for the salvation of our souls.[216] Nevertheless, if it is necessary to speak, one should always be brief out of respect and fear for the hour at hand, also regarding the matter as being to our condemnation.

LETTER 738

Question: "If I do not want to speak, but some of the fathers who are present begin speaking to me, what should I do in order that

216. Cf. 1 Pt 1.9.

they may not be scandalized by my silence, thinking perhaps that it is a matter of scorn?" Response.

If they begin speaking to you, then again respond briefly, regarding this matter, too, as being to your condemnation.

LETTER 739

Question: "My thought tells me not to leave the house continually. Yet there are times when there happen to be many [liturgical] services through the week. Should I attend these or rather stay in stillness at home?" Response.

If you know that when you go out, the conversations are harmful to you, then it is beneficial for you not to leave all the time and not to use the services as an excuse. So attend them only from time to time. For stillness delivers us from many evils.

LETTER 740

Question: "If, nevertheless, I need to leave the house for some need of my own or of the fathers, is it still wrong for me not to attend the services?" Response by John.

If it is truly necessary, namely, [in obedience to] some command of the fathers, then strive to accomplish the matter with godly fear, and do not be concerned about not attending the services; rather, return to your house and, there, remember your own sins. If, however, you leave the house out of indolence or distraction, then it is more beneficial for you to attend the services and avoid distraction by paying attention.

LETTER 741

Question: "Is it a good thing for me to go down to church during the night, or should I remain in my house, keeping my vigil as much as I can?" Response.

It is a good thing to keep vigil in your house; for in church there are frequent conversations.

LETTER 742

Question: "If I want to enter a martyr's shrine or some church, but I enter only to venerate the altar or the holy relics, or else to take Communion, is this a serious sin?" Response.

Entering simply to venerate is not a serious sin; however, you should take Communion together with the rest of the people. Guard yourself, lest [you think you deserve] the honor of entering to take Communion in the sanctuary. Now, if you are called at the command of the priest, decline once or twice; but if he persists, then show obedience. For he knows what he is doing, and if it is a serious sin, then it is ascribed to him. Nevertheless, be careful that vainglory does not arise in you from this. Rather, enter even while condemning yourself as being unworthy; for that is how it is anyway.

LETTER 743

Someone once wanted to associate with another person in some matter, and so he asked the Old Man whether this was a good thing. The latter responded as follows.

This matter is of no benefit either for your soul or your body, but it will only bring you affliction and inconvenience. Indeed, since I am foolish and do not know Scripture, I shall tell you a popular proverb: "If you have an associate, then you also have a lord." Now, then, you may do as you wish; for we do not give any commandments in order not to afflict anyone. So test the matter yourself[217] in order to see whether you are able to bear the affliction gladly or not. May the Lord be with you. Amen.

LETTER 744

Question: "My thought suggests to me that my resources are tight and that I cannot feed myself or my household, and this causes me sorrow. What does this mean?" Response.

217. Cf. 1 Cor 11.28.

This sorrow is human;[218] for if we had any hope in God,[219] he would provide for us as he wills. "Therefore, cast all your anxiety on the Lord,"[220] and he is able to take care of you and your own without any sorrow and affliction. Say to him: "Your will be done,"[221] and he will not allow you to grieve or be afflicted. May the Lord have mercy upon you and protect you with his right hand. Amen.

LETTER 745

A Christ-loving layperson, who was a scholar and friend of the monastic community of the fathers, was asked by the abbot to do something necessary and urgent. For his custom was always eagerly to do whatever they asked him for God's sake. Through the action of the devil,[222] however, it happened that he was indifferent in this particular matter. Afflicted, therefore, the abbot asked the same Old Man what he should write to him. The latter said the following.

Write as follows to that person: "We know that we cause you affliction and that we disturb you about many things, which afflict you. And so you have become indifferent and cause us affliction by not doing anything. Therefore, tell us freely whether we are burdening you, and we shall no longer burden you. For if not through you, can God not fulfill our need by means of someone else? Either, then, strive [to accomplish it] or else tell us [that you cannot do so], and God will take care of the matter. Moreover, pray for us."

When he heard this, it was as if fire possessed his heart, and he became genuinely vigilant about this matter through the prayers of the saints. He, therefore, quickly proceeded to handle the matter. Afterward, he came and made a prostration, seeking forgiveness. This proves the power of the word when it comes from someone who has received the Holy Spirit, inasmuch as it brings about everything in little time. For it is said: "The sayings of the wise are like goads."[223] Behold, then, the matter was arranged, and his soul was corrected from the mother of evils, namely, indolence.

218. Cf. 2 Cor 7.10.
220. 1 Pt 5.7; Ps 54.23.
222. Cf. 2 Thes 2.9.

219. Cf. Acts 24.15.
221. Mt 6.10 and 26.42.
223. Eccl 12.11.

LETTER 746

A brother asked the same Old Man: "If a person despises something that belongs to God, so that it ends up being harmed or destroyed, what is the punishment that such a person receives?" Response by John.

Such a person resembles someone who has stolen or abused something against God's will, and therefore receives the same punishment.

LETTER 747

Question: "If a person strives not to despise this object but loses or damages it involuntarily, will he still be punished?" Response.

That person should blame himself, requesting forgiveness from God for his neglect.

LETTER 748

Question: "If a person argues with another about something relating to God and they find no solution, how long should one persist?" Response.

If the argument gives rise to harm for the soul, then one should not persist at all. If it is not harmful, then one should become neither faint-hearted nor indifferent; otherwise, one will be condemned for indolence. For it is written: "Accursed is the one who is neglectful in the work of the Lord."[224] One should, however, entreat God to contribute to a beneficial solution.

LETTER 749

Question: "When I prepare [to settle] an account with someone, my thought suggests to me that I should become attached to some small detail, through which I might trick him.[225] What should I do?" Response.

Strive on the contrary to give him a little more, which does not place any burden on you, such as an obol, in order that

---

224. Cf. Jer 31.10.   225. Cf. Lk 16.10.

you may avoid evil greed. For someone who strives to give a little more is also removed from dishonest gain. Thus, from small things, one can progress to greater things; just as from small passions, greater passions arise. May the Lord instruct you in his fear. Amen.

LETTER 750

Question: "If I settle my account and afterward discover that I have tricked him involuntarily, what should I do?" Response.

If the amount is large, then return it to him. If it is small, then examine your thought carefully, asking—from the contrary perspective—what you would do if you were tricked by him and were about to receive the amount from him; if you find that you would indeed want to receive it, then you, too, should return it. If you would not in fact receive it, then neither should you give it, unless the person was extremely poor; for in this case, a small amount would actually make a difference. Therefore, you should return to him what is fair.

LETTER 751

Question: "Is it really a sin to work on Sundays?" Response by John.

For those working according to God, it is not a sin; for the Apostle said: "I worked night and day, so that I might not burden any of you."[226] For those working in scorn, greed, and shameful gain, however, it is a sin. Nevertheless, it is a good thing to stop all work and attend church on the Resurrection day and on major feasts of the Lord, as well as on memorial days of the apostles. In fact, this is a tradition from the holy apostles.

LETTER 752

Question: "Is it actually a good thing to give a blessing [received by us] from the fathers to a foreigner or a pauper?" Response.

226. Cf. 1 Thes 2.9.

Do not hesitate to offer a blessing to a pauper; for this is a sign of mercy. Nor again to a foreigner; for the blessing is not harmed at all by the foreigner. Rather, it blesses the foreigner; so it may even happen that through this blessing, which has the power of God, the foreigner, too, may come to knowledge of truth.[227] Indeed, a certain Philemon, who played the flute, who was about to make an offering on behalf of the holy martyr Apollonius, dressed himself in the clothing of the martyr in order to deceive those present. Afterward, through the power of the martyr, he converted and became a martyr himself.[228]

LETTER 753

Question: "My animal is sick. Is it improper to ask someone to read a spell over it?" Response.

Magical spells are forbidden by God, and one should not resort to them at all. For they bring destruction to the soul through transgressing God's decree. Instead, bring your horse to other forms of healing and therapy, as proposed by veterinary doctors.[229] For this is certainly not sinful. Furthermore, sprinkle some holy water over it.

LETTER 754

Question: "If my servant is unwell and visits a sorcerer without my knowing, is this reckoned as a sin against me?" Response.

This is not reckoned against you, but only against him. If you learn about it, however, reprimand him vigorously, advising him not to do this again.

LETTER 755

Question: "Since visiting a sorcerer is outside God's will, if I happen to see someone going there, should I tell him not to do so?" Response.

227. Cf. 1 Tm 2.4.
228. Cf. *Historia monachorum* 19.
229. Lit., "by horse-healers" (ἱπποιάτρων).

If this person happens to be a close friend of yours in Christ, then you should tell him: "Brother, you are harming my soul and angering God, who does not allow us to do this." If he does not accept your word, then the responsibility is his.[230] If, however, it is any other person, then it is not your role to speak to him, unless he asks you about this; in that case, you should tell him the truth. For if you do not speak, you will be condemned. For indeed, when Saul was about to approach the witch, he asked his son Jonathan, who did not permit him to go and condemned him.[231] Therefore, if someone lies within your authority, it is your duty to advise and even reprimand him for this transgression.

LETTER 756

Question: "If one is buying or selling something, is it a sin to agree on a price, whether this should be higher or lower?" Response by John.

If there is no constraint but the matter is freely handled, then it is not a sin to bargain over an agreed price. If, however, one knows that one has gained more, then one should return the amount of one's own accord; for one would be doing something good as well as pleasing the other person.

Now, when one agrees on a price with someone under one's authority, then one should also examine whether the agreement was made by force; for this is a sin. Rather, one should reassure the other person, saying: "Brother, I shall not grieve if you do not do as I say; nor shall I offer you more. Therefore, do as you please and as you want."

LETTER 757

Question: "You teach us that it is a good thing to blame oneself in everything. If I am accused by someone for hurting him, but cannot find any fault within myself,[232] what should I do? For if I wish to condemn myself, then I shall be found to confirm his sorrow against me, as if I have truly hurt him. On the other hand,

230. Cf. 1 Tm 2.4.   231. Cf. 1 Sm 28.
232. Cf. 1 Cor 4.4.

if I wish to defend myself before him, saying that this is not how things are, I am found to justify myself; then, how can I bear the blame? Enlighten me, holy father, as to what I should do." Response.

First, blame yourself within your heart, and perform a prostration before him, saying: "Forgive me, for the Lord's sake." Thus, in humility, and not as one wanting to justify oneself, but rather as one wanting to heal him and remove his suspicion, tell him: "Father, I am not conscious of wanting to hurt or sin against you in any way. Therefore, do not think about me in this way." If he is still not reassured, then say: "I have sinned; forgive me."

LETTER 758

Question: "If I do something against him and he grieves when he hears about it, is it perhaps a good thing to hide the truth in order to end his grief? Or is it better to admit my fault and ask for forgiveness?" Response.

If he has plainly learned about it, and you know that the matter will be examined and exposed, then tell him the truth and ask for his forgiveness. For lying will only further provoke him. If, however, he has not learned about it and will not examine the matter further, then it is not improper to keep silent in order not to give occasion to grief. For when the prophet Samuel was sent to anoint David as king, he was also going to offer sacrifice to God. Yet, because he was afraid lest Saul learn about this, God said to him: "Take a heifer with you; and if the king asks you: 'Why did you come here?' then tell him: 'I have come to sacrifice to the Lord.'"[233] In this way, by concealing one thing, which brought the wrath of the king, he only revealed something else. You too, then, should be silent about that which causes grief, and so the problem will pass.

LETTER 759

Question: "If it is clear that I did not hurt a person, but instead was hurt by that person, how can I blame myself? What happens,

233. 1 Sm 16.2.

for example, if I am traveling somewhere and come across someone along the way, whom I do not know at all and who strikes me
without reason, without my saying anything to him? How can I
blame myself in this case?" Response.

You can say: "It is my fault for coming this way; had I not
come this way, I would not have met this man and would not
have been struck by him." Do you now see how you can ascribe
fault to yourself?

LETTER 760

Question: "If I neither recognize the sin as being apparent nor
is it clear to me immediately how I should in fact blame myself,
then what should I do?" Response.

Well, then, say: "It is clear that I am at fault; however, the sin
is now concealed from me." That is how you can blame yourself
[on that occasion].

LETTER 761

Another Christ-loving layperson would regularly visit the monastic community of the fathers. Once, however, he delayed in going there; so the abbot asked him joyfully: "Do you know the way
here?" He replied: "Abba, had you been praying for me, I would
not have delayed. I entreat you, however, to speak to the Old
Man about this." When the Old Man heard this, he announced
the following.

You have caught us asleep and unable to do anything. Yet
you, too, have not been found to be more earnest than when
you came to awaken us; moreover, you know the example of
the Savior's disciples. For when they were in a storm, they approached him, awakening him and saying: "Master, save us; for
we are perishing."[234] He awoke and saved them.

LETTER 762

When he heard this, again he declared the same. The Old Man
responded as follows.

234. Lk 8.24; Mt 8.25.

Brother, forgive me; for argumentation has no humility.

When he heard this, he was moved to compunction by these words; and so he left edified.

LETTER 763

A Christ-loving layperson asked the same Old Man: "God has created the human person free, but he also says: 'Apart from me, you can do nothing.'[235] How, then, is this freedom maintained while also reconciled with not being able to do anything without God?" Response by John.

God created the human person free in order that we may be able to incline toward good; yet, even while inclining out of free choice, we are incapable of accomplishing this without God's assistance. For it is written: "It depends on neither human will nor exertion, but on God who gives assistance."[236] Therefore, if we incline the heart toward good and invoke God for our assistance, God will pay attention to our good intention and bestow strength upon our work. In this way, both are developed, namely, human freedom and divine power. This is how good comes from God, but it is always accomplished through his saints. Thus God is glorified in all and in turn glorifies them.[237]

LETTER 764

Question: "I have certain relatives in the world, some of whom are influential and reside nearby, while others are insignificant and live farther. Now, it happens that they come to visit us. Therefore, if someone asks me who they are, should I tell the truth or keep silent? For telling the truth grieves the other relatives, who are ashamed of the fact that they are an embarrassment." Response.

Unless necessary, you should not speak openly about this, indeed especially since this creates sorrow in the other relatives. Therefore, if you are specifically asked about who they are, you should respond prudently so as not to reveal the truth. If, however, no one is either hurt or afflicted by this, then, when asked,

235. Jn 15.5.
236. Cf. Rom 9.16.
237. Cf. 1 Sm 2.30.

you should not conceal the truth; otherwise, this would be vain-glory. For all of us are creatures of God, and no one is more important than another, except the one who fulfills God's will. Yet vainglory creates distinctions among people. Nonetheless, one should respect the conscience of the other relatives on account of the weakness of their thought, particularly when there is no need to publicize the truth.

LETTER 765

Question: "I have a servant who is infected with leprosy. Should I keep him or not?" Response.

It is not necessary for you to keep him in your house; for not everyone will tolerate living with him. If they could bear this, then retaining him would be the pious thing to do. Yet you should not afflict others on his account. Instead, send him to a hospice for poor lepers, and provide for his meals and for as many garments as he requires, as well as for his bed, so that he is in no way burdened.

LETTER 766

Question: "If he wants to receive the daily subsistence that you ordered as well as his portion from the external offerings at the hospice, provided by others as well as by myself, should I still allow him to receive them or not?" Response.

You should not allow this; for this would be your responsibility. Nor again, however, should you prevent him; for he will grumble and blaspheme. Let him do whatever he wants. Now, if it is your turn to provide the offering, then give it to him, if he intends to take it.

LETTER 767

Question: "My father according to the flesh always initiates conversations with me about fleshly matters that are of no benefit to the soul; and, although listening to him afflicts me, yet I refrain from putting an end to his conversation. What, then, should I do?" Response.

If you are able to transfer your intellect from the words being spoken by him either to prayer or to remembrance of the words of God and the teachings of the fathers, then this is a good thing; in this way, you may let him say whatever he wants. If, however, you are unable to do so, then strive to put an end to his conversation, gently turning it to another, more beneficial topic, lest by delaying therein, some trap of the enemy may be found. For the devil is able to construct a trap unexpectedly through a single word, if he simply finds you listening with pleasure.

LETTER 768

Question: "When we are gathering grapes, some people come and strip the vine of its leaves;[238] is it improper to prevent them from climbing the vines? If I suspect that they have stolen some grapes, should I search them out? And if I find any, should I take them back, so that others will not do likewise? My thought hesitates in all these matters." Response by John.

It is not improper to forbid them from climbing the vines. If you suspect that someone may have taken some grapes, but are not quite certain about this, do not search that person by chance, lest you be in error and be ashamed. If, on the other hand, you know that someone has taken some grapes and you have allowed him to do this, it is certainly a good thing; otherwise, let that person go without insulting him.

LETTER 769

Question: "When I commit an injustice and then correct the same injustice, my thought becomes arrogant, believing that I have done something good. What, then, should I tell it?" Response.

Tell your thought: "One who commits an injustice is punished; one who corrects the same injustice avoids punishment and receives praise." For it is one thing to do good, and quite

238. Cf. Dt 24.21.

another thing to do injustice. The first serves God and brings about eternal rest, while the second angers God and brings about eternal damnation.[239] This is precisely what David says: "Depart from evil and do good."[240] For without God, we cannot do anything good. He told us: "Apart from me, you can do nothing."[241] The Apostle also says: "What do you have that you did not receive? And if you received it, why do you boast as if it were not a gift?"[242] Therefore, we cannot be arrogant when we do good; how much less so when we simply avoid evil! For it is great foolishness to imagine that there is praise in not sinning. So pay attention to yourself, brother, lest you be deceived by the wicked demons, whom may the Lord abolish[243] through the prayers of his saints. Amen.

LETTER 770

Question: "I am ill, and the doctor has ordered me to bathe. Is this, however, a sin? Moreover, should I even show myself to a doctor?" Response.

Bathing is not entirely forbidden for those in the world, whenever necessity dictates this. Therefore, if someone is ill and needs to bathe, this is certainly not a sin; on the other hand, if one is healthy, then it brings healing and bodily comfort, but also self-indulgence. So we should simply guard what is necessary, namely, the heart and the tongue, in order not to judge or despise anyone, since bathing is not sinful for those in the world.

As for showing yourself to the doctor, it belongs to the more perfect to leave everything to God, even if this is a difficult thing to do; it is the weaker person who shows himself to the doctor. Indeed, not only is this not sinful, but it is even humble; for being weaker, one needed to visit the doctor. One should, however, remember that, without God, not even a doctor can do anything. Rather, it is God who bestows health to the ill, whenever he so desires.[244]

---

239. Cf. Mt 25.46.
240. Ps 33.15.
241. Jn 15.5.
242. 1 Cor 4.7.
243. Cf. 2 Thes 2.8.
244. Cf. Sir 38.9.

LETTER 771

Question: "Some people, influenced by the devil, are well-disposed toward me because I am pious; for I do not hasten to visit the market place and do not become involved in matters. Then, when the time comes and my bodily needs require me to bathe, I am always embarrassed that I might scandalize those who think highly of me, expecting that I would refuse a bath because of my piety. Why is this happening, father?" Response.

This is vainglory. For you are a secular man; and, as we have said, bathing is not forbidden for a layperson, at least whenever necessary. Now, if Satan suggests to some people that you are a prophet in order to mislead your thought toward arrogance, and in spite of this you still want to confirm this lie about you, then it is this that you should be ashamed of.

Those actions which involve transgressing God's commandment, such as fornication, avarice, and the like, are precisely what bring true scandal. In regard to these, one should give account not only for oneself but also for the harm brought upon one's neighbor. Bathing self-indulgently and unnecessarily is sinful and truly scandalous. On the other hand, bathing only when necessary is not a scandal; so the one who is scandalized bears the judgment.[245] If you are embarrassed about this, then this is vainglory from the devil.

LETTER 772

Question: "Father, you have said that the one who truly scandalizes is the one who transgresses God's commandment and therefore also bears the judgment for harming one's neighbor. Then why did the Apostle say to the person eating food offered to idols: 'You are doing well by eating; for no idol in the world really exists. My brother, however, is not edified. So do not let what you eat cause the destruction of one for whom Christ died'?[246] Behold, then, he renders one responsible for harming a brother in something that is not even forbidden by the commandment of God, while at the same time excusing the weakness of the other." Response.

245. Cf. Gal 5.10.   246. Cf. 1 Cor 8.4–11; Rom 14.15.

Brother, first of all, the Apostle has forbidden this, and so no one should question it any further,[247] but instead should submit to his decree as if to God's law. Nevertheless, I shall tell you what I think. In this case, there is a distinction between the place and the act. For the idol was reserved for the worship of demons, while the food was offered as sacrifice to demons. Now, to the weak person, it truly appeared to be food offered to idols; therefore, upon seeing the faithful eating, he, too, was encouraged to eat foods offered to idols, but felt that he was polluting his conscience. Yet the faithful one did not regard this food as an offering to idols, but rather as holy food created by God; therefore, he enjoyed eating it, and felt that his conscience was in fact clean.[248] Nevertheless, since the other brother was weaker in faith, regarding the food to be an offering to idols, this is why the Apostle rebukes the faithful eating food in a manner that is not beneficial, since it harms one's neighbor, which is something foreign to love according to Christ. For eating did not imply fulfillment of God's commandment, just as not eating did not imply its transgression. Yet the Apostle required him to prefer the edification of his brother over the food. Now, in the case of the bath, it is exactly the same thing. Bathing is neither improper nor forbidden; anyone scandalized by this bears the judgment of scandal alone.[249] Therefore, for a layperson to be ashamed of bathing for fear of being blamed by others, especially when necessity demands it, is only vainglory and brings harm to that person. So, whenever necessity demands, bathe with godly fear and not with self-indulgence; for this is foreign to godly fear and harmful to the soul.

LETTER 773

Question: "Since every food contains natural sweetness, is this harmful to the person who consumes it?" Response by John.

God our Master created such sweetness in each food, and there is no harm in eating of this with thanksgiving.[250] But one

247. Cf. 1 Cor 11.16; 2 Thes 3.11.
248. 1 Tm 3.9.   249. Cf. Gal 5.10.
250. Cf. 1 Tm 4.4.

should always guard against attachment; for this is what is harmful to the soul.

LETTER 774

Question: "Is it not improper to do something with cleanliness, whether housework or something else?" Response.

For something to be clean and orderly is not improper inasmuch as it is helpful; however, it should be done without attachment. Even the Lord rejoices in all forms of cleanliness. When you see, however, that you are becoming attached to something, remember how in the end it will become corrupted, and then you will find rest. Indeed, nothing stays in the same shape; rather, everything is corruptible and ephemeral.

LETTER 775

Another Christ-loving layperson asked the same Old Man, saying: "If a Jew or a pagan happens to invite me to a meal during the season of his feast, or perhaps even sends me gifts during that season, should I accept or not?" The Old Man spoke as follows.

Do not accept; for this is against the canons of the holy church; so you should not receive them.[251]

LETTER 776

Question: "What if the person happens to be important or else a friend? For he will be saddened if I do not accept. What should I tell him?" Response.

Tell him the following: "Your love knows that those who fear God are obliged to keep all his commandments. You may be assured of this from your own practices. For you, too, would never consent to transgress a commandment of your tradition on account of your love for me. Yet I would never consider that, in doing so, you were transgressing your love toward me. We, then, also have a tradition that comes from God through our holy fa-

251. Reference to Apostolic Canon 70, as well as to Canons 37 and 38 of the Council of Laodicaea. See D. Cummings, trans., *The Rudder* (Chicago: Orthodox Christian Educational Society, 1957).

thers and teachers, according to which we should never participate at all in any pagan feast. In saying this, my love for you is
not diminished."

LETTER 777

Question: "There are some pagans in the marketplace who sell
various merchandise during their feasts. Is it improper for me to
purchase what I need from them?" Response.

This is not improper; for according to the Apostle,[252] everything sold in the meat market may be purchased without question in order to fulfill one's need.

LETTER 778A

Another Christ-loving layperson, who was a teacher of secular
wisdom, had a son whose life was in danger. He asked the same
Old Man, Abba John, whether he would live or die. The Old
Man replied that he would live. And, indeed, he lived, just as the
Old Man said. After some time, another of his sons was in similar
danger. He visited the Old Man again about this, and the latter
again responded, [this time] in the following way.

We shall pray; however, it is up to God to have mercy on
him.[253] Therefore, cut off your own will and give thanks to him
in all circumstances.[254]

LETTER 778B

When he heard this, since he did not understand the meaning
of the words or the response, he thought that his son would actually live. So he returned to his son, who looked up and saw all
the holy elders standing around and said to his father: "Do you
see the saints who are so close to us?" When his father replied:
"I do not see anyone," he told him: "Behold, they are standing
here and saying to me: 'Why does your father disturb us by coming and going, asking us whether you shall live in the flesh?[255]
Behold, then, we have prayed to God for you, and he said that

252. Cf. 1 Cor 10.25.
254. Cf. 1 Thes 5.18.
253. Cf. 1 Sm 15.20.
255. Cf. Gal 2.20.

the time has come for you to leave the body.'" Having said this to
his father, he added: "Look, father, they have removed me from
the grasp of a certain Saracen who was dragging me, and they
have led me to a place that is brightly illuminated and ineffable.
There, I saw guileless children, who said to me: 'For the sake of
your father's request, we have entreated God that you be sent to
this place.' Indeed, they are already celebrating liturgy and taking Communion."

    After saying these words, he began saying the great prayer—
the "Our Father, who art in heaven"[256] and "Glory to the Father,
the Son, and the Holy Spirit"—and in this way surrendered his
spirit.[257] His father was deeply comforted, being assured of the
salvation of his soul. So he came and reported this to the Old
Man, entreating him to explain why he had not spoken clearly
to him about his son's death, just as he had done about his other
son's life. The Old Man responded in the following way.

I told you to cut off your own will for God in order, through
this, to show you his death in the flesh. As for not speaking to
you clearly, you should understand this from your own experience. Behold, you are a teacher of worldly wisdom and you have
students. Now, if you order one of them to write a letter, would
your student write what you want, or would you let him write
whatever he wants? Surely, he would write whatever you dictate
and not whatever he happens to want. The same applies to the
saints. They do not speak of their own accord, but it is God who
speaks through them[258] as he desires, sometimes in the form of
a shadow and at other times with clarity. In fact, in order that
you may be assured that this is so, the Lord himself said to his
disciples: "It is not you who speak, but the Spirit of your Father
is speaking through you."[259] Therefore, God speaks as he wills,
and not as they will.

LETTER 778C

When he heard this and was reassured, he said: "Why, then, is it
that we find the ancient holy fathers receiving all their requests
from God?" The Old Man responded as follows.

256. Cf. Mt 6.9.   257. Cf. Jn 19.30.
258. Cf. Ps 59.8.   259. Mt 10.20.

They did not receive all their requests from God; but whatever they received was recorded in writing. Let the word of the
Gospel reassure you: "Someone came to him, saying: 'My son
suffers terribly from the demons; and I have brought him many
times to your disciples, but they could not cure him.'"[260] If, then,
the apostles did not receive what they had requested at that
time, how can we say that the saints receive all their requests?
For indeed, the apostles themselves asked him in surprise: "Master, why is it that we could not heal him?" And he told them:
"This kind can come out only through prayer and fasting."[261]

LETTER 778D

Once again, he asked: "Then, why do the saints not receive all
their requests?" The Old Man said the following.

God does everything for our benefit; for he knows more than
anyone else what is beneficial and profitable for us. Since we do
not know what is beneficial for us, this is why he commanded
us not to heap up empty phrases when we pray, asking for one
thing instead of another: "For your heavenly Father knows what
you need before you ask him."[262] Therefore, just as God cares
about you, he also cares about his saints. He cares for you in order that you may not become arrogant by manifestly obtaining
what you requested; he cares for the saints in order that they,
too, may not become arrogant as a result of revelations manifested by them. For they are not greater than Paul the Apostle,
who said: "Considering the exceptional character of the revelations, and in order to keep me from being too elated, a thorn
was given me in the flesh, a messenger of Satan to torment
me."[263] Go home, then, and pay attention to yourself; indeed,
we shall pray that God may grant you a firm heart and unswerving faith. So do not be scandalized by the saints. For the Holy
Spirit of God that speaks in them is never deceived. In them is
fulfilled the following word: "May your good Spirit lead me on
a level path."[264]

---

260. Cf. Mt 17.15–16.   261. Cf. Mk 9.28–29; Mt 17.19–21.
262. Mt 6.8.   263. 2 Cor 12.7.
264. Ps 142.10.

On hearing these things, he was reassured in the Lord and returned rejoicing and blessing God, who glorifies his saints.
Amen.

LETTER 779

Another Christ-loving layperson asked the same Old Man: "A
dog has bitten my slave. Tell me whether my slave will die or not.
For some people say that anyone bitten by a dog will die within
forty days." Response by John.

There is nothing wrong with him. Do not be afraid. Rather,
try to think of what is written: "Not a sparrow falls into a trap
apart from your Father who is in heaven."[265]

LETTER 780

When he heard this, he thought that his slave would not die.
Nevertheless, two days later, he did in fact die. Since, however,
this master had great faith in the Old Man, knowing that he does
not lie, he was surprised and was not certain whether his slave
had actually died. So he came and asked him about this, saying: "We are not sure as to whether or not the slave has died, or
whether he is alive. What do you say, father?" The Old Man responded as follows.

He has died.

LETTER 781

Therefore, the master said to the Old Man: "Then, why did you
say that there was nothing wrong with him?" The Old Man responded as follows.

Since you suspected that he would certainly die from the
dog's bite, I indicated to you that this was not the case and told
you that there was nothing wrong with him. For there is nothing wrong with death that comes from God. In order, however,
to reveal to you that he would die the death that comes from
God, I also added: "Not a sparrow falls into a trap apart from

265. Cf. Mt 10.29.

your Father who is in heaven."[266] For it is not possible for anyone to die without God's decree, even if one is bitten by tens of
thousands of serpents.

ter 782

Question: "Then, why was your answer so unclear?" Response by
John.

Do not be surprised that I did not speak clearly to you about
this. For one should not always speak clearly about such things,
since they are harmful and of no benefit to the person speaking. Do you not know that even the Savior, wanting to show his
human side, used simple words, saying: "Where have you laid
Lazarus?"[267] and: "How many loaves do you have?"[268] or: "Who
touched me?"[269] In this way, he was teaching the saints that they
should not always use lofty words. This is why they respond in
a manner that is beneficial to them. Now if perhaps some people are scandalized, let them hear Paul saying: "For we are the
aroma of Christ among those who are being saved and among
those who are perishing; to the one a fragrance from life to life,
to the other a fragrance from death to death."[270] Now for those
who are faithful, these things are for their understanding and
benefit; however, for those who are not faithful, they are for our
benefit through their scorn.

LETTER 783

Often it happened that this Old Man, John, would be asked a
question but out of humility would convey it to the Great Old
Man, Abba Barsanuphius, especially when it concerned some
great and wonderful matter. And any question that was conveyed
was never left without response. Therefore, a Christ-loving layman once said to the Old Man, John: "Why are you mocking us,
Father John, by sending us to the holy and Great Old Man, Father Barsanuphius, when you have the same power of the Spirit?" He responded as follows.

266. Cf. ibid. 267. Jn 11.34.
268. Mk 6.38. 269. Mk 5.30.
270. 2 Cor 2.15–16.

I am nothing; and even if I were [something], I would not be mocking you. For if I had sent you to him and you had not obtained a response, then it would have been mockery. Therefore, it is to your benefit that there are two people praying for you; for two people are more than one. It appears that even the Lord does the same; for he says: "My Father is greater than I,"[271] whereas he, too, was able to perform the works of his Father. This is why he says: "Whatever the Son sees the Father doing, he, too, does likewise."[272] Indeed, not once but many times would he send his disciples to the Father, saying: "If you ask anything of my Father in my name, he will give it to you";[273] and again: "I will ask the Father";[274] and again: "I do nothing on my own; but the Father who dwells in me does his works."[275]

LETTER 784

There was a miracle that occurred through both of them, and it should become known. An extremely Christ-loving and hospitable layman, who performed the work of Abraham,[276] was in danger of dying from some illness, being condemned by the doctors. Therefore, some of his beloved in the Lord sent a letter asking the Old Man John about him, whether this was his end and whether he should prepare his will.

He responded that this was indeed his end and that he should prepare his will. Having announced this, he told the attending brother the following.

Go up and see the holy [Great] Old Man, asking him to pray for him so that God may grant him additional life for the sake of his good work of hospitality. For if the Old Man asks, he will surely obtain grace.

So the attending servant went up to ask this and persuaded the Old Man to pray; but the latter did not say anything in response. He was again sent there a second and a third time by the [Other] Old Man, John, to the holy and Great Old Man. While the Great Man prayed, however, still he did not say anything. When

271. Jn 14.28.
273. Jn 16.23.
275. Cf. Jn 14.10.

272. Cf. Jn 5.19.
274. Jn 14.16.
276. I.e., hospitality; cf. Gn 18.1–8.

Abba John learned this, he told his disciple: "That man will not yet die from this illness; for the Old Man has obtained grace from God." So the abbot informed those who asked about him of everything.

As for the sick man, he immediately regained consciousness, emerging from this danger and obtaining complete recovery through the prayers of the Great Old Man and of his imitator, the similarly disposed John.[277] After he learned about the miracle of his healing, he made greater and greater progress in the practice of hospitality for the glory of God. Amen.

LETTER 785

Certain Christ-loving laypersons, who were expecting to be done injustice by some important people, asked the same Old Man, John, whether they should approach other more influential people in order to secure their protection financially. He responded as follows.

Do not purchase the protection of any mortal and corruptible person; for today that person is here, but tomorrow he is not. If you give away your property and your protector dies, then you will have lost your property as well as your protection. Do you want to purchase a protection that is incorruptible? Then purchase the protection of the immortal and incorruptible king and God,[278] namely, by [giving money to] the poor; indeed, he receives unto himself whatever is done to the poor: "For I was hungry and you gave me food to eat."[279]

Indeed, you know that, if you purchase human protection, God will not protect you. Now you say: "Then, why is it that we find some of the fathers also having protectors according to the flesh?" Yet these did not secure their protection through a financial deal. Instead, they entreated them for the sake of God's love, and their protectors joyfully accepted them, with faith.

Examine the heart of the matter and you will find that nothing was exchanged as a purchase of such protection; nor did these people ask anything more from the fathers than their prayers to God, which are more valuable than any gold and sil-

277. Cf. 1 Cor 4.16.   278. Cf. 1 Tm 1.17.
279. Mt 25.35.

ver.[280] And what was the result? If the wrath of the Lord comes, then they implore him for their sake. Therefore, observe and you shall see that, from beginning to end, the matter occurred according to God.

LETTER 786

When confusion arose in the holy church of God, certain people, who were not in communion, were about to be ordained at the decree of the emperor. Since a persecution was expected, certain Christ-loving laypersons asked the same Old Man whether they should depart and hide their belongings. He responded as follows.

Is there anyone more powerful than God? If we are in God's hands and chant with David: "Into your hands I commend my spirit,"[281] then what have we to fear? Did not God say that he would destroy the city of Nineveh? Did he actually destroy it? No; instead, for the sake of their repentance, he forgave it.[282] Therefore, let us also repent to God, and he will calm everything. Moreover, is there an earthly king more powerful than Nebuchadnezzar? Yet Daniel and the three children implored the heavenly King and God, and he subjected the king to them.[283] Your question, however, reflects the double temptation of cowardice and avarice. As for us, we are in the hands of God; and he has the authority to do with us as he wills. Therefore, neither flee nor hide any of your belongings.

LETTER 787

The same people again asked the same Old Man: "Then, why is it written: 'When they persecute you in one town, flee to the next'?"[284] He responded as follows.

But we have not yet been persecuted.

280. Cf. Ps 118.72.
281. Ps 30.6.
282. Cf. Jon 1–3.
283. Cf. Dn 1–4.
284. Mt 10.23.

LETTERS TO VARIOUS
BISHOPS AND TO THE INHABITANTS
OF GAZA (788–844)

LETTER 788

A certain priest, who had been elected to the episcopate by the faithful of that city, sent a letter asking the same Old Man whether God wants him to become a bishop. Response by John.

ROTHER, YOU ARE asking me something that is beyond me; for I am the least significant person[1] and have not reached such a measure. Nevertheless, you have abandoned the Apostle and ask me, who have not even begun[2] to be a monk. The Apostle says: "Whoever aspires to the office of bishop desires a noble task. Now a bishop must be above reproach,"[3] and so forth.

Yet Scripture says, as if the person of God were speaking to the sons of Israel in saying: "If you ask a false prophet in my name and are worthy of hearing the truth, then I shall place a word of truth in the mouth of the false prophet in order that he may accordingly speak to you."[4] In this sense, I, too, say to you: "If you have well adorned your house and prepared your heart in order to receive such a fragrant myrrh," then according to the teaching of the Apostle: "It will be prepared for you by God";[5] for he is not lying,[6] who says: "May the Lord grant you according to your heart."[7]

---

1. Cf. 1 Cor 15.9.
2. A copticism also found in *Letters* 55, 266, 276, 493, 500, 560, and 562.
3. 1 Tm 3.1. 4. Cf. Mt 10.41.
5. Cf. 1 Cor 2.9. 6. Cf. Ti 1.2.
7. Ps 19.5.

LETTER 789

A certain bishop in a village[8] asked the same Old Man whether he should abandon his episcopal duties and withdraw to a monastery. Response.

I cannot advise you to abandon the one who entrusted you[9] with the care of the holy churches of God, but only to attend to your own soul according to godly fear. Do not accept gifts from anyone;[10] do not waver in your judgment;[11] do not be ashamed in the presence of any ruler[12] and do not find the guilty innocent nor condemn the innocent. Keep avarice far from you; for it is the root of all evils.[13] Indeed, this is said to be—and is—a second kind of idolatry.[14] Do not be arrogant, so that you may learn from the Apostle, who says: "Do not be haughty, but associate with the lowly."[15]

Do not try to please people; for you know what happens to those who do this. They are estranged from the service of Christ; for the Apostle says: "If I were still pleasing people, I would not be a slave of Christ."[16] Submit to the Lord, who says: "Learn from me; for I am gentle and humble in heart, and you will find rest for your souls."[17] Quench your anger; for this leads to one's fall. Do everything according to God, and you shall find assistance in him. Always fear death; for it must come to us all. "Remember the hour of your departure, and then you will not sin unto God."[18] And if you reach the point of stillness, then you shall find rest with grace, wherever you may happen to withdraw.

LETTER 790

A certain bishop, who used to be a monk, had great confidence in the elders and sent a letter asking the Great Old Man whether

8. The term χωρεπίσκοπος refers to a particular category of assistant bishops, who were responsible for smaller rural regions and also lay under the jurisdictional authority of a local metropolitan bishop.

9. Cf. 2 Cor 11.28.   10. Cf. Prv 15.27; Sir 20.29.
11. Cf. Ex 23.2.   12. Cf. Sir 7.6.
13. Cf. 1 Tm 6.10.   14. Cf. Eph 5.5.
15. Rom 12.16.   16. Gal 1.10.
17. Mt 11.29.   18. Sir 7.36.

he should abandon the world and return to the monastic life. At the same time, he asked for his prayer, blessing, and assistance. Response by Barsanuphius.

This is an opportunity for me to repeat the word of the Apostle, who says: "I have been a fool; you forced me to it."[19] Nonetheless, since we are using words spoken according to God and not according to mortals, allow me to repeat also the words of his servant Moses: "Either lead my spiritual son, who has been inscribed with me, into eternal life with me, or else wipe me also from your book."[20] May I not be permitted to see the face of Jacob the father of Joseph unless I have Benjamin with me.[21] I believe in his holy name, that he shall not refuse my request. For the joy of the Holy Trinity and of the holy angels is the salvation of those being saved. Therefore, I shall not cease praying to God until he grants me the joy of your salvation.

Nevertheless, be careful that these things do not slacken your thought to indolence. In addition to all these things, remember that this world passes; its glory is not lasting[22] and its pleasure is corruptible. Choose for yourself rather: "To share ill treatment with the people of God than to enjoy the fleeting pleasure of sin."[23] Also remember that we shall leave this world, even if involuntarily, and that our life will not be long. For what is the life of any person? You should especially remember that we cannot have any assurance of life in this world, even as to whether we shall live from morning to night. Let us voluntarily renounce things, so that we may receive our reward. Let us choose to be free from earthly cares, since we desire to appear before the countenance of God,[24] in order that we may have the boldness to say: "Bring my soul out of prison, so that I may give thanks to your name."[25] Hurry; run "while it is yet day,"[26] before night overtakes us—that time when the indolent mourn and the lazy repent in vain. Learn that no time remains; and if the hour comes, the servant will not be ashamed. For who has

19. 2 Cor 12.11.
21. Cf. Gn 44.34.
23. Heb 11.25.
25. Ps 141.8.
20. Cf. Ex 32.32.
22. Cf. 1 Cor 7.31.
24. Cf. Ps 41.3.
26. Jn 9.4.

shamed him and been heard? He is a true servant of the true Master, genuinely fulfilling his commandments.

Let us fear that most dreadful day and hour, when we shall not be protected by our brother or relative, by any power or authority, or by wealth and glory. It will simply be: "Behold, here is a man and his work."[27] Let us sell the corruptible things, which drag us down to the abyss of destruction, and let us purchase a wedding garment[28] for ourselves in order to come to perfection.[29] For if we come to perfection, then we shall seize the perfection of perfect love according to God, which casts out fear,[30] and joyfully sing with the Apostle Paul: "Love never fails."[31] My genuine child,[32] may I see you in the kingdom of my God in Christ Jesus our Lord. I greet you in the Lord, in the name of God; I greet you in Christ Jesus; I greet you in the Holy Spirit, most honorable one.

LETTER 791

Another bishop sent a letter asking the same Great Old Man to offer him an exhortation. He responded as follows.

What can I say to your loving grace? Should I say that it is not permitted for a servant to offer exhortation to his master? Nevertheless, I have not yet been delivered of my vainglory in order to regard myself as being the servant of all.[33] Therefore, I am embarrassed, since I cannot defend myself. My only refuge is to tell you: "Forgive me, for the Lord's sake, and pray for me so that I may not be condemned when he comes again, that I may know he is God, and that I may be concerned with his divine commandments and receive mercy."

LETTER 792

There was once a struggle over the faith,[34] and a certain bishop was sent there by the emperor to inquire of the same Great Old

27. Cf. Rv 14.13.
28. Cf. Mt 22.11–12.
29. Cf. Heb 6.1.
30. Cf. 1 Jn 4.18.
31. 1 Cor 13.8.
32. Cf. 1 Tm 1.2.
33. Cf. 1 Cor 9.19.
34. On christology, see *Letters* 536–539, 547, 600–607, 694–702, 734–736, and 775.

Man in the form of a letter, saying: "What should be done?" For he expected to find opposition from certain people of importance in the world but not of sound faith. Response.

From what we have learned through your messenger,[35] we find that, in addition to his resurrection according to God, Daniel also enjoyed the friendship of the king.[36] Nevertheless, in placing his hope in God, who saves his servants[37] and "is near to all who invoke him in truth,"[38] he feared neither the threat nor the stratagem of the royal decree, which did not disturb him at all. Rather, as he was supported by the faith of Christ, God glorified him abundantly through this faith. Indeed, it is true that: "The heart of the king is in the hands of God; he directs it wherever we desire, we who are walking uprightly."[39] Be strong in the Lord. Be strong.

LETTER 793

A bishop was once accused of avarice and other crimes. He was hated for these things by the people and condemned by the synod of the land. After being rebuked, he submitted a written self-defense and was ousted from his throne by popular vote. Thereupon, the inhabitants of the city judged three other men as being worthy of the episcopate, but were not sure which of these three to choose. So they sent a letter asking the Great Old Man, Barsanuphius. Response.

You should choose none; but entrust the choice to the [arch]bishop.[40] Let him give you whomever God assures him about.

LETTER 794

Another Christ-loving layperson asked the same Great Old Man: "Will God surely give them one of these three?" Response.

If they desire this with unity of mind, simplicity of heart, and faith in God, then not only will God give them one of these

---

35. Cf. Rv 2.1.   36. Cf. Dn 6.11–28.
37. Cf. Dn 13.60.   38. Ps 144.18.
39. Cf. Prv 21.1.
40. Reference to the metropolitan archbishop of Caesarea in Palestine.

three, but even an angel from heaven,[41] namely, a man equal to angels, if they so ask. God cannot lie to us; for he said: "Ask, and it shall be given you; for everyone who asks receives."[42] To those who ask wrongly: "You ask and do not receive; for you are asking wrongly."[43]

LETTER 795

Question: "What happens, then, if one of the three is better than the others? Will God give them this one?" Response.

If they offer the choice in this regard to the archbishop, then God will give them the person that he sees will be more beneficial for them than the others. For example, if one of them is strict, and the people still require discipline for their correction, then he will give them this one.

LETTER 796

Question: "What happens if a city is divided in such a way that some of the people want certain candidates on the basis of their faith, while others want another based on attachment? In the case where the candidates of both parties are good, what will happen then?" Response.

To those who ask in faith,[44] God will grant their request; to the others, he will not grant their request. Not because he refuses their candidates, but he refuses their bad request.

LETTER 797

Question: "What happens, then, if the candidate promoted by those who do not ask in faith[45] actually turns out to be better than the one proposed by the others, who ask in faith?" Response.

God knows people's hearts[46] and sees the intention of those who ask well. So he will give them the candidate of those who ask badly. Not because of the way the others are asking; for their

41. Cf. Gal 1.8.   42. Mt 7.7–8.
43. Jas 4.3.   44. Cf. Jas 1.6.
45. Cf. ibid.   46. Cf. Acts 1.24.

intention is evil. But because of their good intention; for they would gladly have accepted the better candidate, whom out of ignorance they did not propose.

LETTER 798

Question: "That means, however, that those who did not ask with the correct intention also end up benefiting, actually receiving the good candidate in spite of their unworthiness. What happens then?" Response.

For the sake of the worthy, God also shows mercy on the unworthy. For "he sends rain on the righteous and on the unrighteous."[47] Indeed, he revealed this to us through sacred Scripture, saying to Abraham: "If I find ten righteous people in the city, then for the sake of the ten I shall not destroy the place."[48] Now, if for the sake of ten righteous people he does not destroy the city, how much more so will he show loving-kindness also to the others for the sake of so many!

LETTER 799

Question: "What then? If all the candidates are proposed in good faith, but none of those proposed is in fact useful for them, will God grant them one of those candidates?" Response.

Since they are worthy of his favor, God overlooks their choice and, when the time comes, he certainly inspires them to elect another candidate or else inspires the one who has the authority of ordination to give them someone else, more useful than the ones proposed by them.

LETTER 800

Question: "What happens, then, to all those who do not ask with correct intention, but who in fact recommend a good candidate? Will their request be granted or not?" Response by Barsanuphius.

God foresees everything. If he sees that they are going to repent, then he grants them the [candidate of their choice]; for

47. Mt 5.45.   48. Gn 18.32.

they are deemed worthy on account of their subsequent repentance. If, however, he sees that they will remain without repentance, he does not grant them their request, on account of their
unworthiness.

LETTER 801

Question: "Father, you said that, even if the city is divided, those
who are unworthy will—for the sake of those who ask properly—
also enjoy the good candidate that will be granted. Then how is
it written in Scripture that: 'If a kingdom is divided against itself,
it shall not stand'?[49] For behold, in this case, the city is divided,
and yet the entire city will stand firm for the sake of the good."
Response.

The division referred to is the deviation of both parts toward
evil. For then the words: "It shall not stand," namely, toward
good, are fulfilled. This good, however, does not create division; for the teaching of the apostles is only one, and the Apostle says: "If the unbeliever separates, let it be so."[50] What, then?
Are we saying that the church was divided for this and shall not
stand? Surely not! For the Lord said: "The gates of Hades will
not prevail against it."[51] Nevertheless, the person who does not
stand on the side of good, that same person is divided against
himself; whereas the person who stands on the side of good is
not divided.

LETTER 802

The inhabitants of the city conformed to the response given by
the Old Man, presenting three candidates, and so a bishop was
offered to them, who was both holy and pleasing to God. The
former bishop, however, confident in the riches that he had acquired, ran off to Byzantium in order to request that the throne
be returned to him. Therefore, rumor spread that he had
achieved his goal, and everyone grew anxious again. So they sent
a letter, asking the Old Man what they should do. For they were
afraid of appealing to the emperor for fear of failure and of the

49. Mk 3.24.   50. 1 Cor 7.15.
51. Mt 16.18.

further harm that this might bring to the church. The Old Man declared to them the following.

Send a supplication, through which you reassure the emperor about the deposition of that bishop, mentioning that it happened properly, attaching also a copy of the written protests and the expressions of thanksgiving at the election of the new bishop, in order to demonstrate that this is due to God and not to people. In this way, the emperor will be sufficiently reassured to withdraw his confidence from the former bishop. Those who wish to deal with the matter in an evil manner will only lose their money and later be sadly put to shame. As for the money spent [by the former bishop], as Scripture says: "Samson died with the foreigners [Philistines]."[52]

LETTER 803

When they heard this, they neglected to send a supplication, and the former bishop seized the metropolitan diocese and reassumed office by means of a royal decree to the magistrate. When great commotion and confusion ensued in the city, they sent another letter to the Old Man, entreating him about this. He declared the following to them.

You were wrong in neglecting to inform the emperor, and God despises negligence. Nevertheless, in the name of the Lord, I tell you that, even if he should reach the gates of the city, yet he shall not enter it. For God will not permit him to do this.

After the Old Man had said this, the magistrate forcefully entered the city in order to fulfill the royal decree, so that everyone was filled with worry and fear. Suddenly, however, rumor spread about the emperor's death[53] and all the expectations were dispelled. So the former bishop left [Byzantium] without success, having spent in vain all of his money, just as the Old Man had predicted. For the inhabitants, on the other hand, the prophecy was confirmed in the events themselves. Indeed, according to the word of the Lord: "Whatever was bound on earth was also bound in heaven."[54]

52. Cf. Jgs 16.30. 53. Reference to Justinian I (527–565).
54. Cf. Mt 16.19 and 18.18.

LETTER 804

The newly ordained bishop considered himself unworthy of the priestly ministry and incapable of the administration of ecclesiastical affairs. He was thinking about leaving the office, when he sent a letter asking the same Great Old Man about this. Response by Barsanuphius.

Rejoice in the Lord, servant of God and celebrant of sacred mysteries. You know that the holy Paul the Apostle wrote these words: "In whatever condition each of you was called, brothers, let him remain in it with God."[55] I, too, believe that you were made bishop by the will of God; you are not a mercenary but a pastor.[56] Therefore, do not wish to withdraw, in order not to provoke the anger of God. For he said: "Heaven and earth will pass away, but my words will not pass away."[57] Therefore, do not be a coward; indeed, it is written that after Moses had died, when Joshua, son of Nun, was afraid of leading the people to the promised land, the angel told him: "Be strong and of good courage; do not be afraid; for just as I was with Moses, so also shall I be with you."[58] Therefore, listen also to the same words from me, the wretched one: "Be strong and of good courage in the Lord."

LETTER 805

The same person asked the Other Old Man: "Father, whom should I ordain to the priesthood, and what sort of life should they lead?" Response by John.

You should ordain people worthy of God and good in character, in order that these might minister at the sacred altars of God; they should especially be recommended by many other people, in accordance with Scripture.[59] It is such people whom you should strive to ordain, admonishing them upon ordination that God will demand the judgment of the church from them, should they depart from it. In so doing, you are also showing God your

55. 1 Cor 7.24.
57. Mt 24.35.
59. Cf. 1 Tm 3.7.

56. Cf. Jn 10.12.
58. Cf. 1 Chr 22.13; Jos 1.9.

intention and desire to ordain good people for the churches of God.

Question: "If certain holy fathers recommend someone as worthy of ordination, should I not be satisfied with their testimony, or should I still demand the approval of the majority?" Response.

You should be satisfied with the testimony of the fathers; for they are speaking in accordance with the will of God, and of such a kind are the ministers whom God desires.[60] Now, if, after receiving such a testimony, you notice that your thought is troubled, then such a tare is sown only by the devil.

Question: "What happens, then, if, after the testimony of the fathers, the candidate refuses to receive ordination or else relinquishes his ordination?" Response.

If the candidate refuses ordination, then he must be forced to ordination. If, after being forced, he leaves, then this does not constitute any cause for blaming those who offered testimony about him; it is, however, cause for blaming the candidate for abandoning the will of God. For he is obliged to undergo testing and to labor in the matter. Then, if he should observe that he is incapable, he should again ask the saints about this, those salted by the grace of God,[61] and he should do whatever they tell him. After all, many of the saints resigned [from candidacy for ordination] but were still obliged by God [to accept]. Even Moses said: "Choose someone else,"[62] and Jeremiah said: "Truly, I cannot speak, for I am only a youth."[63] Other fathers, too, fled from ordination; yet, once forcefully seized and ordained, they bore their ministry for the name of God. One who is obliged to approach ordination and then resigns, however, is avoiding obedience; and Scripture says: "Obedience is better than sacrifice."[64]

---

60. Cf. Jn 4.23.
62. Ex 4.13.
64. 1 Sm 15.22.

61. Cf. Col 4.6.
63. Jer 1.6.

Now, if someone is considering others, who lead a life of stillness and meet no person at all, one should not think about ordination for these, obliging them to come into the midst of people. If, however, there is someone who does meet with other
people and will not reject an invitation to visit towns and cities[65] whenever such need arises, and if this person is also recommended as being good and skillful, then it is precisely such persons whom the bishops should seize for ordination. For these
can benefit not only their own souls but also the souls of others.
This is why the Apostle ordered Titus: "Appoint presbyters in
every church,"[66] clearly ordering him to appoint those who were
worthy of such a task, such as Timothy was.

The holy Gregory, too, and others like him, were ordained
by force.[67] Indeed, if we investigate, we shall also discover many
other servants of God suffering in the same way, even in our own
times. Nevertheless, although they were greatly afflicted, they
endured the labor, fearing to reject the will of God. If someone
resigns from his candidacy to ordination without any consideration, then that person needs to pray that his resignation does
not afflict his own soul. For it sometimes happens that, for the
sake of some pretense to rights, Satan will trip up a person; may
the Lord banish Satan far from our souls and from all those
who fear God. Amen.

LETTER 808

The same person desired in godly fear to ordain deacons in the
church and promote certain others to ecclesiastical offices. Not
knowing, however, whom to choose according to God, he sent a
list to the same Old Man with the names of the clergy, so that he

---

65. Cf. Lk 13.22.   66. Ti 1.5.

67. The critical edition of Barsanuphius and John's letters in *Sources chrétiennes* observes that this refers to Gregory the Theologian, who left the throne
of Constantinople after the Second Ecumenical Council (381); see *SC* 468, 272
n.1, and Gregory's lengthy apologetic regarding his flight to Pontus in *Oration* 2
(PG 35.408–513). Since, however, the reference here in *Letter* 807 is to ordination realized "by force," rather than ordination followed by flight, another obvious possibility is Gregory the Wonderworker (d. ca. 265), who hid in order to
avoid being ordained to the episcopate and was ordained *in absentia*. The Gaza
elders would have been familiar with both historical examples.

might choose those whom he wanted. When the Old Man selected from them some who in fact appeared by human standards
to be incapable of administration, the bishop was surprised and
asked him about this. The Old Man said the following.

Do you imagine that I said something of my own accord? We
prayed, and whatever God inspired me to say, I spoke. It is not,
however, because of any competence of my own that this response was given through me;[68] whenever necessary, God can
even open the mouth of an ass.[69]

LETTER 809

Question: "The same person sent a question to the same Old
Man, John: How can such people even be involved in their affairs or be charged with any important responsibilities? For they
are simple, without any skills in speaking, and so they might easily be despised by people." Response by John.

Tell the lord bishop: If you become like Abraham, then "God
is able to raise children for you from these stones";[70] indeed, if
you strive to focus all your hope on God,[71] even if you appoint
people unable to speak or think as administrators and advocates,
yet God will render these more impressive than any secular magistrates. If you should charge these with important responsibilities, you will obtain anything that you want through them to the
glory of his name. Otherwise, even if you send an advocate who
is skilled in rhetoric, he will return just as he left. The sons of Israel were remarkable warriors; when their hearts were set on the
right path,[72] they would conquer their enemies; but when they
overlooked their salvation, they were defeated by their enemies.

LETTER 810

Question: "Then, how can I become like Abraham?" Response.

I did not say that you should become like Abraham in everything, but only insofar as cutting off your own will, as he did,

68. Cf. 2 Cor 3.5.
70. Cf. Mt 3.9.
72. Cf. 2 Chr 12.14.

69. Cf. Nm 22.28.
71. Cf. Acts 24.15.

when he sacrificed his own son voluntarily.[73] For Abraham's achievements were many, and, while we cannot be like him in everything, we can do so at least in those things which are obvious to us.

LETTER 811

Question: "I am convinced that whatever you say is from God, and so I must certainly act accordingly. Since, however, I believe that everyone in church will be scandalized when I do so, and since my thought is actually weighed down by this, what do you order me to do? Should I ordain everyone or only those whom I consider useful in dealing with church affairs?" Response by John.

The Lord said: "Whoever does not hate father and mother, wife and children, yes, even life itself, cannot be my disciple."[74] Hating life itself means cutting off one's own desires through ascetic discipline. Such a person will pay no attention either to people's words or to people-pleasing, but only to sacred questions and answers that come through the lips of his saints. The person asking should, therefore, believe that God will place [the response] on the lips of the person asked, according to the heart of the former; for it is said: "May the Lord grant you, according to your heart."[75] We have proved unable to bear the insults and afflictions of others. Even if a person wishes to edify everyone, this would be impossible; for not everyone wants the same thing.

You also asked about perfection; this implies casting the matter entirely before God so that he might choose those whom he wishes. Yet, upon hearing, we were not able to endure the response and did not realize that God does not see in the same way as people see. For human beings inspect the externals,[76] even mingling their own will with this. God, however, looks beyond the externals[77] to the depths of the heart;[78] and he is able to see the future as present.[79] Nevertheless, it is very beneficial for us to recognize that there still remains within us that human element, so that we may come to know our limitations, namely,

---

73. Cf. Gn 22.1–19.
75. Ps 19.5.
77. Cf. 1 Sm 16.7.
79. Cf. Rom 4.17.

74. Lk 14.26.
76. Cf. Jn 7.24.
78. Cf. Jdt 8.14.

where we actually are, and be humbled in order to receive the grace of the humble.

Therefore, we entreated God that he might condescend to the will of our weak nature, just as he gave to the prophet Ezekiel "cow's dung instead of human dung,"[80] and a king to the Israelites,[81] when they saw that they desired one. For behold, his goodness has condescended and cut off his own will for our sake. Therefore, if only we blame ourselves, saying that we are still only eating vegetables, then God will deem us worthy of solid food, which is reserved for the perfect in Christ.[82] Amen.

LETTER 812

Question: "I have a pious secretary, who is quite capable and highly recommended, but I hesitate to ordain him, lest I scandalize some people for promoting my own. What do you order me to do?" Response.

In regard to your secretary, you have not been thinking correctly. For if he were corrupt and useless, without the recommendation of anyone, then you would have hesitated, and rightly so. If, however, he is good and useful, with the recommendation also of others, then you should not, for the sake of your pretense to rights, transgress the commandment of the Apostle, who tells us to appoint such persons.[83]

You should also know that, if someone does something with godly fear and does not incline the heart to human considerations, even if scandal should ensue, it will not last or harm anyone; for such a scandal arises from the envy of the devil.[84] A bad tree does not bear good fruit, just as a good tree does not bear bad fruit.[85] I entreat you, therefore, to forgive me for the Lord's sake and to pray for me.

LETTER 813

A monk, who was formerly an academic, sought to be ordained as a priest in the church of the Holy City [Jerusalem]. Influenced

80. Ezek 4.15.
82. Cf. Heb 5.12.
84. Cf. Wis 2.24.

81. Cf. 1 Sm 8.5–22.
83. Cf. Ti 1.7.
85. Cf. Mt 7.18.

by an assembly of certain people, the bishop ordained him to the diaconate, in consideration of his title as an academic, and was entreated [by others] to ordain the same person to the priesthood as well. Regretting what he had done, however, he sent a question to the same Old Man, asking whether he had done the right thing in even performing the first ordination to the diaconate, and whether he should proceed to make him a priest. Response by John.

In regard to the past, what has happened has happened. Therefore, do not be sorrowful about this; for God is able, according to his will, to lead this brother to the knowledge of truth.[86] As for the priesthood, this time do not be influenced to ordain him. If he should manifest fruits worthy of this purpose,[87] then God will reassure you about him; for God is never far from us.[88]

You should not, however, pay attention to the academic's title or to his secular wisdom alone. For if a person does not possess the heavenly or spiritual wisdom,[89] then the secular one is in vain. If, however, one has both one and the other, then that person is truly blessed. For it is said: "Every scribe who has been trained for the kingdom of heaven is like a master of a household who brings out of his treasure what is new and what is old."[90] Be careful not to be carried away by every wind that blows to and fro;[91] for "bad company ruins good morals."[92]

LETTER 814

Question: "If I am unsure as to whom to ordain for village churches, what should I do?" Response.

Those in the villages should give testimony. So you should trust their testimony and cast upon them the judgment of this testimony, ordaining those recommended by them. The responsibility is theirs,[93] and you will in fact be innocent.[94]

---

86. Cf. 1 Tm 2.4.
88. Cf. Acts 17.27.
90. Mt 13.52.
92. 1 Cor 15.33.
94. Cf. Ps 17.26.

87. Cf. Mt 3.8.
89. Cf. Jas 3.17.
91. Cf. Eph 4.14.
93. Cf. Mt 27.4.

LETTER 815

Question: "If a particular town has sufficient clergy but its inhabitants recommend others whom they would also like ordained, should I accept them, too, and ordain more clergy than required?" Response.

If that church has sufficient clergy, then there is no need for you to ordain any more, so that there may be no confusion. Furthermore, where there are enough clergy, there is no need to accept people's recommendation of others. What for? If a town happens to have another ten worthy people for ordination, just because the people recommend these, does a bishop have to ordain them? No! Everything must be done in an orderly manner. If, however, they truly require another clergyman, and they happen to recommend someone, even if this person refuses, you should still ordain him.

LETTER 816

Question: "A town that required a clergyman recommended two persons. One of them was twice married but wealthy; the other was poor. Which of the two, then, should be ordained?" Response.

You should not ordain the person who is twice married, because this is against the canons;[95] however, you should ordain the poor person and give consideration to the means of supporting him a little on account of his poverty for the sake of God.

LETTER 817

Question: "There are certain ordained clergymen in our diocese who also happen to be civil servants. There are other clergymen, in fact ordained elsewhere, who are nevertheless assigned to our diocese at the demand of the town's inhabitants, and these, too, are civil servants. Finally, there are also others, assigned to the diocese at the imposition of certain people in authority or at the

---

95. Cf. Ti 1.6. See also the 17th Apostolic Canon.

request of others, without actually being worthy of this. Should all of these depend on secular professions [for support], whether physical or financial, or should they not?" Response.

Those who have been ordained or assigned worthily by the town should not depend on any other physical or financial profession. Those who were assigned at the imposition of some people, or else at their request, should also not depend on physical labor, but should have some financial support [of their own], even if rumor spreads that they were ordained for a bribe. An ordination for God must be honored in some manner; and this is the responsibility[96] of the one who bears the judgment.[97]

LETTER 818

Question: "In ordaining someone, I overlooked another person who had caused me grief. Now I am afflicted inasmuch as I do not know whether or not I have actually done the right thing." Response by John.

If you were truly caused grief on account of his negligence or some other fault, then you did the right thing. If, however, you acted in reaction to some fleshly sorrow, then you should repent and ordain that person of your own accord.

LETTER 819

"Since I have been caused much trouble by various people requesting ordination of certain individuals, I thought it best up until now to ordain no one. Yet now, a certain Christ-loving and genuinely beloved layperson and friend of mine, who labors a great deal for the sake of God and on my behalf before powerful people, has asked me to ordain a particular layman, recommending him as being a good person. Should I ordain him for the sake of my friend?" Response.

Had you focused all of your hope on God,[98] then you would not have been concerned about anyone else. Since, however, you still depend on people, then you, too, are obliged to return

96. Cf. Mt 27.4.   97. Cf. Gal 5.10.
98. Cf. Acts 24.15.

a favor for a favor.[99] For it is said: "Do to others as you would
have them do to you."[100] Nevertheless, if the person asking you
happens to be good, as you say he is, and the one whom he
recommends is also good, then you should not look unfavor-
ably upon this testimony or the ordination; after all, it is he that
bears the judgment.[101] If, however, you know that the candidate
for ordination is not good but has been discredited in some
way, then you are not obliged to accept him for ordination; otherwise, you shall bear the judgment.[102]

LETTER 820

Question: "Since it was revealed that some people were Manichaeans, and, in order to avoid the threat of persecution, they
went elsewhere to be baptized, but without any preparation, what
do you order me to do?" Response.

In regard to the confessed Manichaeans, you should write[103]
in order to prevent this and inform those who wish to baptize
them that they are in fact Manichaean. Then, it is up to them
whether they baptize them or not; for not everyone pays attention as necessary to these matters. Furthermore, they do not
know that such people require much study and long preparation, together with the hearing of sacred words and catecheti-
cal instruction by holy priests in order to be received; therefore,
this should not happen immediately and haphazardly. For the
matter is awesome. Indeed, wherever there is no desire for God,
we should in that instance recall our Master, who says: "Do not
give what is holy to dogs; and do not throw your pearls before
swine,"[104] and so on.

LETTER 821

Question: "The emperor issued a decree, ordering pagans no
longer to adhere to their customs;[105] the same applied to schis-

99. Cf. Jn 1.16.   100. Lk 6.31.
101. Cf. Gal 5.10.   102. Cf. ibid.
103. That is, he should write an encyclical letter.
104. Mt 7.6.
105. Issued by Justinian around 529. The Archbishop of Jerusalem, who is
writing to Abba John, is Peter.

matics. Some of these, however, approached after holy Pascha
either to be baptized or to receive Communion. Should I accept
them? And when should they be deemed worthy either of Baptism or of holy Communion?" Response.

Those who wish to be illumined should be received and
granted holy Baptism during holy Lent or else at the holy As-
cension of the Savior; then, they shall have an entire week for
celebration. Now, if one of them intends to be received out of
custom or simply out of fear for the decree, then say: "If you are
here on account of the decree, it is a sin. If you are approaching
with godly fear for the sake of your life, then you will actually receive two benefits, namely, the salvation of your fleshly life and
your true life." The same should be addressed to those who wish
to take Communion in church. And if they say: "We are here for
the sake of God," then receive them at once; for they are Christians.

Question: "A certain pagan has been captured in the territory of
the faithful, and many people say that he should be murdered or
burned. Is this good or not?" Response.

He should be neither murdered nor burned; for this is not
proper for Christians to do. Rather, he should be whipped and
fined; for these measures are effective with people. Then one
should entrust him to someone who fears God,[106] in order that
he might be instructed in the way of God[107] and thereafter illumined.

LETTER 823

Question from the same person to the [same] Great Old Man:
"Father, I have encountered ill temper from people who are hurrying to cause injustice. When I correct them, I become their enemy and cannot find any support from anyone. So I grieve and
want to leave the church." Response by Barsanuphius.

106. Cf. Acts 10.2.
107. Cf. Mt 22.16.

Tell me, is it a sin to transgress the commandment of the Apostle, or is it not? It is quite clear that it is a sin. Now, if it is a sin, the Apostle says: "Are you bound to a wife? Do not seek to be free."[108] You, then, have taken the church as a wife; do not seek to be separate from it; otherwise, you shall be greatly tempted, and you shall repent of this. Therefore, endure with courage everything that comes to you, and you shall afterward find mercy from God. For it is said: "The one who endures to the end will be saved."[109]

So resist wickedness, and the Lord will bring your enemies to your feet; in fact, your opposition shall become your friends. Struggle unto death for the sake of truth, and God will battle on your behalf.[110] Furthermore, do not seek any assistance from people; for one who hopes in human beings[111] falls quickly. Assistance that comes from God is much greater than assistance from tens of thousands of people. For it is said: "With the Lord on my side to help me, I do not fear what mortals can do to me."[112] Therefore, establish your heart in the Lord, be brave and strong,[113] and the Lord shall be with you.

LETTER 824

Request from the same person to the same Great Old Man: "Master, if you so order, I shall not refuse to obey; but pray for me, that I may acquire God's assistance and be protected from temptations that assail me." Response.

I know that I am nothing[114] and that I do not pray in the way that God wants. Someone who asks another's prayers, however, must also join that person's prayer with a little of one's own toil. For it is written: "The prayer of the righteous is very powerful," but he added: "and effective,"[115] namely, when it is assisted by the [prayer of] the one requesting prayers. Your angel should know, therefore, that you have not received just a little protection from God, and he protects you through the prayers of the

---

108. 1 Cor 7.27.　　　　109. Mt 10.22.
110. Cf. Ps 109.1.　　　　111. Cf. Jer 17.5.
112. Cf. Ps 117.6.　　　　113. Cf. Dt 31.6.
114. Cf. 2 Cor 12.11.　　　115. Jas 5.16.

saints. Look at how the deacon is praying for you,[116] repeating the word of the Apostle: "rightly teaching the word of truth."[117] So teach it rightly, neither being ashamed of anyone nor trying to please anyone, and you shall find grace before God and people.[118]

Have no human thoughts; for every human affair is abominable before God.[119] Let the church not be unfair to anyone; rather, let it be an example[120] of the right way for everyone. Then God will be in you and you in God, and he protects you from every evil[121] and every trap of the enemy. May our Lord Jesus Christ be with your spirit and with me. Amen.

LETTER 825

The same person overlooked certain rules of the church for the sake of pleasing some people. For this reason, then, God allowed him to be subjected to a temptation that grieved him. So he sent a question about this to the same Great Old Man. The Old Man replied as follows.

You were not delivered [into this temptation] for no reason at all or without God's consent. Therefore, let us examine our hearts in order to see which commandment of God we have transgressed, and we shall learn why we were delivered [into such temptation].

LETTER 826

Request from the same person: "Holy father, I know that I have harmed both my own soul and the holy church of God, so that now harsh things have arisen against it. For those who oppose the church are many and powerful;[122] if I should wish to resist, harm will surely ensue. And as far as human beings are concerned, there is no solution; whereas 'with God, all things are possible.'[123] Therefore, I fall down in prostration before you,

---

116. Reference to the liturgical commemoration of the bishop by the deacon in the Divine Liturgy.

117. 2 Tm 2.15.   118. Cf. Acts 7.46.
119. Cf. Prv 17.15.   120. Cf. 1 Pt 5.3.
121. Cf. Ps 120.7.   122. Cf. Ps 55.3.
123. Mt 19.26.

master, in order that you might request forgiveness on my behalf; come to my own assistance as well as to that of the church,
and revoke the affliction, as you will; for you are able to do so."[124]
Response.

If everything is possible with God, and we believe that it is indeed so, then let us do our best for his sake, and he will wipe out
those who assail us. "The Lord brings the counsel of the nations
to nothing; he frustrates the plans of leaders. But the counsel of
God stands forever."[125] Affirm the truth, and strive for its sake,
and God will do battle on your behalf against its opponents.
These oppose it in fleshly manner; you should affirm it in spiritual manner, namely, by offering prayers and supplications in
regard to everything, asking for assistance from God. Reprove
with boldness, discipline, and encourage,[126] as is appropriate for
a spiritual teacher; and do not fear them; "For there are more
with us than there are with them."[127] They are with the devil and
with those people who have the same passions; we are with God
and his saints. We place our hope in God, who says: "I will never
leave you or forsake you."[128] He always accomplishes "far more
than we can ask or imagine,"[129] so that these words are fulfilled
in us: "Happy are those whose help is the God of Jacob, whose
hope is in the Lord their God."[130] They, however, place their
hope in mortals, from whom there is no salvation.[131]

Therefore, if some small harm ensues, let us overlook it and
not react or be ashamed of anyone; otherwise, we are provoking
God's anger. Rather, let us stand firm in the truth; then, your
opponents will not delay in falling before your feet, and so God,
who is always glorified by his servants, will be glorified. Have
the saints, then, as your allies through their prayers to God for
your sake. Rightly teach, as you have already heard, the word
of truth[132] as a bishop of God, and people will fall before you
as before a genuine servant of God, with fear, trembling, and
love. For those who fear God are feared by people, just as his

124. Cf. Mt 8.2.
125. Ps 32.11–12.
126. Cf. 2 Tm 4.2.
127. 2 Kgs 6.16.
128. Heb 13.5; Jos 1.5.
129. Eph 3.20.
130. Ps 145.5.
131. Cf. Ps 145.3.
132. Cf. 2 Tm 2.15.

angels are feared by demons. Therefore, do not be afraid; for God and his grace are with you.[133] Receive the "strength that is from on high,"[134] which the apostles received through the grace of Christ our God. May his grace remain with you until your last breath. I greet you in the Lord, spiritual father; I greet you with a holy kiss;[135] I greet you in the Holy Spirit, entreating you to pray for me for the sake of love.

LETTER 827

Question: "Father, through your holy words, the church has received much assistance from God, and several of those who have brought injustice to the church and insulted its representatives are now asking for peace, promising to help us and to correct the injustices against us as well as to control our opponents. So what do you order? Should I accept them or not?" Response.

If they are entreating you, then receive them for the sake of the one who tells us to forgive one another.[136] Allow them time to be corrected, but with proper care, neither without care nor without compassion. Furthermore, some document should be signed in order for all to protect their own rights.

LETTER 828

Question: "Is it a good thing to keep the accounts of the church?" Response by Barsanuphius.

If you keep the accounts of a church, you are actually keeping the accounts of God. For you are God's steward.[137] Therefore, you are obliged to keep the accounts in such a way as to feed the poor and the orphans, should there be any surplus. After all, God is their Father and nurturer, and you are administering their goods. If there is no surplus, you should do whatever you can to produce one. Otherwise, you are not keeping the accounts of a church but only intending to take care of yourself. If that is what you are doing, then you are no longer actually

133. Cf. Is 8.8–12.
135. Cf. Rom 16.16.
137. Cf. Lk 12.48.

134. Lk 24.49.
136. Cf. Col 3.13.

keeping the accounts for God, but for the devil. Do everything, then, according to God, and you shall find your reward in him.

Question: "The damage that occurred has been aggravated for various reasons, and I am afflicted inasmuch as there is no money left in my hands. What should I do?" Response.

Scripture says: "Whoever does you injustice does not do so to you but to the Holy Spirit that lives in you."[138] Therefore, do not grieve over any human damage; the Lord will not deprive you of what he knows that you need. For he said: "Your heavenly Father knows what you need even before you ask him."[139] But "seek first the kingdom of God,"[140] performing its works, and "all of these will be given to you as well."[141]

If you are suffering a little for lack of resources, you will surely find good things generously before you through God's will. Remember that it was written: "All who want to live a godly life will be persecuted."[142] And again, it is said: "Rejoice in the Lord always, whenever you face trials of any kind."[143] Behold the persecution, and behold the temptations; however, bear them courageously and faithfully, so that God may be glorified through you. For patience leads a person to character; and character produces hope; and hope does not disappoint.[144] Pray for me.

Question: "There are many so-called tax collectors who come to this city, always expecting contributions from the church. I do not know what to do. Should I contribute? Sometimes [I feel that] I am offending God by wasting what belongs to the poor. Should I perhaps not contribute? Then, however, I am slandered before the magistrates. What do you order me to do?" Response.

Tax collectors are servants of human authorities. Conceding to contribute is a sign of human fear. Therefore, if we do not

138. Cf. 2 Tm 1.14.
140. Mt 6.33.
142. Cf. 2 Tm 3.12.
144. Cf. Rom 5.4–5.

139. Mt. 6.8.
141. Lk 12.31.
143. Cf. Jas 1.2.

want to fear them, let us stand firm in the truth, with godly fear, and we shall hear the Apostle saying: "Do you wish to have no fear of authority? Then do what is good, and you will receive its approval."[145] Do not worry about slander; for it is said: "When you are maligned, those who abuse you for your good conduct in Christ are put to shame";[146] and again: "If I were still pleasing people, I would not be a slave of Christ."[147]

LETTER 831

Certain farmers from the province were being abused by the soldiers of the governor,[148] being forcibly removed from the boundaries of the holy churches. So the city authorities, together with the bishop, decided to inform the emperor, although they were afraid of the harm that the governor might bring upon them. They sent a question, asking the Great Old Man about the matter. He told them the following.

If you believe that God truly cares for the poor, then take a courageous stand on this matter. For the one who cares for the poor will certainly lead those who struggle on behalf of the poor. We also have his assurance, when he says: "Just as you did it to one of the least of these, you did it to me."[149]

LETTER 832

Response by the Great Old Man to those who were neglectful in this matter.

Be on watch, so that the following words may not be fulfilled in you: "Having started with the Spirit, are you now ending with the flesh?"[150] Do you not know that this is a work of God? Indeed, you are not alone in your struggle concerning this matter; for there are many others who are struggling with you in their prayers.[151] Be careful, because if you betray the work of

---

145. Rom 13.3.   146. 1 Pt 3.16.
147. Gal 1.10.

148. The term for "governor" here (δουκός) derives from the Latin word *dux*, which, from the fifth century onward, signifies a military administrator in command of a province.

149. Cf. Mt 25.40.   150. Gal 3.3.
151. Cf. Col 4.12.

God, then God himself will betray you. As for the authorities,
let no person frighten you; for no one is able to resist the will of
God.[152] Always remember to struggle for the sake of truth until
death, and the Lord will battle on your behalf.

LETTER 833

Response by the Other Old Man to the bishop, who asked about
the same matter concerning the governor, but kept silent.

Pay attention to yourself. For neither governor nor emperor
will redeem you on the day of judgment. Therefore, do not relax in this, so that you may have boldness to find mercy before
God. Moreover, do not be afraid; for you are not the ones bearing the weight of this matter; rather, God and the Old Man [are
in fact bearing the burden]. Therefore, if you do your best, you
will share the reward. Otherwise, you shall later bear the judgment.[153] Pray for me.

LETTER 834

Question from the same person to the same [Old Man]: "Since
the governor has recently embraced Christianity on account of
the zeal of the Christ-loving emperor, do you order us to address
friendly letters to him? For he [has the power] to correct the injustice that was done against us. And, if it seems good to you that
we should do so, then will you dictate the letters? For there is a
different power in the words that come from the Holy Spirit that
dwells in you."[154] Response by John.

Write to him as follows: "There was no small joy inspired within us as well as within all those who fear God,[155] as a result of your
reception into the faith of Christ. This joy is further increased
when we see spiritual fruits blossoming within you. For truly, it is
a joy for us to observe the evangelical words fulfilled in you: 'In
the same way, let your light shine before others, so that they may
see your good works and give glory to your Father in heaven.'[156]
"As your majesty well knows, young plants bear plentiful and

152. Cf. Rom 9.19.
153. Cf. Gal 5.10.
154. Cf. Rom 8.11.
155. Cf. Acts 13.26.
156. Mt 5.16.

beautiful fruits. Therefore, since you, too, are newly planted, you should demonstrate your plentiful, beautiful, and spiritual fruits for the edification of all,[157] for the glory of the holy and consubstantial Trinity, as well as for your own honor by the Christ-loving emperors, through whom you were deemed worthy of this great gift of illumination. What else are the spiritual fruits, other than struggle for faith in Christ[158] and the establishment of Christianity? For while these are certainly supported by God himself, nevertheless God wants to test people's intentions, in order ultimately to reveal their inclination.

"Indeed, it is impossible for the Christian faith to be dissolved; for such is God's promise: 'On this rock, I will build my church, and the gates of Hades will not prevail against it.'[159] Good must certainly arrive; and blessed is the one through whom it comes! Therefore, Christ-loving people, seize this beatitude. I only want your honor to know this; even if a pagan had been in authority and opposed our faith, for whatever reason he did it, we would need to do nothing else but to close the churches and wait until they are later reopened by the Christ-loving emperors."

LETTER 835

Question: "Certain very illustrious citizens wish to introduce an innovation into the church during my tenure and demand that we accept a certain tax for their ship, which will dock in our harbor. Indeed, some people advise me to accept the entire tax, assuring me that this will prove very profitable. Do you, then, order me to accept the tax or not?" Response.

It is not fitting for the church to receive taxes; for this matter belongs to secular authorities. Tell them this. If we are all Christians, we do not need to listen to mortals, but let us follow the Savior himself, who says: "Do to others as you would have them do to you."[160] Consider also that whatever is donated to the church is dedicated to God; therefore, it is not beneficial for us to diminish anything at all. Indeed, woe to the one who causes any injustice to the church!

157. Cf. 2 Cor 13.10.
159. Mt 16.18.
158. Cf. 1 Tm 6.12.
160. Lk 6.31; Mt 7.12.

LETTER 836

Question: "The church has certain rules that forbid going out at night to theatrical presentations as well as to pagan festivals. But the magistrate wants to violate these. What do you order us to write to him?" Response.

Write to him as follows: "According to the Apostle, you are a servant of God[161] and have been ordered to keep his commandments,[162] just as I, too, have been ordered to do the same. Therefore, we are obliged to protect the privileges of the church, for the glory of God and for your own honor. Out of love for you, then, as being our friend and soul-mate, I am simply reminding you that it is not proper for Christians and pious laity such as you to prefer human pleasures, which are harmful to the soul, rather than divine worship."

LETTER 837

Question: "There is an important person, a very influential citizen of ours who lives in Constantinople, who is trying very hard to conduct such theatrical presentations. What do you order me to write to him? In addition, should he wish to conspire against us, pray that he may not be successful." Response.

Write as follows to him: "My child, our entire prayer is that God will increase the faith of the Christians according to his fear so that he might exalt the power[163] of his church; for he is the hope of our salvation. Consider this, too: In time of need, whence do we have our help? Where else but from the church and the prayers of the saints? So whoever inclines toward these shall discover them at the appropriate time. Now, theaters are workshops of the devil; and someone who tries to establish them falls outside of the flock of Christ, becoming associated with the devil.

"We know that you are a child of Christ's church and always endeavor to do what pleases him.[164] So you are in no need of any teaching,[165] but only of a reminder not to communicate

161. Cf. Rom 13.6.
162. Cf. Ps 118.60.
163. Cf. Lk 1.69.
164. Cf. Jn 8.29.
165. Cf. 1 Jn 2.27; 2 Pt 1.13.

with those who hurry to support the theaters of the devil. For in time of need, this cannot be of any profit to, but will only plunge into depths, all those who run toward them. Yet whosoever have their hearts turned toward God and wish to support that which pleases him, these same people will boldly invoke him in the day of affliction,[166] and God shall hear them; for 'he grants to all in accordance with their deeds.'[167] You know that 'the present form of this world is passing away,'[168] but the faith of God lives forever."[169]

Write these things to him and do not fear anyone's conspiracy; indeed, you are struggling for the sake of God's faith,[170] and you have him as your helper. Whoever resists him is drowned like Pharaoh in the Red Sea;[171] whereas whoever believes in him without hesitation stands firmly on solid rock.[172]

LETTER 838

Question: "Father, I try to fast each day [from morning] until evening. Tell me whether this is good, and whether I should pray before I do anything." Response.

As for fasting, examine[173] your heart to see whether it is deceived by vainglory. If not, then examine it again to see whether this fasting renders you weaker in the troubles of practical matters; for such weakness is not beneficial. If you are not harmed in this way either, then your fasting is good. Prayer resembles light, and every Christian should pray before doing anything, especially if one happens to be a priest of God.

LETTER 839

Question: "Master, for the Lord's sake, pray for me. For I have all my hope in God[174] as well as in your holy prayers." Response.

---

166. Cf. Ps 19.2.
167. Ps 61.13.
168. 1 Cor 7.31.
169. Cf. Ps 116.2; 1 Pt 1.25.
170. Cf. 1 Tm 6.12.
171. Cf. Ex 14.27.
172. Cf. Mt 7.24.

173. The term translated as "examine" on both occasions in this letter is ψηλάφησον, which literally implies "groping" or "handling in the dark," as well as "blindly feeling one's way."
174. Cf. Acts 24.15.

May the Holy Spirit assure you that you are firmly established in my prayer, day and night. . . .[175]

LETTER 840

A Christ-loving layperson, who had traveled abroad in order to struggle for the sake of God on behalf of the church of God against certain people who had harmed the church, sent a question, asking the same Great Old Man for a word of life[176] and a word of advice. Response by Barsanuphius.

Hold on to the love of God and to truth and freedom. And do not be afraid of helping as much as you can. For the affairs of the church are dedicated to God; and woe to the person who brings any harm to the church. Furthermore, always have God in your mind, praying to him about everything, and follow the ways that you have chosen. Do not try to please people in any way,[177] and you will receive the grace of God. For such people are strangers to God,[178] and the Spirit of God does not dwell in them. Possess the Spirit of God, and it will teach you everything properly; for without this, you are able to achieve nothing.[179]

Guard yourself from turmoil and anger. Do not fear anyone, but always remember these words: "The Lord is my helper, and I shall not fear what mortals can do to me."[180] And again: "All the nations surrounded me; and in the name of the Lord, I cut them off,"[181] and so on. If someone happens to be troubled against you, then respond to that person with humility and love, speaking the truth with prudence; and God will calm that person through the prayers of the saints. You have the counsel of the fathers, and with God this will protect you from the evil one.[182] Therefore, be brave in him and always be strong.[183]

175. Cf. 1 Thes 5.17. A fragmentary *Letter* found in Manuscript 192 at Panteleimon Monastery on Mount Athos.

176. Cf. Jn 6.68.   177. Cf. Gal 1.10.
178. Cf. 4 Mc 11.8.   179. Cf. Jn 15.5.
180. Cf. Ps 117.6.   181. Ps 117.10.
182. Cf. Ps 120.7.   183. Cf. Dt 31.6.

LETTER 841

Question: "If I am unsure as to whether or not I should in fact do something, tell me what to do." Response.

If a matter should occur to you, then pray about it to God three times, asking that you may not be deceived. And if the thought still persists firmly within you, then fulfill this thought; for it is happening to you from God and not from yourself. When, however, you are not reassured in this regard, then ask the fathers.

LETTER 842

Question: "When the fathers tell me to do something that appears contradictory [to what I think], I am sometimes tempted not to trust them; and so I always tell my thought that it must happen just as the fathers say. Is this a sign of faith or of faithlessness?" Response.

Responding to your thought in this manner is a sign of faith. Strive hard, however, to reach the point of accepting [the words of the fathers], even when they tell you that darkness is light. For they say nothing without God. Nevertheless, you require much vigilance, because God asks us to do something at a particular time, and this must always be done immediately. For a little later the circumstances may change; and if one is not established in the faith, then one will be scandalized.

The same occurs with the saints [who direct us]. Those, however, who are ignorant about the fact that God's power and providence are effected through the saints always say: "Why did the saints not inform us about the changes in our circumstances?" Yet they are always speaking about the present moment; if they are asked after the change in circumstances, they will speak differently,[184] as in the case of their teacher, who said that he would bear his anger against Ahab; but, when the latter changed, God, too, was changed with respect to his anger, saying: "I shall not bear my wrath in his days."[185] What, then, would these foolish

184. See *Letter* 363. 185. Cf. 1 Kgs 21.29.

people say? Is God ignorant, too? They are deceived, not knowing that the judgments of God are like a deep abyss[186] and incomprehensible. For these mysteries are entrusted to the faithful; not
everyone can understand them.[187] Therefore, brother, you should
truly know that the genuine fathers are not in fact afflicted, even
when they are considered to be liars by those who do not know
the mysteries of God. Indeed, even if this is not in itself beneficial
for them, yet it is certainly not harmful to them; for they do not
claim glory for themselves, but only for their Master.

LETTER 843

When God's wrath came upon mortals, many people [were pos-
sessed] by impure spirits and began to sound like dogs; others
would utter prophecies that deceived those who believed that
they were actually speaking the truth. Then some Christ-loving
laypersons sent a question to the same Great Old Man, asking
about this. He said the following.

God foresaw our weakness and faithlessness. So he told us:
"False messiahs and false prophets will arise and produce great
signs and wonders, in order to lead astray, if possible, even the
elect."[188]

LETTER 844

Response by the same Great Old Man to the bishop of the city,
who asked him to show him what he should do, as well as to pray
for the people who were afflicted on account of the impending
wrath.

Your holiness should suffer excessively with those who are
afflicted. For this is the task of a spiritual father and teacher.
Moreover, a good shepherd cares for and is vigilant over his
sheep. Therefore, train people to cooperate with the supplication and prayer offered for their sake; for in this way, they shall
be able to achieve great things, according to the Lord's commandment.[189]

---

186. Cf. Ps 35.7.   187. Cf. Mt 19.11.
188. Cf. Mt 24.24.   189. Cf. Mt 17.20; Jn 14.12.

LETTERS TO VARIOUS LAYPERSONS
AND A BROTHER (845–848)

LETTER 845

A Christ-loving layperson asked the Other Old Man: "Is it good for me to suggest to the lord bishop whatever I feel may be beneficial for him?" Response by John.

HIS IS a good thing, and it is proper for a love that is according to God. Hold your heart in purity before God, and this will not cause you any harm. Now, having your heart in purity means not saying anything against anyone out of vengeance, but only for the sake of good itself. Therefore, do not imagine that such a thing is in fact slander; indeed, everything done for the sake of correction is not slander. Nothing good results from slander; whereas, in this case, the result is actually good. That is why it is not slander.

LETTER 846

Question: "What is hesitation[1] of heart, and what is duplicity?"[2] Response.

Hesitation of heart is contemplating or continually calling to mind whether or not God will actually have mercy on one. If one believes that the answer is "no," then this is faithlessness. If you do not believe that he desires to have mercy on you, even more so than you are expecting, then why do you approach him in supplication?

Duplicity is not completely giving oneself over to death for the sake of the heavenly kingdom, but instead being wholly concerned about one's fleshly life.

---

1. Cf. Mt 14.31 and 28.17.
2. Cf. Jas 1.8 and 4.8.

324 BARSANUPHIUS AND JOHN

Question: "What does this sentence mean: 'A city located on a hill cannot be hidden'?"[3] Response.

The city is the soul, while the hill signifies the height of virtue, whereupon those who have ascended "shine as stars in the world, holding fast to the word of life so that they might boast for themselves on the day of Christ."[4]

Question: "What does this sentence mean: 'Rejoice always; pray without ceasing; give thanks in all circumstances'?"[5] Response.

These three things in fact contain our entire salvation. The way of righteousness is the preservation of rejoicing always; for no one can truly rejoice unless one's life always appears righteous. Praying without ceasing is the aversion of every evil; for this allows no room for the devil to act against us. Finally, giving thanks in all circumstances is clear proof of our love for Christ. If our life is properly regulated by the first two, then we shall give thanks to the Lord.[6]

3. Mt 5.14.
4. Cf. Phil 2.15–16. In place of "for themselves" (ἑαυτοῖς), the standard text of the NT has "for me" (ἐμοὶ), referring to Paul, in verse 16.
5. 1 Thes 5.16–18.
6. For an analysis of this *Letter* by Vamvakas, see bibliography.

INDICES

INDEX OF NAMES AND PLACES

INDEX OF SUBJECTS AND KEY WORDS

332   INDEX OF SUBJECTS AND KEY WORDS

fear, of God *(cont.)*
201, 203–4, 206, 217, 224, 228–
29, 232, 234, 239, 245, 250, 266,
270, 280–81, 291, 301, 304, 309,
312, 315–16, 318

fever, 89, 150, 220

fire, 22, 35, 42, 54, 88, 94, 102, 107,
180, 182, 200, 232, 268

flesh, 22, 24, 34, 49, 81, 83, 93, 98,
115, 118–19, 129, 132, 167, 173,
190–91, 194, 225, 235, 241, 276,
282–84, 288, 307, 309, 312, 315,
323

food, 17–18, 72, 74, 89, 95, 109,
111–12, 115–16, 118–22, 130–31,
166–67, 190, 193, 200, 212, 239,
256–58, 279–80, 288, 304

force, oneself, 76, 118, 120, 172

foreigner, 132–33, 261, 270–71

foresight, 25, 119, 161

forgetfulness, 2, 36, 62, 155–56, 262

forgiveness, 1, 4, 6, 24, 29, 38, 41, 62,
77, 79, 148, 151, 173, 205, 253,
262, 265, 268–69, 273, 312

fornication, 12, 20, 73, 76, 103, 105,
185, 194, 230–31, 246, 279

freedom, 16–18, 31, 172, 189, 275,
320

friendship, 223, 294

fruit, 18, 39, 42, 67, 70, 101, 135,
154–55, 181–82, 199, 207, 218,
225, 247, 304–5, 316–17

garden, 224

garment, 39, 104, 114, 169, 276, 293

Gehenna, 3, 122

gentleness, 68, 114, 150, 213, 216,
229

gladness, 15, 73–74, 111, 147

gluttony, 76, 104, 185, 193

Gospel, 66, 78, 128, 167, 180, 183,
190, 213, 245, 284

governor, 315–16

grace, 6, 22, 29, 46, 54, 68–71, 74,
103–4, 112, 126, 149, 156, 160,
188–89, 214, 219, 224, 233, 253,

287–88, 291, 293, 300, 304, 311,
313, 320

grapes, 277; *see also* wine

Greek, 133, 165, 181, 192

grief, 96, 158, 273, 307

guilt, 236, 291

Hades, 297, 317

handiwork, 60; *see also* manual work

harbor, 47, 52, 144, 317

hardhearted, 102, 137

heal, 14–15, 24–25, 29–30, 41, 59,
61, 70, 72, 78, 89–90, 106, 108,
114, 116, 119–25, 132, 138, 149–
50, 175, 205, 207, 221–22, 242,
271, 273, 278, 284, 288

health, 29, 41, 70, 114, 116, 119,
121, 150, 175, 278

heart, 7–10, 14, 21, 24, 34, 36, 38,
41–45, 48–56, 62–65, 68, 70,
74, 84, 87, 91, 94, 96–103, 107,
110–12, 115–16, 123, 126, 128–
29, 134, 137–38, 143, 150, 153,
155–57, 160, 163, 166, 168, 172,
181–90, 195, 199–204, 213–16,
219, 221–23, 231, 236–39, 243–
49, 252–53, 255–56, 258, 262,
268–69, 273, 275, 278, 284, 288,
290–91, 294–95, 302–4, 310–11,
319, 323

heaven, 3, 5–6, 22, 25, 27, 29, 65, 67,
90, 101–2, 122–23, 130, 135, 139,
145–47, 154, 157, 159, 161, 166,
168, 173, 180–81, 185, 191, 203,
207, 211, 213, 242, 248, 283–86,
289, 295, 298–99, 305, 314, 316,
323

hell, 78, 179–80, 182, 184, 190, 205

heresy, 126–27, 180, 182, 249, 251–
52, 264

hesitation, 6, 122, 319, 323

hippodrome, 67, 223

holiness, 109, 133, 153, 188, 322

hope, 6, 22, 26, 31, 33, 55, 77, 79,
97, 101, 108, 122, 128–30, 151,
153–55, 171, 198, 203, 237, 241,

INDEX OF HOLY SCRIPTURE

Numbers refer to the *Letters* of Barsanuphius
and John appearing in this volume.

New Testament